the ninth life of a diamond miner

GRACE TAME

the ninth life of a diamond miner

a memoir

MACMILLAN
Pan Macmillan Australia

Pan Macmillan acknowledges the Traditional Custodians of country throughout Australia and their connections to lands, waters and communities. We pay our respect to Elders past and present and extend that respect to all Aboriginal and Torres Strait Islander peoples today. We honour more than sixty thousand years of storytelling, art and culture.

First published 2022 in Macmillan by Pan Macmillan Australia Pty Ltd
1 Market Street, Sydney, New South Wales, Australia, 2000

A catalogue record for this book is available from the National Library of Australia

Typeset in 12.5/17 pt Minion Pro by Post Pre-press Group, Brisbane

Printed by IVE
Illustrations by Grace Tame

The paper in this book is FSC® certified.
FSC® promotes environmentally responsible, socially beneficial and economically viable management of the world's forests.

To Christian, Kelly, Janet and all the children whose lives were taken, even in part, before they were able to live them to the fullest, on their own terms.

Telling your stories will make us whole again.

Contents

Prologue

The Diamond Miner

In the European summer of 2014, when I was nineteen, I spent six weeks living in a ramshackle share house in Portugal.

That's where I met Jorge. One front tooth, a barely live circa 1985 Peugeot 205, stacks of overstuffed photo albums and an equally overstuffed chihuahua named Pirate were his only material possessions, besides the clothes on his back. His jeans were tattered and his white T-shirt had long surrendered its whiteness, but it looked bright enough against his deep olive tan and warm brown eyes, which also offset his shock of salty hair. Whether he was 67 or 76, I can't remember. He may well have been neither.

Jorge lived in the attic. His entire life was up there, hanging in the high humid air that clung to a treasure trove of memories and time-warped talks. Without moving, he was at once above and part of all the rest of us young passing guests.

He knew the meaning of life. How could he not, having lived it over and over, in seven different languages, no less?

Although he was asset poor, Jorge was story rich. He really had lived nine lives, or thereabouts. He had played soccer, and been a springboard diver. He had performed in a band that toured through Europe. He had become involved in a cocaine cartel – 'The size of bricks, I tell you!' He had lived in New York, fallen in love, and married a Jewish-American heiress to a fortune worth millions. And he had mined for diamonds in Brazil.

In the end, though, he would leave all that behind for the simple pleasure of having nothing more than a wealth of vivid memories and real friends. He would return to his native land, with man's best friend, burdened only by freeze frames of his freedom in Kodachrome.

Jorge's irreverent authenticity helped reinforce for me what is truly important in life, and what has genuine value. People. Places. Experiences. Love. And connection.

At least in my naive eyes, he lived and breathed the underrated, overlooked commodity of simplicity.

Looking back as a healthily jaded adult eight years later, it occurs to me that Jorge might have been a conman, which makes him even more of a badass, and adds a delicious layer of irony to this attempt at sentiment.

Then again, some things in life are ultimately what we make of them. There are forces we can control, and others we can't. Pain and joy are inevitable in equally unpredictable measures. Our power lies in how we respond to each, and the meaning we derive from our experiences.

Some of you might already know my name because you're

familiar with a part of my story that has been magnified and scrutinised publicly; how when I was fifteen my 58-year-old Maths teacher groomed and repeatedly raped me at my high school. Yet, while child sexual abuse and the lasting effects of it are undeniably traumatic, that time hasn't defined my unfinished experience of life. That man is just one man, among a crowd of people whose paths have intersected with mine. Jorge, the Diamond Miner, is also in that crowd. The value of his connection is such that, despite its brevity, on its own it pervades the darkness. When bundled together with the other similarly positive experiential souvenirs I've collected over my 27 years, their combined weight overwhelms the bad.

Perhaps the biggest blessing and curse of my life is the open-heartedness and humour I retain to this day. For everything it has cost me, I've regained it all and more by stubbornly refusing to cut myself off. There is great strength in vulnerability. I've met my fair share of monsters. I've met some angels too.

I originally wanted to call this book *Diamond Miners and Rock Spiders* but my editor wouldn't let me. Nor would she let me call it *A Diary of Daddy Issues.* Satire is dead and you can blame it on the mainstream. ('Stop attacking me,' begged my editor. 'I am going to release a director's commentary,' she threatened.)

As far as I see it, we are all to each other a passing ship in the night, a cross-section of humanity, moving through time and space, leaving impressions and sharing lessons. Here are some of mine. Raw. Real. Uncut.

Chapter 1

Princess Buildings Parade

Integration

It might not be a coincidence that a baby girl born into instability was trying to find her feet as early as possible. I was walking by the time I was ten months old. For as long as I can remember, there's been little consistency in the short but fulfilling time I've so far spent on this earth. I've found myself soaring at the highest of heights and crawling in the deepest, darkest depths. It's standing still on firm, middle ground that's foreign to me.

Some might say that since day one I was – and still am – happy-go-lucky, with an emphasis on the happy, but even more so on the go. Hard and fast is how I've always lived. Mostly on others' terms.

So much so, in fact, that it's been hard for me to form a strong sense of self. In the early days, it got trampled on.

This could be because I was carted back and forth between two houses my entire childhood, which was too much for an undiagnosed autistic child. My parents split when I was two, so I'd spend three or four days in one place, before having to uproot and leave again for the other. My clothing had to be kept separate – the first thing I would do when I got home was shed all my layers including my underwear and dress again. I never questioned why.

Maybe it's because I was psychologically abused by someone in my life from the age of two onwards – 'bitch' and 'cow' were names I'd been called by the time I was six. The same person would stick her rude finger up at me in front of my father, and tell me, 'You've got a pretty face, but it won't last.' When I was only a child. All of this – and there was so much more – chipped away at my self-esteem.

Both of my parents worked full-time, so they weren't always around. Some mornings I was dropped off at school as early as seven o'clock and left unintentionally unsupervised, confused and in tears, starting when I was four and all the way through primary school. I didn't say anything at the time, that was just the way it was.

Or it could be that I have both autism and ADHD, which nobody knew back then. My undiagnosed neurodivergent three-year-old quirks were sometimes met with a smack instead of patience.

Or that at six I didn't understand what was happening when an older child told me to get undressed in a closet, before molesting me and forcing me to touch him too. There were four of us, it turns out. We've since spoken about what happened, and made peace with it. My memory is cut with visions of earlier incidents, but there's only so much that's worth holding on to.

Like the poignant relevance of the Nobel Prize–winning Austrian poet Peter Handke's words about children not knowing they are children juxtaposed against the disturbing fact that Handke himself is an absolute fuckhead who publicly came out in support of a war criminal – it is possible for two opposing things to be true at once. Like how, in spite of the painful turbulence of my upbringing, I am eternally grateful for all of it; for the invaluable lessons it continues to teach me, and the ways it continues to shape me.

I also had many opportunities that a lot of children don't have growing up. Both of my parents were raised in a very different time from me, in working-class families. They fought hard to make sure I didn't miss out. I got to spend blistering-hot summers camping for weeks in the Tasmanian wilderness, giggling uncontrollably with my cousin Eloise, and trading showers for swimming in the ocean or eel-infested lagoons. When I was eleven, my mum and three of her sisters took six of us kids on an overseas family holiday to South East Asia, where we travelled to five countries in two weeks – all ten of us. (Herding cats? No, herding *cars*.) For four years I attended a private high school on two scholarships, where my mum still paid almost $8000 in annual fees. (Not that that ended well . . . Fuck me – too soon?)

They sent her a bill after I disclosed, by the way. No, she did not fucking pay it.

There is darkness and there is light. Good and bad. Each unable to exist without the other. How else do we have perspective on anything? The taste of food after a gruelling sub-three-hour marathon race. The feel of your mother's warm embrace after two years apart. The sound of truth after eight years of silence. I wouldn't want to trade a thing, not even the worst of the horrors I've seen. There are also unique gifts born of adversity that I am fiercely protective of. Like resilience. Hard-won grit. An open heart and an open mind. Compassion. The ability to move in spite of fear. Humour. And an appreciation for the raw beauty and transience of life.

It's nearly impossible to pinpoint exactly why people are the way that they are. Some say nurture, some say nature; perhaps it's both, perhaps it's neither. Some of us never stop to think about it. Some of us never have the luxury of free time to think about it. Some of us don't want to.

On average, it's 23.9 years after the contact offending stops that survivors of child sexual abuse disclose their experiences. Before being named Australian of the Year at the beginning of 2021, I used to think this silence was because of the re-traumatisation that results from reliving the abuse. That certainly is a factor. I have been battling it chronically in the public eye. Under a microscope. In front of cameras.

But what I am also living – privately, simultaneously – is a totally bizarre, unnatural, accelerated unpacking and processing of my entire life to date. One that is playing on a loop. Because my work, the questions from the media and public regarding it, and my life – these are all inextricably linked. Here I was thinking I'd already made peace with most of my past. I could almost feel my hands wrapped tightly around some solid answers, only to look down and see vapour misting through my fingers.

'*Switch off*,' you say. Life doesn't have a pause button.

'*Stop being a victim.*' Nah, that's not it. Context is important. Without the precipitating and predisposing factors, an abuse survivor's story makes no sense. The absence of context – I have also come to realise – is perhaps the last frontier of protection for perpetrators. The devil, as they say, is in the details. Child abusers are among the most sophisticated of criminals. They use their victims' family secrets and closet skeletons like an insurance policy. They bank on the fact that the worst of their offences will remain hidden because they knit them into your past.

'*Where were your parents?*' That's not it either. My parents are two of the greatest, most kind-hearted people I know. Two people who did their best with what they had. Two people who had *two meetings* with the school before any contact offending ever took place because they were very concerned about his inappropriate behaviour. I never hid the fact that one of my teachers was talking at length to me in his office. The school, on the other hand, hid a lot. We would later discover there were other victims dating back to 1992, whose experiences were *common knowledge*. In any event, predators are relentless. They do not stop until they succeed.

To be clear: the only person responsible for a child abuser's behaviour in any circumstances ever is *the child abuser themselves*. They can try to shift blame onto others all they like, but ultimately they are the instigating, orchestrating party.

Child abusers groom through isolation, fear and shame. Through manipulation of our entire society. All of us, to some extent, have been groomed. You included. Yes, you. You have been groomed without even realising it. Groomed to reinforce the mythology that child sex offenders' actions can be somehow intellectualised, minimised or deflected onto someone else. There may be sympathisers, enablers and inactive bystanders who are complicit to some extent, but the bulk of the burden of guilt belongs to the perpetrators who *enlist them* in the first place.

While child abusers for so long have used their victims' past abuses and vulnerabilities as deflections, I believe doing so actually incriminates them further. Almost every case of child sexual abuse is preceded by abuse, neglect, family separation, dysfunction, or trauma of a different kind. That someone could be so cruel as to prey on a person who is not only physically and mentally less powerful than them, but also has a known history of trauma – to me this is the epitome of evil.

The general public knows only a relatively whitewashed version of my story. Not necessarily because I have hidden it from view, but because to honestly reflect on one's own life, especially the most painful parts of it, is incredibly confronting. And to a child, everything you live is normal until someone outside your world tells you otherwise.

Until 2022, the freight train of my entire existence had never stopped. So many of my firsts were in front of you; you just didn't know it because I had to grow up too quickly. To have to suddenly face and swallow the true oddity of your own existence live on national television, because a reporter unwittingly framed your life in a way you'd never even considered it before, is a surreal experience.

If it weren't for my autistic mastery of 'masking' and 'mimicry', last year might have been a hell of a lot harder than it already was.

I'd never even heard of these concepts until the end of 2021. There I was – the accidental presenter; the autistic artist who finds everyday socialising harder than calculus, but walking on stage as easy as kindergarten maths; the all-but-dead parrot who feels more comfortable addressing an audience of thousands than a private dinner function of ten – sitting opposite a psychiatrist, dumbfounded, as they put another giant piece of my life's puzzle into place, where before there was a gaping hole. Mimicking and masking, they explained, are survival strategies particularly common among autistic women. A lot of what we see we 'copy and paste' – as these behaviours are sometimes described – and we tend to be especially empathetic. This is part of why it can be harder to diagnose women. Our idiosyncrasies can fly under the radar because we learn very quickly to fit in, albeit at the expense of our own identity and needs.

I now know why I don't get nervous in interviews. What many neurotypical people are terrified to do for a brief moment is what many autistic people are doing every moment of their entire lives. I am five-foot-three and weigh fifty kilos. I have to make myself big in other ways.

My best friend is an openly gay autistic man, who I met when we were seven. Dom, his name is. We don't even have to speak to each other when we are together. We just are. Our connection swallows time and space. Neither of us knew the other was neurodiverse until we were adults. Not that it mattered to us. Our own private nonverbal world remained as perfectly imperfect as ever. I have watched others assume things about us throughout our friendship. They tell, instead of asking us, what we must be. I can't speak for Dom, but there is much to be said of the insidiousness of these presumptive projections. Isolation and invalidation have certainly been at the core of my experiences of autism and of life in general.

I am unfiltered, and intensely empathetic. These traits have made me especially vulnerable to predators because I've always had such porous boundaries. Ever since I was little, in lieu of strong attachments, I've sought connection from others and have often been told that I overshare without realising. While most people are good and greet this with compassion and an understanding of how to help me see what I am doing without inducing shame, there are a rare few who are more calculated and opportunistic.

When we were eight, my friend and I were left alone with three teenage boys at a property in Primrose Sands, while Mum and their parents went for an afternoon walk. They tied us up with ropes and taunted us while we cried. I can't remember how long it was before our parents came back and untied us.

I was nineteen years old, asleep in a foreign country, when one of my exes broke the door of my one-bedroom apartment off its hinges because he was looking for a knife to fight someone at four o'clock in the morning. We broke up because he cheated on me while I had been away for a week-long work trip, but he still tried to make me feel bad about it. 'I was tired of jerking off,' he said.

I've been love-bombed by former partners who've promised me the world but delivered hell.

I'm no saint, and trauma sparks trauma, but if there is a holy tenet I subscribe to it is that actions speak louder than words. The moment I was spat at in the eye by a pack-a-day smoker is when I knew I was staring domestic violence square in the face. Since then, I've seen fists through plaster and dinner plates smashed into walls. I've been pushed and shoved, backed into corners, choked with the hood of my jumper from behind, had hands put over my mouth to silence my cries for help, and felt the full force of an open palm smack to my head.

I do my very best to manage the ongoing effects of complex trauma, autism, ADHD and the ways in which they intersect; to practise mindfulness and gratitude; to feel peace; and to stay open and care for myself and others by staying grounded in the simple pleasures of ordinary life: family, friends, nature. And love.

Thankful and aware of my privileges though I am, it's worth remembering that I didn't ask to be given a national platform. I have just gone with the flow and done my best to make the most out of it. I was unemployed and living with my aunt when I learned I was nominated for Australian of the Year over the phone. It wasn't until my now-fiancé, Max, and I arrived in Canberra for the ceremony and saw Cathy Freeman's 1998 poster in the hotel lobby that I realised how serious the honour was. (My dad only decided to go to the ceremony when we told him the betting odds were in my favour.) I believe public policy advocacy is important work. Being a billboard is a by-product.

I have always been an object of other people's *projections*, just on a much smaller scale. An expert at making adults feel better about their own shitty behaviour, even as a young child; even after being subjected to it. I've lost count of the number of hats and labels I've worn as I've tried to find myself through the fog, mainly because they were given to me by other people who don't know me from Adam.

At fourteen, when I was involuntarily hospitalised for six weeks with acute anorexia, I had already started to numb from mounting trauma. I was here but not there. Whatever connection to the present that remained would soon be lost to fear-induced adrenaline.

At fifteen, as many of you now know, I was preyed upon by a 58-year-old serial child abuser. He had taught me during the very same year my mental health began to decline. The very same year I was admitted for eating disorder treatment. He said I taught him more than any student in all his years of teaching, and masterfully groomed me into believing that I loved him.

'I had boy trouble in high school too,' the school principal said to a then-sixteen-year-old me in April 2011, just moments after I disclosed to her outside her office as we waited for the police to arrive. The psychologist who was called to the scene and overheard was horrified.

'I just can't believe you've had sex' was another great line I would hear later that day when I disclosed as much as I could manage for the second time ever. At that stage, I still hadn't had a chance to talk to my mum yet. 'I just can't believe you've had *sex*' they kept saying to me, over and over, as I sat there in hysterics, still in my fucking school uniform, fumbling my way through stabbing images of a six-foot-two beast looming over me. 'I just can't believe you've had sex.' There's a special place in the Victim Blamers' Hall of Fame for that one. The same person would later say to me, when I received victims of crime compensation, 'Not everyone who gets raped gets paid.'

Until very recently, I didn't have the developmental capacity to comprehend my alienating experiences of hyper-vigilance, detachment and dissociation. I didn't know that these states of mind were the true places I lived in for most of my life, alone. I didn't know that I was on the spectrum until I was twenty. I didn't know what boundaries were, what the concept of autonomy was. I always just followed everyone else's rules, constantly toeing jagged fault lines, desperate not to misstep. Forever fighting, freezing, fleeing and fawning for fear of falling. And when I moved halfway across the world at eighteen to escape my past, the stakes only grew; the canyons too.

To this day, the longest I have ever lived under one roof is one whole year. As quickly as I form attachments to people and places, they seem to break. Either that, or I break them early, in anticipation of them being broken without warning. Having never formed proper bonds to anyone or anywhere since birth, self-preservation by default became both a force of habit and habitat. All I ever wanted was a single place to call home, and a person with whom to share it. Our own turf, on our own terms. Free of the fear of leaving or being left.

It wasn't until eight years after the trauma at my high school, as I sat in a therapist's office, in the throes of yet another short-lived, volatile, violent relationship, that I learned one of life's most tragic truths. Survivors of child sexual abuse are five times more likely to be victimised again later in life. Women with autism have three times the odds of being sexually abused.

And although I have always tried to keep my feet on the ground and head out of the clouds through it all – just like my pop Wally used to tell me – all I have ever really known is this feeling like I'm running on a landslide. That is my familiar territory. That is my normal. On even ground, I stumble.

Separation

I was born on 28 December 1994 at Calvary Hospital. Three days after my parents named me, there was a band playing the bagpipes outside. All of a sudden 'Amazing Grace' bellowed through the windows. Mum tells the story so sweetly, like it was some kind of divine sign, as if the odds of a band playing that song outside were impossible. I love her, but they were clearly just doing a New Year's Eve gig at a Catholic joint. On the fucking bagpipes.

I'm aware I've opened this with heaviness, but on the whole I have pretty happy memories of my childhood. Although I don't remember my parents being together, what I have to substitute for that are photographs and imagined scenes of an unfamiliar faraway time. A family I never knew as one, now fragmented. Photographs of Mum, Dad and little me with my hands in the air, laughing. On Princess Buildings Parade.

I was, reportedly, one of the happiest babies. Equal parts placid and active. Instead of waking distressed in tears, I used to click my tongue in my bassinet. If you spend long enough with me, you'll discover that I still do it to self-soothe. Minus the infant-sized bed.

The first house I ever lived in was in Rokeby, Tasmania. 'Preston', it's called, with a bright white roof to offset the name, horrendous mustard weatherboards, and the only toilet was an outdoor dunny. It shared a backyard with the house my father grew up in – the pale-yellow brick house my pop built for their family in the 60s. He and Nan lived in it for the rest of their lives.

Like the perfect metaphor, I have always been so near to my first home and that time, without ever being able to actually claim it. Growing up I played in and outside of 'Preston', because I spent a lot of time with Pop and Nan. My aunt Jenny and three cousins also lived in it for a while. Then Nan's brother, Graeme, and his male 'roommate', Ta, moved in after they left. It remained in the family until Graeme passed. But I always walked through the hallway and sat on the furniture in the same way I walk through my own memories of that place – like a passing guest.

Despite their volatile chemistry, Mum and Dad's separation was amicable and there was no custody battle. They both found partners who they've happily been with ever since, so I know my parents as individuals. I am glad of that, for all our sakes, because they are two truly irreconcilably different people. Theirs was not the healthy kind of opposite pairing. I credit them both for doing their best to refrain from badmouthing each other in front of me when I was younger, but I've copped 'you're just like your mother' and 'you're just like your father' as ammunition enough times to know. They're both, for the record, decent people with pure hearts, whom I love, and whose love for me I have never doubted for a second. All relationships have their complications, of course. But love – love transcends every one.

It has been the only constant for me.

So that's me – the product of a creative, empathetic pacifist, and a self-sufficient, independent, analytical rebel – forever trying to reconcile such dissonant roots from a rocky, quaking base that never finished being built in the first place.

This has worked in my favour, it seems. I certainly didn't grow into the spotlight. I was thrust into it, suddenly, out of obscurity. It's been a steep ascent onto a sizeable platform. Thankfully, my fast and loose has given me solid sea legs and drowned any fear I had of heights.

Chapter 2

The Matriarchy

Girls, Girls, Girls

Wildly untraditional, imperfect but unconditional is my maternal extended family. Even though some of us now live in different states, we all still – and always will – call Tasmania home. The *mother*land. Our mothers' land.

My mother, Penelope, Penny, is the youngest of five sisters. When she was born, the eldest – Shelley – was only five years old.

Shelley arrived in February 1959, followed only sixteen months later by Wendy in July 1960; then Jenny in November 1961; Denise in October 1963; and finally, Penny in December 1964. There's only one whose name doesn't half-rhyme, so we call her 'Neesy'.

There was another, Jane. She was born before them all but tragically lived only six weeks.

Their mother, my nan Patricia Watkins, whom everyone including her own children calls 'Nanny Pat', says she washed cloth nappies every single day for eight years straight.

Raised for the most part by Nanny Pat and her mother, 'Nanny Beulah', there's little need to state either the five sisters' closeness, or their ability to testify to female strength. All five of them are brightly blue-eyed, brilliant, and objectively – indisputably – beautiful, from the inside out. But each very much in her own way. I adore them all equally, but for very different reasons.

The first, Shelley, is the boss. Assertive. Adventurous, if at times aloof – we call her 'Secret Squirrel', after the 1965 bulletproof trench coat–wearing cartoon rodent spy. She's by far the most well travelled of us, having lived in both Japan and China for a combined three years, and visited countless other countries across all but the two polar continents. A lover of language, she speaks Mandarin, Indonesian and Japanese with near fluency. She is fiercely intelligent, unimpressionable but always understanding. She carries a pepper grinder in her handbag because she covets the spice and has no faith in restaurants.

The second, Wendy, is the eternal mother – ethereal, gentle, petite and patient – always putting others first and capable of soothing everyone's sadness. She is quiet but a quick thinker, equal parts conventional and creative. Hers is the tightest hug and the fullest pantry. She was panic-buying before it was mainstream. Tim Tams. Iced VoVos. Monte Carlos. Scotch Fingers. She keeps Arnott's in business. Mum says it's a hangover from when they were growing up and had nothing. When I was five, Wendy and her family stayed with Mum and me for a while. Mum had previously never allowed Coco Pops in our house, but Wendy let me have them for second breakfast after Mum left for work.

The third, Jenny, is the wild one; the entertainer. Uninhibited – in the best way. Open-minded. Freethinking. And almost always available at any time of the day or night – whether to yarn about something whacky or stage an after-hours rescue. No, really; as soon as my two-week post-international travel quarantine stint in early 2020 ended, she was outside in her maroon Toyota RAV4 at midnight on the dot, ready to roll. She's less of a black sheep than a vividly multicoloured one. A prankster. A tomboy. With boundless energy, spirit and style. Striking. Sharp. Eccentric, eclectic and electric. Some say that we are very alike. I can't argue. We certainly have a lot in common, both in terms of taste and life experiences. I lived with her during the first coronavirus lockdown, which we spent listening to Lou Reed and playing dress-ups, watching cult classics like *Paris, Texas*, *True Romance* and *Bad Boy Bubby*, and threatening to Glad Wrap each other. 'Be still!'

The fourth sister, Denise, is the comedian and confidante. Almost always laughing, and loyal to a fault. Dennis, I call her – and she calls me Graeme. Devoted, dependable Dennis. All year round, even in the dead of Tasmanian winter, she braves the cold and swims in the ocean. She's as soft and serene as Wendy, but she'll make you howl harder than anyone. That's part of her warmth – she's cheeky, discreetly. She's charming and positively disarming, with a smile as warm as her heart. She is simultaneously shy and stupendously silly. She wouldn't have an enemy in the world.

And finally, the fifth: Penny, my mother. She's the warrior. They all are, really, but there's just something about Mum's tenacity, her stalwart willingness to sacrifice herself for others, that stands out to me. Maybe I'm just biased. Like Denise, she swims in the ocean every day – but in just her bathers. Mum is poised and polite, but persistent. A courteous, conscientious conciliator. Committed to uncovering, understanding and upholding the truth at all costs, she has quietly campaigned for social justice her whole life. In 1975, when she was all of ten years old, she wrote a very angry letter to the editor of the local newspaper because they had printed an article that disparaged First Nations people. She never posted it, but she still has the letter somewhere. More recently, Mum has devoted over a decade to supporting me personally, as well as to the ongoing fight against child sexual abuse, and other systemic injustices.

That's them: 'the girls' – Shelley, Wendy, Jenny, Neesy and Penny Wright; the wonderful, wise women who helped take care of me and my many cousins. Bastions of independence, selflessness, openness, humour and fortitude respectively, but not exclusively. Collectively, they've helped teach me that there is, unquestionably, nothing more important or more powerful than love and connection.

Role, Over

Fifty years ago was a different era, with more polarised gender stereotypes. I know what you're thinking; I wasn't alive. But I've watched *Monty Python's Flying Circus* and two-and-a-half episodes of *Mad Men*, so I'm all across it. Tradition had it that men predominantly won the bread, managed the money and took on the manual labour, while women did the housework and were decorative novelties, apparently. Nan, Beulah and the five girls, however, had little choice but to do everything themselves. And they didn't just rise to the occasion. They rose above it.

(I did also study history, by the way. I just had to get that off my A-cup chest.)

Nan worked full-time as a secretary at Commonwealth Industrial Gases, which is now the site of Woolworths in New Town, just outside of Hobart. She also taught herself how to handle finances, and prepared every meal – almost – despite not being the best of cooks. In her defence, the era of 'deb potato' had just dawned. She was swindled by the marketed convenience of freeze-dried peas and carrots; a victim of 'one-pan dinner in a box – just add meat'.

'It would be chops,' Mum recounts with the same lack of confidence I imagine she felt when she was actually eating them. 'Chops or mince with cabbage and . . . some kind of noodle soup?'

Every one of the five girls could bake, sew and crochet thanks to Beulah, herself a milliner and 'good with her hands', Wendy says, who took them all 'under her wing'.

And they taught themselves how to do just about everything else. Nan would have two tonnes of wood delivered at a time and they chopped and stacked every load. They mowed the lawns. Lit the fire. Repaired things. Jenny – who was a gymnast – did the guttering. In contrast, Mum had a friend, Andrea, whose parents never even let her ride a bike because they were afraid she would fall off.

Nan had a younger brother, Kevin. If you couldn't already tell by looking at them, their gentle hearts, patiently listening ears and softly spoken words were all the evidence you needed that they were related. In his later years, Kevin walked with a limp. He lost half his leg when he was unexpectedly caught beneath the fall of a truckload of iron while working in Mount Isa. Sadly, he and his adoring wife, Sue, have both passed away. My memories of them remain as bold as the burgundy streaks Sue put through her shock of grey hair to match her acrylic nails. Christmas lunch was incomplete without their symbiotic company, and the taste of Sue's famous trifle.

They had two children, Carrin, born in 1963, and Kent, born in 1965 – who later became Kelly in the 1980s. Like her parents, Kelly is sadly no longer with us. Carrin has since come out as gay and lives happily with her partner, Helen, and to this day maintains with lightness that she and Kelly must have been born in the wrong bodies. You are who you are is how I've always seen it. So long as your freedoms aren't impinging on someone else's.

(Don't get me started on women's sport. Forget the years of pain and suffering; men just want to become women so they can beat us in the pool. Sure.)

Although they grew up in Mount Isa, Carrin and Kelly often travelled down to Tasmania to spend time with Mum and her sisters when they were little. According to Mum, all Kelly ever wanted to do was dress up in Nan's black tulle ballgown, and she would 'go crazy' in the car whenever they drove past the local shoe shop. Carrin, on the other hand, was only ever interested in army games. A motorbike – that was what Carrin wanted. While she learned to weld, Kelly sewed all the costumes for their high school's play.

Growing up as a part of this family, I never questioned a person's worth or rights based on their sex, gender identity, sexuality, colour, race, religion, creed, wealth, nationality, ability or politics. I was raised to be inclusive. It was entrenched. It's in my blood. There are few things I won't tolerate, one being intolerance. That said, I do believe in constructive criticism, and being able to laugh at oneself. Self-deprecation and punching up are one thing; punching down is out of bounds. My humour is certainly dark and dry, and usually at my own expense. The best jokes, of course, are when no one gets hurt, and we're all just laughing together as one.

Three-year-old me has a confession to make, though. Legend has it that in 1998 I had already decided that the One Nation Party was not what I was about. Clearly I had been absorbing some adult conversations that I probably wouldn't have been able to elaborate too much on at the time. Nevertheless, my mind was made up. They were the enemy.

Back then, Mum was living alone down at South Arm, having not long separated from my dad. One night, she was looking after me and my cousin Griffin.

While Mum was preparing dinner in the kitchen, Griff and I were quietly entertaining ourselves in the adjacent ensuite bathroom. Our quietness gave Mum no cause for concern.

Like Wendy, Mum has a tendency to stockpile things as a hangover from running out of supplies when they were kids, only Mum's thing is toilet paper, not biscuits. What she didn't realise that night was that we had discovered her stash of toilet paper rolls and had unravelled every single one. We were wading ankle-deep in the stuff. We'd covered the whole floor and filled the shower cubicle, too.

Tasmania is a long way from Queensland, but when Mum eventually came to fetch us for tea looking less than impressed, I apparently assured her flatly that 'Pauline Hanson did it', without batting an eyelid. In all fairness, we were standing in a sea of whiteness; it was worth a shot.

Everything and Nothing

When I asked Mum and her sisters separately where they think their strength comes from, they each told a different story that nevertheless wound up at the same conclusion: each other.

Solidarity. And lots of love. A bit of drama, too. Just a bit.

They didn't have money, but they did have love. Love and wicked, wicked laughter. And a shared wealth of life lessons born of hardship. Most importantly, though, they had the most prized gift of all on this earth: connection. They still have it, and every single one of us cousins is blessed to have inherited it. We are inseparable and indestructible because of it.

Jenny remembers bailiffs knocking on the door and men coming to repossess the television. Denise dropped out of school early to help Nan pay the bills. Wendy is the eternal mother because she was a mother then too. Shelley was the only one who went on to university.

After finishing school, Mum had several service industry jobs and lived like a nomad. She came and went, just like me. Technically her first job was in Year 8 working for 'Pete the Greek' selling groceries. Since then she's been a hotel receptionist, a croupier, a corporate DVD producer, and a righthand to a knitwear near Detroit. Then she became a television newsreader.

There's no such thing as fame in Tasmania; nobody lets anybody get too big for their boots. Besides, it's a fucking island. We all know each other. All 67 of us. I remember seeing Mum's first live broadcast as a newsreader when I was six and just being miffed because she didn't say hello back. For the ten years that she was on television as an anchor, her salary was less than my father's. He was a public high school teacher, who started out teaching PE and Home Economics, then ended up teaching English to higher-needs kids.

Mum has long retired from reading the news. It's been over ten years now. Today she works as a youth worker, caring for young people aged between twelve and eighteen, whose parents have relinquished responsibility for their upbringing to the government. My parents might hang and fold their washing in opposite ways, and insist how they do it is the way it must be done, but at the end of the day, their hearts are one and the same.

Huntsman spiders – they're Mum's only obvious nemesis. To be fair, they're probably most people's nemesis. And us humans – what with our straw brooms, rolled-up newspapers, vacuum cleaners, Mortein, glass jars, tea towels, six-buck servo thongs, and backyard DIY blowtorches fashioned from matches and some of your big brother's Lynx deodorant (for all you pyromaniacs out there) – are probably theirs. Jenny picks them up with her hands. So do I, but that hasn't always been the case. They have had to earn my respect. I see the way they run. It's beautiful.

Mum and I have a sixth sense for them. Denise will testify. She has it, too, apparently. We can feel when there's one in the room even when it's pitch dark.

One time at Mum's South Arm house, she shot up in the middle of the night. I had been asleep next to her until I heard her whisper harshly, 'I know there's a spider in here.' Sure enough, when she turned on her bedside lamp in trepidation, the distinct shape of a huntsman was visible on the wall opposite us. It had clearly been startled by the sudden shock of light and the sight of one-and-a-half humans boring their four eyes into its eight. You can tell when they're uneasy by the way they bend their legs into their body, as if that will make them seem smaller.

For the next three nights, we slept on the couch. Mum refused to go back into the room. It wasn't until Dad came over to pick me up that the door was even opened.

Mum remembers this story for a different reason. On our first night in exile, when all was still and quiet, as we lay there snuggled into each other, I whispered, 'Mummy, I am you and you are me.'

That's it. That's our family's strength; we are each other's everything.

Recently, I had a special moment with my father, too. Out of respect to him, the details of what was said will stay between us. But the sentiment was the same.

Despite all that has come between my parents and me, which has made forming bonds a test at the best of times, we will be each other's family forever. Forever and all time.

Love is a form of attachment in and of itself.

The family *we choose* is everything. Nothing else matters.

Cousins Are It

It's time for some more lightness. Some more lightness and likeness. The cousins.

1. Leah – October 1978 (Wendy's)
2. Alie – November 1985 (Shelley's)
3. Chelsea – July 1987 (Jenny's)
4. Morgan – July 1989 (Jenny's)
5. Ryan – September 1989 (Denise's)
6. Eloise – September 1990 (Wendy's)
7. Maddie – January 1993 (Denise's)
8. Griffin – December 1994 (Jenny's)
9. Grace (Me!) – December 1994 (Penny's)
10. Millie – May 1995 (Shelley's)
11. Oscar – May 2010 (Penny's)

As your plane nears the runway, fast approaching Hobart Airport, it might just seem to graze the tops of a deep-green line of pine trees, chasing water and sand, in a place called Seven Mile Beach.

Surf Road runs from Lewis Avenue, where 'the shop' is (yes, the one and only), all the way past the tarmac to Pittwater. When I was one, in 1995, my parents bought number 5. My uncle Tony, Wendy's husband, built one a few blocks down. He also helped my uncle Gary, Shelley's then-husband, build one a few down from that. Denise and her then-husband Brad were living around the corner from us on Winston Avenue, and Jenny was fifteen minutes – if that – up the road in Howrah.

Until I was fifteen and my dear, darling baby brother Oscar joined us, I was an only child on paper. But there's no denying that the connection shared between my cousins is more akin to siblinghood. For starters, we all grew up on the same street. We were always over at one another's houses, getting up to all sorts of mischief in the backyard or at the beach. We were the last generation before the advent of mobile phones and iPads, thank Darwin.

By the time Millie was born five months after me – she remained the youngest until Oscar – the eldest lot were of babysitting age. Of the eleven of us, eight are girls. Ryan and Griffin seemed indifferent to that, though – if anything, I was more fearless than the two of them combined, swallowing bouncy balls and two-dollar coins, climbing trees, jumping fences, and unconvinced that there was such a thing as top speed on a PeeWee 50. There's an element of courage that all of us cousins have that our mothers gave to us. You don't grow up like they did without it.

One time when I was five, I had an argument with Dad and ran away from home. Really I just ran to Millie's 500 metres up the road and insisted on being taken in by her and Gary. With our matching long blonde hair and twin tiny frames, we could almost pass for each other. Only, Millie is far more knowledgeable, worldly and well travelled than I am. When she was two, her family lived in Japan for two years and she came back speaking fluent Japanese. When she was ten, she spent a year in China, and she is near-fluent in Mandarin. She went to Italy on exchange in high school, and diligently kept up her commitment to language studies throughout university where she completed a bachelor's degree in Global Studies. Ironically, she is as down-to-earth as they come.

There are graphite marks on a wall in her paternal

grandmother Sylvia's house that her late poppy John drew. He insisted on measuring our height every time we went over there to play in their sprawling backyard, with the apricot tree that meets the edge of the River Derwent on Tranmere's rocky bluffs. Like Sylvia, who is a nimble 95, those marks haven't faded, and neither have my visions of Millie and me when we were little, playing there together without a care in the world. And I will never forget how we had each other when we walked through the fire at fifteen, in the face of a man only she and I met.

Griffin, the gentle giant, is aptly named. He is something of a mythological creature. Nobody in our family is tall enough to play basketball, yet somehow he grew to be over six foot. With his sandy mane, broad stature, loyal nature and pure heart, he is lion in part. It's his otherworldly humour and creative imagination that also makes him a legend. We have covered more ground than a few toilet rolls' worth in our time. Playing up in the treehouse at Princess Buildings Parade, woodworking with Pop in his shed after school, and camping in the backyard at Narang Street in Lauderdale. The 25 December is also known as 'Griffmas' in our family. Griffin was born three days before me in a room just down the hall.

When Millie's family went to Japan, Jenny moved into their house in Seven Mile, so Griff and his two older sisters, Morgan and Chelsea, spent time growing up in the suburb, too. One of Griff's old friends from high school ended up being the roommate of my first ever boyfriend in a place at the top of Barrack Street in West Hobart. After we broke up, my friend Georgie and I used to just go and hang out there with Griff and listen to music or watch something silly on TV. He was very protective of us both, without ever imposing, interfering or assuming that we even needed protecting. He was just a tranquil ally, standing by.

Maddie is almost two years older than me, but because she was born in January 1993 and I was born in December 1994, she was only one year ahead of me in school. Maddie is butter soft, and honey sweet, with saucer-wide blue eyes and a Colgate smile. She's pure, kind, mild and modest, but she'll split your sides with her brilliant wit. There was a game we used to play where we pointed to pictures of people's bizarre facial expressions in magazines and made the noise we thought they were making. Failing that, we could always just laugh at the shapes we could contort our own elastic faces into. We both went to the same primary school from 2002 onwards and would catch the bus or a ride home together, if I didn't go home with my best friend Dom – who also happened to live in Seven Mile when we first met, and whose older sister, Anna, was in Maddie's class.

Oh, the days before endless hours were swallowed by screens. Putting every condiment in the pantry on a single spoon and double-dog-daring each other to eat it without blocking our noses – Worcestershire sauce, seeded mustard, mayonnaise, wasabi, Tabasco, peanut butter. Pulling faces in the bath in butter-yellow shower caps. Playing chasings up and down Denise's carpeted staircase. Or even just bumping giddily from step to step in our flannelette pyjamas before bed, howling at the sound of our vibrating voices. Isn't it funny how little you need when you're a kid, with the comfort of a companion?

I missed my parents, but always wished sleepovers went a little while longer. They always ended too soon. I didn't want to go home, back to the grown-up world of fitting in with fickle rules.

When I was five, that dream became reality, albeit very briefly, when Wendy and Tony sold their place on Surf Road and went to stay with Mum in her place in Bellerive Bluff, while they were building a new house. Their eldest daughter, Leah, was living in Queensland at the time, but angelic Eloise (Weasy), who is four years older than me, moved into my room. The rest is a sisterly history.

It was matching outfits, Coco Pops for breakfast, bouncing on the bed and low-key organised crime. There were family fishing trips and dress-up parades. There were water fights on the trampoline under Mum and Wendy's washing, and not while it was wet. Our trampolines were not those fancy, new-age helicopter-parent giant beekeeper veils like they have now. These were the steel-spring launch pads of death, whose only safeguards were piss-weak borders of inch-thick blue foam that usually got chewed up by the dog on the first day. Admittedly it wasn't Weasy's golden labrador, Buddy, who was to blame for the bite marks all over the matting on mine, though. I take full responsibility for that.

For a while I wrote letters to the tooth fairy, who wrote back, only for me to discover they had very similar handwriting to Eloise. That fraud was made up for by word-for-word choreography to 'Stop' by the Spice Girls, watching *Little Rascals*, and an unforgettable introduction to Robin Williams through his hotdog impressions in *Mrs Doubtfire*. On weekends I would climb into Weasy's red-painted wood-framed bed, which had worn-out springs and sank in the middle. The two of us would roll into the dip, tuck ourselves under the covers, and giggle about anything that could possibly be giggled about.

Even after Eloise and her parents moved out, there was no separating us. We have camped, surfed, swum, travelled and walked through just about everything side by side. We've supported each other through half-marathons, marathons and an ultra-marathon, holding each other's hands with tears in our eyes, blood on our feet and nothing left but love to fuel our bodies. And now, Eloise has Nick, her husband, to join us as we go.

For my first three years of education, I went to a small school called the Cottage School, which was a short walk from Mum's house in Bellerive. After that, I moved to Cambridge Primary, not far from Seven Mile Beach, where Eloise, Millie, Maddie and her brother Ryan went, although he had already left by the time I got there. Griffin, Morgan, Chelsea, Alie and Leah all went to Cambridge too, although Griffin finished at Lauderdale Primary.

There was no separating any of us. My photo memory catalogue is overflowing with innumerable cousin birthday dinners at the Shoreline Hotel drinking raspberries through our noses, school holidays with the whole family up at Swanwick, running amok on the goat track golf course, wild weddings that didn't seem to end, a dozen hot Christmases in Seven Mile that wound up with everyone in the ocean, and all kinds of spontaneous gatherings we didn't need an excuse for that continue to this day.

Along the way we've welcomed new members like Scott, Steve, Nick, Lilly, David, Dylan, Max, Reyne and Dave into the fold with open arms. Ryan, Morgan, Chelsea, Alie and Leah are a bit older than me, but I still have plenty of clear memories with them growing up, and in recent years adulthood has nullified the age gaps.

Alie lived with Mum and me for a little bit at the Bellerive house when I was younger. It must have been while her parents and Millie were still in Japan. I was only four years old, though, and most of what I can picture from that time is overlaid with broken *Rage* clips of a hyper-sexualised underage Britney Spears in a school uniform asking baby to hit her one more time. All I can remember clearly is that at some point Alie got a haircut that she didn't like and was upset because it was too short, and Mum was trying to reassure her that it was 'just hair' and it would grow back – a memory that doesn't do her justice at all. Al-pal – whose hair has well and truly grown back now and who is always ready to let it down – is equal parts easygoing and energetic. She's a loveable and lovesome badass. Just like me, she's mad for hip-hop and belly laughs, and her hugs will reset you amid all of life's conditioning.

Like Griffin, Ryan is another gentleman. He's also our breakout home movie star, most famous for his early appearances as Batman in the driveway, and greeting every species of native animal in the backyard with a determined 'wise and shine' alongside his sidekick Eloise in a non-speaking role. His passion today remains local wildlife, with a soft – or rather, scaly – spot for reptiles, which he rescues and relocates. He's got two Tasmanian-themed coloured-ink tattooed sleeves in progress, complete with an open-jawed Tassie Devil in all its glory. His kind heart has been passed down to his adorable son, Franklin, and he has found a keeper in his partner, Reyne, who shares his love of cold-blooded creatures.

A few buildings down from the local television station where Mum read news, there used to be a dance studio, Strictly Ballroom, named after Baz Luhrmann's 1992 Australian cult classic film. My cousin Chelsea used to go there, and her talent was the show-stopping kind. If ballroom wasn't a pre-existing global tradition, you might think that Baz Luhrmann himself invented its diamanté-bedazzled aesthetic for his Baz Luhrmann production directed by Baz Luhrmann. For some reason Mum thought that a goofy seven-year-old me would look and move as effortlessly as glamorous fifteen-year-old Chelsea if she just put me in a homemade purple lycra outfit and the same amount of fake tan. Alas, she's not wrong about many things, but that was one of them. Even though Chelsea's trophy-winning feet were far out of my league, she made time to be my dance partner. She towered over me back then, but she made me feel big and special. From flawless foxtrots and fruit flans at four in the morning as a baker's apprentice, to becoming an award-winning executive PA on the national stage and getting a master's degree – all while keeping fit running, tough-muddering, and mothering two of the most adorable little cherubs, Finn and Evie, with her lovely husband, Steve – Chelsea remains one of the most selfless yet self-determined people I know.

Morgan, Chelsea's younger sister, has their mother Jenny's eccentricity, but is herself entirely. She is magical. A creative genius with an extra hunk of spunk and funk. She went to Box Hill Institute and RMIT and the clothing patterns she designs are transcendentally mental, in the best way. She sewed my wedding dress in 2017. Most of her own outfits are handmade, as are her dream journals. She's on a different level of feeling and healing. She can sense your energy, babe. Not just through tarot, or in the waters. If there's someone you need to turn to for a cry-laugh, who'll ease your soul, not just your blood pressure, it's Morgs. At the risk of a defamation suit, I think she might also be an even better rug-cutter than her sister. (But Griff's robot is undefeated.) Like both her siblings, Morgs is wildly hilarious. She's also a savvy powerhouse; a businesswoman of the world.

Like Leah, who's a real estate agent extraordinaire, and hasn't aged since she was twenty-something. Last, but definitely not Leah-st. In fact, she was the first cousin. Wendy had her when she was just eighteen. There's a sixteen-year age difference between us, and until I was in my teens, she was mostly up in Queensland from what I remember. She lived in Tasmania on and off, and has been down here permanently for less than a decade. She's strong, driven and striking to the eye. When I was about ten, her and Weasy's parents built a Donut King in Kings Meadows in Northern Tasmania. They rented a place nearby in Launceston, and on weekends Weasy would catch a bus up after school to help them out at the shop. Sometimes I would join her for the three-hour Friday night road trip, and cling to the faint sound of 'Don't Look Back In Anger' playing through a single earphone as the coach engine grumbled its way up through the midlands. Leah was in Tasmania then too, and she was pregnant with her first daughter, Lilli. I can still see us all sitting on the living room floor of the Launceston house before she was born, and now she's in her last year of college. Her little sister, Maya, is in her last year of high school.

I don't think our family's sixth spidey sense has anything to do with huntsmen. It's not just a few of us who have it. It's a special kind of familial intuition. Even though Leah and I didn't spend a lot of time together as kids, and didn't talk all that much, she could tell something was wrong when I fell of the rails in America when I was nineteen. I'd unexpectedly found myself with no place to live, no job and only a few hundred dollars to my name. All my belongings were in my car, so I drove from Los Angeles to San Francisco, couch-surfing with friends, and found myself in a bit of trouble. I stopped communicating with friends and family back home in Australia. It just so happened that Mum was visiting Leah in Queensland at the time. Mum's intuition kicked in, too. I might not have survived otherwise.

Chapter 3

Mothering over Othering and Smothering

Nanny Pat is the embodiment of humility. She's among the kindest, most patient humans I've ever known. She is a stranger to extreme behaviours; a passive pacifist who never discriminates. She says we can never know what's going on in someone else's world, and she dislikes gossip. By example of her modest life and language, she taught each of her children – and in turn all her grandchildren and great-grandchildren – the virtues of non-judgement and mercy. Her good graces extend beyond civil tolerance of others, too. She is actively accepting and welcoming. She taught us all to think more deeply about everything – especially the words we choose. The things we say can't be unsaid. That is something I know I can improve on. Most of us at some point will utter a regrettable remark or two – who am I kidding, we usually *yell* them.

Mum recalls listening to Nan and Nanny Beulah talking about the many wars that have been waged in the name of religion. Mum makes particular note of Nan's belief that religion has no place in politics; that in her eyes the meaning and purpose of religion should be more concerned with how people live their everyday lives. Personally, I'm not religious. Spiritual, definitely. But not religious.

'All religions are manmade and therefore subject to fallacy' is a favoured line of my eternally sceptical father that I reckon hits the nail – ahem, pardon the pun – on the head.

Like my dear Nan, I'm wary of signalling *absolute* calls on anyone or anything. I try to keep an open mind that grows in step with an open heart – as much as *humanly* possible. I must disclaim that there are certain people who I will NEVER negotiate with, namely child abusers and their sympathisers. Not that I should have to, but I will give you my reasons that go beyond personal 'beef' in due course – I mean, it's really the main, meaty course of this book. The eye fillet. Rare. Bloody. And cut against the grain.

It's worth pausing here, as I walk you through the thicker side of my familial forest. Before we go any further, I want to clarify the lens through which I see the world. There were blessings in disguise that my unstable childhood fostered, including the complementary gifts of an inquiring mind and non-attachment. More importantly, though, amid the physical toing and froing, I was shown that strong values withstand the tests of time, distance and chaos. Indeed, strong values are *created by* those tests. One being intrinsic motivation. Others being authenticity, integrity and the ability to own one's shortcomings.

My parents may have been emotionally incompatible, but they are cut from the same philosophical cloth. And in life when we can't agree, we can agree on what something is *not*. Neither Mum nor Dad imposed any of their ideologies on me, which has been one of the most impactful lessons of all. Because the trouble with human error is its humanness – the blessing that curses itself. You can't have evolution without devolution, and nothing living stands still until it stops.

No philosophy, no institution, no public figure has avoided imperfection throughout the course of history, nor can any claim the moral high ground. No matter how humble its beginnings, or how pure and intact its core remains, every single one has flaws as true as life itself. Including me. Me especially.

If you play the ball and not the player, it's possible to respect people and condemn some of their mistakes. Although if the player keeps doing fucked-up, harmful things, they're probably the ones with the issue, not the ball. And some actions are simply inexcusable and unforgivable, no matter how you try to spin them. Raping a thirteen-year-old girl, for example – I'm looking at you, Polanski.

Optometrist Dr Fred Hollows said, 'Every eye is an eye. When you're doing surgery [in third-world countries] that is just as important as if you were doing eye surgery on the prime minister or king.' Although I agree with the sentiment insofar as I believe that neither a person's wealth nor status should determine their worth – at the end of the day, not all eyes should be trusted. For apparently Prince Andrew didn't see things quite the same way as Virginia Giuffre.

While it's true that I lived in another country for almost six years, that country was the United States – close in culture to Australia. I did stay in Portugal for almost two months in a communal residence with locals during the European summer of 2014, and after saving up a year's worth of pocket money when I was thirteen I travelled alone to Los Angeles to meet my mother's friends, before joining them for a month in the central highlands of Mexico. Still, that's hardly any travelling at all in the grand scheme of life. What I have seen of the world is nothing compared to what I haven't.

And although I do try to read and absorb as much as I can, and favour the immersive low-budget traveller's experience over the tourist's, I'm still very young and can't possibly have insight into the extent to which my inexperience affects my perspective. That is to say, I'm aware of my limited awareness – but only as far as I'm aware!

All I know is what I know. And that is what I can tell you. That is what I can speak to; the truth of what I have lived so far.

To paraphrase Bernie Taupin, I'm a juvenile product of the middle class. Both of my parents worked their way up from next to nothing. They made good, but they weren't loaded either. I spent more years in the public school system in a rural district than I did in the private, and, in fact, the public system is where I ended up.

I was raised with a doting Lutheran step-grandmother; who was also a white Christian survivor of the Second World War, who was separated from her parents as a child and spent time in refugee camps. I have visited beautiful Buddhist heartlands of South East Asia, and also watched my uncle's proudly gay Thai partner die from liver cancer in his fifties because his religious beliefs didn't allow transplants. I have law-abiding American friends who own guns, and I remember Elliot Rodger driving right past my roommate and me the night he killed four women in Isla Vista. I have racked up hundreds of kilometres running alongside one of my best friends, who wears a hijab, and roomed with a girl in Santa Barbara who had a violent boyfriend who converted to Islam, used to yell at my friend and me in our apartment, and was later arrested for stabbing someone in a dispute over a drug deal. I went to an Anglican high school where I learned and grew, and where I lost my virginity via rape to a South African Catholic child-abuser ex-soldier, who sat me on his knee and molested me in his local church – which invited him back to play the organ immediately after he served only seventeen months in jail.

I don't know what else to tell you. There's only so much you can reconcile with future promises without denying the truth of the past and present.

Don't say, '*It's not all bad*,' like I don't know happiness and humour. Don't blame it on the free will of man, like I don't know my theology. Don't tell me to have faith or that I need to forgive. I have faith, but maybe you'll forgive me if my faith's just not in this stuff.

I say these words without judgement or an agenda to convert you (except to stop defending child abusers – I mean, right now, stop it. Seriously, stop doing that). They are the words of someone who is being honest with you, and with themselves.

The outward system of forgiveness as we know it, which is built into religious and other institutional frameworks, would seem to be broken, in my experience. And I think it might just be helping to drive and reinforce abuse the world over. The sentiment of 'turn the other cheek' testifies to a time before assault rifles and atom bombs.

But who the fuck am I to speak for Jesus? I've never even met the guy.

Many of the best causes start out with a singular simple, clear message. Over time, however, as more and more minds are drawn to it, the forces of community and consensus can sometimes butt heads. The original message begins to wane beneath the weight of competing egos, motives, interpretations and the sheer number of *human* beings.

Thanks to the superior (debatable) intellectual capacity that the evolution of our prefrontal cortexes has afforded our dominant (laughable) species, human beings have a unique ability to co-opt, repurpose and weaponise even the most innocent ideas. From the fearless figures of feminism all the way to the overtly false idols of fascism – and every five-minute fad founder in between – everyone is *flawed* (some moustachioed painters more than others).

Broad-church terms are as they sound: broad. They can apply to everyone, almost to the effect of pointlessness. Even agnosticism, it could be argued, is a cop-out. Sometimes I tell people I'm a different star sign out of curiosity to see if they correctly misdiagnose me, because power and perception, like beauty, really are in the eye of the beholding mind. Then when I break it to them that I'm a Capricorn who doesn't buy into astrology, they usually tell me that is 'typical', and there is almost always laughter. To each their own, I say. No harm, no foul.

If anyone ever bothered to ask me directly what my politics are, rather than assume them or take Rupert Murdoch's mastheads as gospel, they'd know I'm not a diehard leftist on every issue. Or even a leftist at all, really. I'm more of a centrist if you really must box me in. And cool your jets on the Greenie slurs. (Although what is wrong with environmental conservation?) Dare I say it, every Australian should be grateful to John Howard for instituting the gun buy-back scheme following the Port Arthur massacre in 1996, if nothing else. Actually the GST, too (although John Hewson proposed that, and I often find myself agreeing with him). Yes, that's right – John Howard, and both of his George Pell–defending eyebrows.

Punk icon Johnny Ramone was a rip-snortin' hardcore right-winger who thanked George W. Bush when he was inducted into the Rock & Roll Hall of Fame in 2002, and among his top ten favourite Republicans are Ted Nugent and Sean Hannity. This isn't about right versus left, and I mean no disrespect, but those aren't even proper conservatives, Johnny!? What about Eisenhower? Or Teddy Roosevelt? For the record, I am not promoting either, I'm just trying to restore some dignity to the conservative name.

And yeah, I have a T-shirt with Johnny's face on it.

Nothing maps out neatly into pure good and pure bad. Everything is complicated and messy. There are abusive feminists, there are dirty, sick, child-molesting priests. Thanks to the inevitable flaw of their human design, institutions provide cover for human corruption. If you commit to a label or an ideology, you have to be prepared to commit to its entirety. You have to be comfortable with the fact that your faith might be someone else's fraud. That's not to say that what others do is necessarily a reflection on you – unless you're an active accomplice! – but personally I'd rather remain as independent as possible. It's not always easy; sometimes you don't even realise you've been claimed.

I understand that's why so many people cling to universally celebrated ideologies in the first place. Sometimes coincidences are too extreme to seem real. My mother, by the most impossible odds, was once sat on a plane travelling from Hobart to Sydney next to the child abuser who abused me. Thankfully, he didn't recognise her as he slapped his religious magazines down on his lap. With cold-running blood she got up and asked the flight attendants if she could move seats. There are few reasons better than the one she had.

However, to *choose* to define yourself by something external is to surrender your identity to another person's experience of that thing. Moreover, if that thing is suddenly taken away or invalidated, what then?

Hail Marys don't hide the truth. And others will define you regardless. They are always going to make different interpretations and projections; you may as well make your own. You've got one confirmed shot. Fucking go for it.

It's not that I am a noncommittal, causeless rebel, a fraud or a fake; I really just don't like being labelled. Even in advocating for survivors of child sexual abuse, I make it clear that I am an advocate of the community, not *for* the community. One in six boys and one in four girls is sexually abused before their eighteenth birthday. The crime of child abuse is as disturbingly common, cruel, indiscriminate, unjust and indeed unforgiving as life itself. No single individual could possibly be a representative for every diverse, intersectional experience.

Despite having been called divisive, I don't like polarity. Nor do I like the inevitable othering and negative identity formation produced by the isolated group mentality. In other words: I'm wary of inclusion that perpetuates or is based on exclusion – instead of substantiative, constructive, positive reinforcement. And if 'inclusion based on exclusion' isn't one of the two commandments of the Trumpian wrecking crew political model, I don't know what the rootin' tootin' heck is.

Binary thinking puts me off. All or nothing–ism of any kind erodes the middle ground, and perspective and proportion along with it. You might be beginning to think that I'm just a lousy, agnostic fence-sitter; an anti-establishment 'woke' anarchist who has no respect for the way things are and always have been. ('*How do you think you got here, you ungrateful little girl?*')

Sure, I can be aggressive and blunt. I know that. I'm a fierce anti-autocrat who sees flaws in democracy, but ultimately a pragmatist who knows that it's the best we have right now.

I do think the two-party system is royally fucked and that the political elite are beholden to corrupt forces, on all sides, universally. Politics is a dirty game played by those with little or no stake in the results.

('*What do you know about the law and politics, little girl?*')

Why are you reading my book, OLD MAN? You're right, I am certain of nothing. I am not absolutely sure about almost everything. I'm a tame punk. A contradiction in terms. A human, simply being.

A PEST.

I've been called all manner of things, from a feminist hero of the fourth wave (what are the first three waves, I have no freaking clue?) to a transgender child abuser who 'grooms children for the autogynephilic'. For all intents and purposes, I'd rather be neither. Not because I don't agree with the principles of feminism, but because I am just me. I am flawed. Both of those titles were bestowed upon me by people I've never spoken to, let alone met. And unchecked idolatry creates distance and distortion. Having heroes is okay, so long as we don't forget we're all human. It's putting people on pedestals that's the problem, for both the sender and receiver.

I spent a lot of time entertaining myself as a kid. Robin Williams was someone I connected with on a number of levels. Like me, he spent a lot of time alone growing up, was a child of divorce, and battled deep darkness. Part of me died with him on 11 August 2014. If suicide is selfish, what the hell is passing judgement on it?

He is adored by millions, if not billions, of others – for his kindness, generosity and compassion, as well as his humour. Anyone familiar with his electrifying stand-up will know that he was as savage and sour as he was sweet; a fierce – and by all accounts fair – critic of George W. Bush's 'reign of error', and bold enough to send up Prince Charles and his wife Camilla right in front of him at the future king's sixtieth birthday celebration event.

It was a condition of Robin's contract that at least ten homeless people had to be employed as crew members on every film he worked on. If you watch the special features of *Patch Adams*, you'll see footage of him playing with the real-life cancer patients who participated in the project – not for B-roll either. This is in the background of other cast members' interviews. On the flip side, he also spoke candidly about abusing cocaine and alcohol, and was married three times. I've gone through a divorce. That shit isn't easy – for either party. Neither is coming down off booze and blow if a person is already predisposed to feeling low. Robin swore like a sailor, and was anything but quiet. He was nothing short of a perfectly imperfect human.

That said, he was an actor, not an advocate for survivors of sexual abuse. He had a booming, deep voice, and forearms thick with hair. He was a man. I don't begrudge him any of that. It's just interesting to see the double standards at play when I make a clean joke that's barely subversive at all. I have often wondered if it's seen as proof of deviance or guilt; it contradicts the conventions of how an abuse survivor is allowed to conduct themselves in accordance with the 'perfect victim' narrative.

Sadly, still today, many professionals are discouraged from disclosing their trauma publicly on the grounds that it will limit their career opportunities. It's as if we are forced to choose: keep your trauma and lose everything else, or lose your trauma and keep everything else. Trauma, as we know, is non-negotiable. It also doesn't exist in a vacuum, and it isn't a black mark.

It's not just stigma and systems that silence; it's stereotypes upheld from a time gone by. They define us, confine us and consign us. I hope we can abandon these. I also hope we can abandon the idea that survivors are anything other than human beings, just like everyone else. Another fatal flaw of binary thinking is the common predicament of being damned if you do and damned if you don't. We can't please everyone, just as we can't always make everyone laugh. John Cleese told me that. He has since shown public support for J. K. Rowling's baffling anti-trans rhetoric, which I suppose proves his own point.

If we live life on other people's terms, we will inevitably be paralysed into inaction. Into silence. And we definitely won't laugh. Living on other people's terms, in silence, certainly isn't my style. Not anymore.

It's possible to be a survivor of child sexual abuse and have a sense of humour. We shouldn't be resigned to suffer all the time.

The conventions of *organised* religion, to me, have long seemed counter to the very concept of faith itself. The idea of believing in and worshipping higher, *controlling* omnipotent power/s, with all these restrictive particulars about the beliefs and how to practise them, just seems a bit paradoxical considering the limitlessness of the human imagination. I mean, honestly, a geriatric old man wearing a robe in a gilded sky mansion? The pursuit of pleasure? Seventy-two virgins? What is this, *Playboy*?

That was definitely a joke.

There is a principled and proactive side of faith that I admire. It's the reactive absolution element that I take issue with. Although well intended in theory, in practice I think it falls short. In the same way that one can be a law-abiding citizen and still be immoral. Shouldn't we be encouraging kindness for the sake of kindness, not in return for reward, or for fear of punishment? Shouldn't we be encouraging unity for the sake of unity, not in return for compliance, or for fear of rejection? And what is the point of the availability of limitless redemption that is vulnerable to repeated misuse? Where does the buck stop?

I'll tell you. That last one was not a rhetorical question. American journalist Adam Davidson, remarking on the prolific abuse history of Jeffrey Epstein, says that institutions sell 'reputation recovery' to disgraced men, and it's called 'the Halo effect'. Davidson goes on to qualify this Halo effect as a vital factor that becomes part of a perpetrator's grooming and offending arsenal. You don't need me to tell you about the cover-up culture within the Catholic Church and society at large. The community is crawling with rock spiders. They aren't cartoon monsters on the outer fringes; they're everyday citizens walking among us. The prevalence of survivors can only mean one thing: a prevalence of abusers. It's no surprise I get a lot of resistance. Child abusers are sub-creatures of shadows and silence. But I'm bold. And loud as fuck. And Mum, well, she taught me to vacuum spiders.

If only responding to actual child sex offences was that simple. The prison terms are laughable, and most laws aren't fit for purpose. What's more, it would seem almost every profession, at every level, is infected. Society by and large isn't comfortable with ugly realities. We'd much rather *tidy them up*. Even if that means sweeping the truth right under the carpet. In any event, forces rarely bend to truth; rather, they usually have little choice but to bend to power and wealth. Those who've fought a seasoned child abuser mastermind and their army of enablers will know that the impact of their wrath often outweighs the cost of legal justice. When truth, power and wealth do align, positive change is possible, but that seldom happens. That's why child abusers seek the solace of online rings, renowned institutions, and malleable systems. They almost always have allyship and resources greater than themselves – long-established public redemption being among them.

So there you have it: the buck stops with innocent lives. Real people – real children – are abused, raped and in the worst cases, murdered. Child sexual abuse is the most under-punished crime in Australia. That is a fact. Needless to say, its ripple effects are immeasurable. Enough with this near-sighted out-of-mindedness. Enough with this wiping hands clean of other people's blood on someone else's behalf. It doesn't work like that. Would you let a serial child abuser babysit your child overnight? Would you go camping alone and off the grid with a convicted axe-murderer?

It's convenient that you can't look a dead child in the face. Yet you can hear a child abuser's contrived confessions. Hallelujah, if there's a heaven up there. But unless a hard line is drawn somewhere, we will just keep going around in hellish circles here on earth. Allowing abusers to continue to operate effectively unscathed in a world they are taught can be adjusted to accommodate their needs is pointless.

Back to Nan. Nan, who sits at the opposite end of the morality spectrum, calm and peaceful in her throne-like recliner chair. The matriarchangel, surrounded by her flock of doting kin. All the more reason to divert from the devil's work. Although, she's not without sin. One time she started the giant Sunday crossword without me. I can forgive her for that. She doesn't travel very far. There are exceptions to almost every rule in my book.

And as incongruous as this sounds, in my own imperfect, evolving view, if Nan has one flaw it might just be that she is sometimes *too* forgiving.

I prefer to think of forgiveness as an inward state of being at peace with the past, as opposed to an outward practice of permissive relief of guilt. Therein lies my disconnect with organised religion and certain schools of academic thought. Yes, this thing that I think is a bit broken, is broken in the secular world too: forgiving the unforgivable.

Ideas – pondered in the private confines of a mind – are safe. They're inconsequential thoughts. But as soon as you externalise them, they become real. They become a readily available resource to be misappropriated as a defence for the indefensible. Like Nan said, be careful with your words. They can't be unsaid.

The thing is, in reality, each and every fraction of understanding that society gives to extremists is a gift they can misuse – no matter how small and seemingly insignificant. Nothing is harmless in the hands of the harmful. Every offering of forgiveness enables them, and endangers the rest of us. Every philosophical attempt to rationalise their behaviour. Every over-egged humanisation of their character. Every subversive academic paper and controversial opinion piece written by pioneers of research desperate to bring new ideas to the marketplace – if only for the sake of doing so. Sure, these pan flashes might make stimulating subject material for the dinner conversations of the insulated intellectual elites with no skin in the game. But beyond the logic vacuum of hypothetical discussion, people die. Children are abused.

There is a point to understanding the behaviour of child sex offenders and other psychopathic criminals, insofar as it informs prevention methods. Beyond that, every bit of redemptive sympathy we give them with our precious intellect comes at the expense of innocent lives. Our forgiveness is part of the abuse cycle. They take it and run. They use it to play the victim and play dumb. To deny, deflect, distract and distort the already distorted.

Call it balance, fairness, integrity, equality – call it whatever you like – devil's advocacy in this context is exactly that: advocating for the devil. The worst part about it is how the concept, ironically, *hides in plain sight*. It is so often proffered as a neutraliser. Well, it fucking isn't. It's usually a bloody time waster, in my opinion. And in case you haven't noticed, in the real world, devils do a fine job of advocating for themselves.

It's easy to be an armchair commentator. It's hard to get accurate data in this field. Resources are limited. Survivors' memories are affected by trauma, and prolonged abuse is usually remembered as a singular experience, or in the form of jagged visions, as opposed to chronological incidents, which is why my story is told the way it is. Perpetrators, on the other hand, by their very nature, are among the most sophisticated narrative manipulators. While there is no singular representation of a child sex offender, in the same way that there is no singular representation of a survivor, there are common pathological behavioural patterns presented by child abusers that can make it especially difficult to acquire honest information from them. Skilled forensic psychiatrists and undercover operatives are able to identify and decipher these patterns, even through layers of deception. However, as for confessions and descriptions of crimes, it is not typically in the interest of the guilty party to admit fault. Alternatively, it is in their interest to feign remorse, minimise responsibility, and reapportion as much blame as possible to others.

Like minds, even the rare data can be manipulated. Especially when those producing and consuming it are far removed from its source and consequences. Research can be warped to make a new argument to the detriment of humanity, under the credible guise of factual information.

From the one-time viewers of online child exploitation material who are in their early twenties, to the fifty-something 'textbook' serial psychopaths who keep folders of their students on their home computer for nearly two decades – child abusers come in all shapes and sizes and it is important to remember that there is a spectrum of classification. However, in saying that, child abuse itself is very black and white. It's the exception to my all-or-nothing rule. It is a crime against humanity. Much like the urge to kill someone, the urge to harm a child should not be tolerated under any circumstances. It is simply unforgivable. We must starve perpetrators of every possible excuse. Our main focus globally as a society should be on education and prevention rather than accepting child sexual abuse as a reality that we react and respond to.

Certainly, by far the most terrifying thing about my experience of child sexual abuse was not being aggressively penetrated on the floor by a man more than twice my size, who was older than my father, on the first day of maybe my fourth menstrual bleed ever. Nor was it being told to undress in a closet after dark in a tiny storeroom in the dead of winter, and being struck by the gut punch of adrenaline because I thought we were just going to chat. It was listening, day in, day out, to the uncut thoughts of a psychopath who was convinced he would never get caught. And then piecing together the histories of all the other survivors in the years that have followed since the day I reported him.

He knew what he was doing. And he knew that it was wrong. All of it. It was so carefully planned. It was a game to him. I still remember him laughing as he told me stories about pretending to be – in his word – 'retarded' so that he didn't have to give up his seat for a pregnant woman on a bus; about 'pissing' on his primary school classmates; about deliberately jamming the staffroom printer in the mornings before lessons started so he could watch the mayhem and then brag to his students; about feeling sorry for himself because he had to be in the same room as the sister of a student he had slept with the year before I was born; about hazing rituals where freshman boys were made to straddle memorial war cannons, naked, and then left outside overnight in the freezing cold so their penises would become stuck to them; about a man seeking revenge on a woman by digging her eyes out with a spoon. And I can still see my hands holding an envelope full of blonde hair, which the police gave me after the investigation, along with other items they'd seized from him and assumed were mine.

Scholars use untouchable high-brow social justice discourse to couch such obscene arguments as incest being a positive form of sexual gratification for people living with disability. I'm not making this up. In 2021, Ryan Thorneycroft wrote an actual paper called 'Cripping incest discourse(s)'. He did so without being an advocate for disability rights, or accountable to any organisation in the sector. Incest is among the most common forms of sexual abuse experienced by disabled people.

There are some who are radical for the sake of it, at the cost of human lives. Then there's the exclusive structure of academia itself, which pigeonholes researchers into an ever-shrinking pool of ideas. In order to write a PhD, you have to present a new hypothesis (says me, who doesn't have so much as a bachelor's degree). This forces candidates to focus on novel ideas, not necessarily important ones. Not to mention the inaccessibility and inapplicability of some experimental abstracts proposed by siloed theorists writing for their peers in papers, and not for the people they're writing about (irony, where art thou?). While there are certainly fields of study with huge tracts of arable land yet to be claimed, new is not always synonymous with good. Save your thought experiments for climate science and stem-cell research.

There are some mysteries in life that can never be answered, and they don't need to be. Others have crystal-clear answers staring us right in the fucking face. But along with the perpetual, innate needs to belong, understand and control, humans seem to have this perverse need to over-complicate things that don't need to be over-complicated. This often results in overlooking the obvious. We can't help being too smart for our own good sometimes.

There are some academics who have gone so far as to advocate for de-stigmatising – and even *decriminalising* – child abuse. Child sex offenders lick their lips at these literal Get Out of Jail Free cards. An attraction to children is not an orientation. It's a distortion that involves causing harm to innocent victims who are unable to consent.

I refuse to platform any specific child-abuse advocates because they are silly. And so are their silly ideas. To the naked eye. In the wrong hands, however, they are in fact dangerous. Such is the *emperor has no clothes* effect of the thought bubble of chronic scholarly inquisition. In this case it's all of society that's undressed, and child sex offenders are gleefully plucking off children right under our noses while we inexplicably come up with new ways to cover for them. We are the ones at a loss here, people! We're the ones being fleeced! COVER YOUR OWN ARSE! NOT THE KIDDIE FIDDLER'S! DO YOU HEAR ME?!

I'm not so naive that I don't understand that there will always be a degree of chaos and violence in this world. There can never be total order, total peace, total equality and total justice. No, I'm not a cynical defeatist either (if you think that, we definitely haven't met). Perhaps my naivety is that I am just yet to see the need for this kind of radical, intellectualised, institutional justification and forgiveness of plain and simple evil. It is extremism. It is bullshit. Extremism is not cool. Except for total, unbridled hatred of child abusers – I'll let that slide.

No doubt being surrounded by formidable women since birth is a big part of why it never occurred to me to refer to myself categorically as a feminist. Not because I'm not a feminist in principle, but because I am one innately. I have lived feminism my entire life within a tight maternal sphere, without stopping to think about it. In my personal life, women have always been in the overwhelming majority of leaders. Inclusive leaders, who are empowered and powerful without being dominant. Leaders who've always operated on the same plane as others, not above. Or so I thought.

Another factor is that, very early on, I unwittingly became a carbon copy of my father, chewing through sun-stained copies of John le Carré's espionage thrillers, listening to Ry Cooder and watching old Bertolucci and Bond films. Before I was twelve, I could recite the whole four minutes of Adrian Cronauer's first broadcast from *Good Morning, Vietnam*.

Incidentally, gender dysphoria is apparently quite a common experience for people with autism. I was eight when I declared that I was allergic to pink, insisted on wearing boys' clothes, and only ones that were oversized. There was little tiny me, in hoodies that went over my knees. I played every sport that my free time allowed and was often the only girl at boys' birthday parties all the way through primary school. I kept my long hair, though; my long blonde hair that still now grazes my tailbone. I've often wondered if it's the last part of my childhood I can't give up.

In all honesty, it is a privilege to call oneself anything at all. To take stock and sort your life out neatly in such definitive terms. To be able to go to a public hospital in your own country and pay nothing at all to be treated, even if you don't have healthcare, and not just hope for the best after waking up at four o'clock in the morning on the side of the road to the sight of two women pulling a man off you who you met briefly at a bar you'd been to with friends but couldn't remember leaving. To not be living pay cheque to pay cheque with everything you own in the back of a car, which you bought for $1500 in a car park in Glendale. To not have to wait for your mother to wake up to figure out what to do next after your partner just hit you in the head while all your family are on the other side of the world.

I have been called privileged by some seasoned journalists and commentators as if to invalidate a story they don't even know, and which they never did. By people in ivory towers of irony sitting on six-figure salaries. I recognise that I have privilege – to an extent I am sure I'm not even aware of. To now have a voice and a platform, especially as a survivor, is a very rare gift indeed. I do not take these things lightly. Many experiences of child sexual abuse remain unheard, under-represented and unjustly unresolved. First Nations people, people of colour, people living with disability, the LGBTQIA+ community, refugees, migrants, low-income earners, the homeless, ethnic minorities and other marginalised groups face even harder – if not impossible – paths to justice due to added layers of systemic disadvantage that will take generations to dismantle and rebuild. It is true that I have had many opportunities, strokes of luck and good fortune. However, it is also true that I have fought my way through a lot of hardships that not many people realised the depths and complexities of – including me, until very recently. I say this not to compare to or detract from anybody else's truth. I am simply speaking my own in full. One person's suffering does not invalidate, diminish or overshadow another's. Nor does their success. Progress is not a deficit model. To hell with this winners-and-losers shit.

The media detests nuance. You're either rich or you're poor. An idiot or an expert. Left or right. And Darwin forbid you try to straddle a debate, lest both sides point the finger at you for not being one of them.

Truly, honestly, for many years I was just surviving. I was clawing my way from one moment to another. I have no greater academic qualifications than two associate degrees from a US community college – don't be fooled by my vocabulary. I'm a kid on a looping rollercoaster that you're watching from the side. You see me through a filter of your own design. What I know, I know reasonably well, and what I don't, I don't. And I'm proud of that: my rough edges, my knuckle tattoos, and my leopard-print furry dice wrapped around the rearview of my 1995 Buick Regal bomb, swaying with every swerve through peak hour on the 405 South.

'Private school' is not the same thing in Tasmania as it is in, say, Sydney's upper echelons. Still, to have such an experience is one I am grateful for in some ways. The most important takeaway I have from my time in private institutions, though, is that being a good student is nowhere near as important as being a good person. Upholding traditions might teach you the values of discipline and respect, but if those traditions include putting the institution ahead of individuals, its policies before its people, we must ask ourselves if they are really worth upholding. You are not your uniform. You are not where you went to school, your grades or the subjects you chose to study. You are not your profession. Who gives a shit? I got a lot more out of head-banging to Black Sabbath B-sides, drawing freely in the art room at lunchtime in Year 12 with my friends Ben and David, and watching Jan Švankmajer stop-motion animations with our teacher Wayne than I did getting pumped full of wet-lettuce we're-better-than-you workshops.

That we should all be treated fairly, regardless of background, has always been fundamental in my mind. Equity is preferable to equality, and the sheer force of relativity renders the latter nearly impossible in any event. In accordance with the limitless variance in individual perception, there is no way that eight billion people are ever going to see eye to eye. The spectrum of human experience remains as imbalanced as it is vast. And, ultimately, equity and equality will always be pipe dreams so long as we fawn over fashion moguls and celebrity apprentices.

It wasn't until I was in school and learned the horrors of history that I had a barometer for darkness, that put my own private world in relation to the outside one. And it just so happened that it was in school that these two worlds collided. I was certainly no stranger to pain and by no means sheltered, but nothing comes close to the way the earth shatters when you lose your innocence. Fuck virginity – I don't mean that. (Fuck virginity; get it?) The way in which it happened, sure. We'll get to that later, along with the premature loss of womanhood. I'm referring to the jarring, ice-cold, organ-piercing moment when your whole being realises that this 'evil' thing you've read about in books and seen in films isn't just a fiction, but is standing right in front of you, blocking the doorway, asking you to take off your clothes, holding a yellow piece of paper with the words 'yes' and 'no' written on it.

People do bad things. They make mistakes. All of us do. I have run a few red lights in my time. I am a serial jaywalker. (Hot tip, Australians, if a cop in the States pulls you aside for crossing the road on foot when you shouldn't, just tell them we don't even have traffic lights back home yet. I learnt that from my friend Gary. Nice, Gary.)

Full-blooded, undiluted evil, though, is not something you see every day. You'll know it if and when you do, because you can't *un*see it. It's in another league of hauntingly sadistic cruelty thankfully reserved for a very rare subset of humanity. Not that humanity enters into it.

I can't overstate what it took to play for him. To go head-to-head with a psychopath at fifteen. To be a lone pawn on his full chessboard. I have been told I am not a bad actor. Well, that was by far the hardest performance of my life and it was to an audience of one. There is no need to exaggerate any detail of what happened. In its raw state it was pure terror.

In the years that followed, my gratitude has only increased with age: in some ways, I am thankful I was so naive when it happened. Faces bandmates Ronnie Wood and Ronnie Lane wrote a great line in a frequently covered song called 'Ooh La La' about wishing they knew then what they know now. Well, I don't. When I told my ex-husband about the time this man asked me if I knew where my clitoris was and then laughed when I said I didn't, my ex went to the bathroom to vomit. Rewatching those days through an adult's eyes made me realise what it means to be naive. Rewatching those days through an adult's eyes made me realise what it means to be free.

That's not to say I'm now jaded or that the impact of my family's strong maternal influence has been dulled – quite the opposite – but there are some truths that you can only see in the dark.

Like the hereditary infection of *internalised* misogyny. Of *subconscious* subservience. Of preconditioned passivity to the pervasive patriarchal paternalism that reigns supreme even in our most liberal democracies. Sadly, most of the female leaders in my life were never actually elected as such. So while they are symbols of strength and hope, they can't really be cited as symbols of change. Truth is that they are leaders by default, and many of them bent and continue to bend to the will of men. Still *afraid* of men; still desperate for their approval. Much as I was, without being aware, until it was too late.

It is therefore likely that my not calling myself a feminist had as much to do with an underlying fear of rejection as it did with inherently believing in inclusivity and equity. I wonder if I am still subconsciously living in pursuit of male validation. I wonder if there is an unconscious bias that I can never reconcile because it's so deeply rooted in pain. There is still dormant trauma I am yet to dislodge from my cells. How can I know for certain these are not factors that still influence my behaviour and decisions?

I haven't had babies yet. Paper qualifications, as I've said, are no measure of worth or life experience, but I know I'm not very well educated in the traditional, institutional, academic sense. I don't always know the correct language to use when talking about a lot of subjects. I can't quote from textbooks. Much of what I know I have learned simply through living. It's all been less than three decades.

In the face of fear, human beings are no different from any other species. Our prefrontal cortexes that house logic are overtaken by our emotions. We are reduced to the capacity of our amygdala or 'animal brain' as we are driven by the instinctive impulse to avoid pain at all costs. Most of us have heard of the fight, flight and freeze responses to perceived threat. There is a fourth response, but it rarely finds its way into everyday conversation. One reason is that it is more nuanced. Another is that it is more confronting and confusing. It has nothing to do with it being uncommon. It is perhaps the most common of them all.

'Fawning' is a maladaptive coping strategy often seen in children who've been abused or neglected by a non-nurturing caregiver. If a child doesn't attach to its caregiver, or have its needs met, it will most likely respond by suppressing its needs and identity to appease the caregiver's needs instead. For obvious reasons, a child is rarely able to escape abusive circumstances. It is forced to do whatever it can just to survive, while avoiding conflict and minimising pain. It will fawn in the vain hope that, by showing love, it will receive it in return. Moreover, as human beings, our tendency is towards the forgiving – sometimes to our own detriment.

Fawning is also known as 'people pleasing'. Although helpful in simplifying it, this language is problematic because it makes it sound superficial. Fawning is a painfully tragic, universal phenomenon. Have you ever seen a puppy desperately vying for the attention and approval of an older, unfamiliar, larger, intimidating dog? This is an example of a scared animal surrendering for connection and closeness.

How about the demeaning stereotype of women who 'love' men who treat them badly? Not only is this offensive, it disregards the reality that many people – not just women – unconsciously respond to abuse by being submissive to protect themselves. Bullshit like this makes a mockery of women, of domestic violence, and of the people who believe in it.

Fawning can also be used to explain the tired trope of corporate hierarchies wherein blatant bully bosses are worshipped by their subordinates. Not because they're liked, but because fear induces *fawning*, which in this example likely translates to feelings of 'walking on eggshells', and the compelling need to impress and appease those who wield superior power and authority.

Fawning is one of our most basic safeguards. We've all had the perfect speech worked out in the shower, yet been inexplicably disarmed in the presence of power.

We are also indoctrinated to have faith in institutions like schools, banks, churches and governing bodies supposedly designed to unite and protect us; whenever they abuse us we find it very difficult to believe. Even in the face of physical evidence so obvious that everyone cannot help but see it, as plain as day, we're at pains to abandon our hardwired, core beliefs. Even *during* abuse, we choose not to believe it.

Instead, we *fawn*.

Why? Because abuse – whether at the hands of an individual or an organisation – is something none of us want to be our reality. Denial comes from a very honourable, human place. It's the final frontier of our trauma-driven desperation to preserve our childhood innocence in the face of *fear*. It is the final frontier of our trauma-driven desperation to preserve our belief that nobody would want to hurt us, and that we are worthy of love.

We downplay and learn helpless tolerance of abuse not because we like it, but because the narrative that someone could be so cruel as to intentionally hurt and abandon us is much harder to reconcile than the alternative. In the face of fear, we are so often shocked into a state of childlike denial. We are at the mercy of our unconscious defences, which, although protective in the short term, can prove devastating in the long term.

And power-abusers are shielded by this. Worse, they thrive on it. They're at an advantage when we're left collectively traumatised, whether we're fighting among ourselves, fleeing from the scene, frozen and helpless, or *fawning* over them despite their wrongdoings. In all four cases, the truth is irrelevant, because logic is no longer in play; *trauma* is. In all four cases, we're distracted. Our attention is diverted away from them, while we are reduced to our survival instincts, and fear reigns supreme. Power-abusers weaponise our vulnerabilities and our tendency *to forgive.*

I was fawning from a very young age. I come from a family of fawners who have had to find their way through the flames of some of the worst kinds of hell imaginable. It's in our blood to not bite back at the hands who are feeding us, even if they are also mistreating us. 'The disease to please,' my mother calls it. The odds of me inheriting it either through DNA or experience were fixed. Almost everywhere I turned, I was being burned.

And I can't stand the feeling of letting anyone down. When you have no solid base, rejection is a truly dark place. Worst of all is being cast out by your own.

The person who emotionally abused me throughout my childhood was a woman. When I got my first proper boyfriend after the abuse, I was seventeen and he was twenty-three.

'Isn't he a bit young for you?' she said.

There was another time she cornered me without warning when I was fourteen, right before I went into hospital with anorexia: 'You love it, you love the attention of being thin.'

I didn't say anything. I just stood there. Jealousy is stranger than fiction. I was down to about forty kilograms and chronically depressed. The whole reason I struggled with food was because I was so destabilised. One of my classmates was caught mocking me after a Biology lesson where we'd been taught about how malnourished animals grow downy fur on them to keep warm. Rarely in life are bullies caught in the act but the Head of Middle School just happened to be standing right behind her.

One of the most bizarre castings of me – the tomboy whose best friend is a man, whose closest friendships remain with men, who advocates for child sexual abuse survivors, many of whom are men – is that I am somehow a man-hater? Sexual assault experienced above the age of eighteen is a much more gendered issue; child abuse is not. One in six boys and one in four girls, as I've mentioned. The statistic is horrific. When I started detailing my story to the media on my terms for the first time back in 2017, I was put in touch with another survivor. I had never even heard of 'grooming' before. I was 22. Seven years it took me to even learn the word. It was a man, not a woman – a middle-aged, burly man – who after seven years of isolation made me feel like I wasn't alone. He was still in Tasmania, but I would stay up until 3 am with my knees tucked into my chest on my tiny concrete balcony talking on the phone, smoking Marlboro Lights, equally saddened and soothed by the sound of someone sharing a past that was so much like my own.

I remember a conversation I had with my paternal nan when I was nineteen and had found myself a job working at an art store in Los Feliz, just east of Hollywood. Good old Nan. My pokie-playing, lifetime-Liberal-voting, ball-busting nan, who sent me an email after a quick trip home to say she was glad I made it back to LA without being 'blown up'. I was telling her about getting a side gig illustrating for my friend's weekly column in a pop culture magazine called *Galore*. After five seconds of soul-crushing radio silence she said, 'Aw, Grace, you're not a feminist now, are you?'

The woman who nominated me for Australian of the Year has publicly shamed me too. After five years of friendship, after I had donated large sums of money and done all I could. I know I've made mistakes, and will no doubt make more. There's a lot of complicated context and I have received an apology. But I would be lying if I said that being torn down in the open by an ally didn't have a profound impact on me. After a year of living my already tumultuous life in a way that was suddenly and unexpectedly heightened beyond my control, it capped off a lifelong feeling like I was always paying rent but had no place to go.

If you complain, you're told you're ungrateful. If you stay silent, you're shamed for not speaking up. Well, I spoke up, and it helped put a child abuser in prison. Twice. But yeah, I still sometimes listen to Eminem.

It doesn't matter what you call yourself. It matters what you do. What matters is what you think of you. Stop telling me what you think I am. I am just the way I am.

Chapter 4

The Cliff's Edge

My Own Myopia

Until I was eight, I wore glasses. I'm terribly farsighted, which is uncommon. Without correction, everything looks blurry up close, but clear from far away. Funny that; it's always been the opposite in real life. I'm a bigger-picture, greater-good kind of person philosophically, with an eye for detail literally.

When you stop moving, like I finally did not long ago, and play back all your life's raw, unfiltered rushes – without being a player in someone else's distorted narrative, improvising your way from scene to scene – everything starts to crystallise. You can begin to see what fits, what doesn't, what is missing, and where to go next. You can also retrace your steps, all the way back to the start.

While replaying and reliving trauma is a trauma in and of itself, it is also inevitable, and necessary in order to see clearly and move forward. There is light to be found in the process of reflection. After all, that's how light travels.

The best way to get perspective is to distance yourself from yourself; to be an observer, rather than a participant, in your own life. Total objectivity is, of course, impossible. We will always be cursed by the unconscious bias of our subjective survival instincts, and subliminal external influences. The problem is that nothing is a shock to you when everything is shocking. You can't feel the temperature of the water you're swimming in – the boiling water.

My brain is a thoroughfare for the competing thoughts and emotions of others, who perhaps don't realise theirs aren't the only ones being thrust at me, on top of my own coalescing ones. Perhaps as a product of autistic neurodivergence, I tend to think and feel everything intensely but nonspecifically all at once, before suddenly, sharply, it all comes together. Without knowing how, an explanation distills itself in an expedited process of compartmentalisation. Once I've arrived there, I can walk back through the piercing logic, but I can't understand how I got there so quickly through what was previously a mess of distressing, indistinguishable emotions. This is not for lack of trying, nor for lack of comprehension skills; I seem to be able to analyse other people's predicaments with ease.

Acclaimed autism activist and author of *Safety Skills for Asperger Women* and *Pretending to be Normal* Dr Liane Holliday Willey was once asked, 'How can you be so smart and so stupid at the same time?' This about sums up my own bafflingly contradictory brain, which is undoubtedly alienating to others. Other disability advocates often remark on the polarised reactions to certain autistic behaviours, citing this among a long list of reasons for the need for increased awareness and education. I can understand how it would be hard to sympathise with someone who appears to be put together, but in reality has incredibly large, debilitating gaps.

Some autistic traits are mistaken as narcissism, for example, such as in those of us who become intensely fascinated by a certain subject matter and can't stop talking about it. Like the migration habits of European and African swallows. Although I present a tough exterior, my brain is always working overtime. When I am uncomfortable, I revert to mimicry. There are people who like me because I reflect them to themselves. Equally, there are people who don't like me because I reflect them to themselves. That's a symptom of autism, not inauthenticity. It is a symptom of fawning; a symptom of fear. I said before that I played my hardest role to an audience of one. I earned stripes in hell, through a trial by fire.

I have a photographic memory. I can remember random dates out of thin air. I do sums with licence plates and house numbers without even trying. But no matter how many times people tell me to stop playing with my hair, clicking my tongue, rearranging items by colour, or that the older man I'm talking to is not my friend – I can't seem to understand it at the time. And believe me when I say that this is as frustrating to me as I'm sure it is to you. My sudden rushes of emotion are jumbled by an inbuilt processing delay; a mix of wiring and a default for fawning that I didn't know I was born with.

My father is a lot like me, although arguably even more blunt (if that is possible). The apple didn't fall far from the metal pole. Although Dad and I are both more like jellybeans, with soft centres, sweet hearts and a sense of humour that is sometimes black. Michael Tame speaks fluent banter. If you watch us in conversation, it's a symphony of synchronicity. If you see us fight, we're each other's mirror. There's no point in asking who's the chicken and who's the egg if both parties will never yield.

Dad presents as being so charismatic and incisive, with a style of his own that he wears with confidence. From the outside you'd assume there's no deep trauma behind him, that he is invincible and invulnerable, the way he talks with such conviction. Then again, when you assume, you make an ass out of you. And me.

The Sound of Silence

Unlike the grey concepts of 'good' and 'bad', which are so subjective that in certain cases they're interchangeable, when I learned about the concept of 'child grooming' it fell so organically into place.

In 1964 – the same year my mother was born – legendary folk rock duo Simon and Garfunkel released 'The Sound of Silence', a sorrowful, soul-stirring classic that is perhaps best known as the background track to the opening scene of *The Graduate*. We hear it begin as a fresh-faced and unassuming Benjamin Braddock, played by a fittingly fresh-faced and unassuming Dustin Hoffman, boards an airport escalator headed straight for the projected fantasies of completely cooked culture. A culture that glorifies sexual initiation between a young person and an older one, and casts the villain as a predatory female seductress. I know, I know; it's just a film. It's a good one, too. And I like it, I appreciate the art of it, don't get me wrong. I even dyed my hair like Anne Bancroft once, with platinum streaks to offset a brunette bob.

Apparently Paul Simon wrote the 'The Sound of Silence' in his bathtub, about our inability as human beings to communicate properly, which in turn has made us unable to love and understand each other. It was as hauntingly relevant in the 60s as it is today. With perfect irony, its lyrics probe the pillars of sociopolitical inaction and tokenism. But it's not the song's eternally profound poetic prose, or even its audible eeriness, that haunts me.

It's that every time I hear it, the present gets chewed up. The cold walls of a small, musty room close in on me. There's a photograph of a man in a dog collar with a crooked smile to my left. The darkness of the song is his hollow laughter. He is sitting right in front of me. 'The Sound of Silence' was a tool of control used by my abuser, who was almost always playing it in his office throughout the grooming and offending. Yes, you bet, he made me watch *The Graduate*.

He told me he wanted to take my virginity because he just couldn't bear the thought of someone else having their way with poor little me in the back of a truck somewhere. As if that was worse than on an old grey carpet, in my school uniform, in a building built before that Mike Nichols film was even made. I can still see my own blood, and the wooden statue of Jesus on the shelf above my head – who I'm sure loves me more than I know. Whoa, whoa, whoa.

'I'll lose my job if anyone hears about this, and you wouldn't want that, would you?' Abusers use veiled threats and intimidation to scare you into keeping their secrets.

Thus it was both literally and figuratively 'The Sound of

Silence' that underscored my experience of grooming and child sexual abuse.

The Six Phases of Grooming, coined by Dr Elizabeth L. Jeglic, are the calculated stages of psychological manipulation that perpetrators undertake in order to prepare an environment for child sexual abuse. Child abusers don't just groom their child targets; they groom everyone to create an entire ecosystem of abuse that allows them to operate unchallenged in plain sight. If ever there was a teachable example of someone who executed every grooming phase flawlessly, it would be the man who abused me. And if the shoe fits – he was a teacher. And well qualified to boot.

Below is a list of the phases – followed by explanations – which I have adapted from Dr Jeglic's work:

1. *Identifying a vulnerable target:* by virtue of their age, all children are vulnerable. Perpetrators often prey on children with added vulnerabilities including: existing trauma, mental illness, family instability, disability and/or social insecurities. (Ding ding ding!!! My buzzer is broken.)
2. *Gaining trust:* early on, perpetrators position themselves as trustworthy. They act as a confidante for children to disclose private details that will later be weaponised against them. Perpetrators do this by sharing their own anecdotes – real or fabricated – to encourage conversational reciprocity. Meanwhile, the child unconsciously becomes attached to their abuser.

3. *Filling a need:* to strengthen their hold, perpetrators look for gaps in their target's existing, possibly weakened support network. They will then assume the role that fills that gap, giving them added appeal among the child's authority figures.
4. *Isolating:* by undermining their target's true support network and/or already tenuous relationships, perpetrators insidiously, disingenuously, make themselves the sole source of comfort and positive reinforcement. They do this by discouraging the child from contacting others, fuelling conflict, casting aspersions, and by requesting that the child spend more time with them.
5. *Sexualising:* stealthily, perpetrators will erode their target's boundaries and gradually sexualise the 'relationship' without their victim even realising it. No child can consent. Their brains are not fully developed. As such, they have no autonomy. Nor do they intellectually have a complete concept of the destabilising physiological changes they are undergoing (despite how much they tell you they think they know at the time – guilty as charged, Your Honour). Therefore, the fact that child abusers knowingly manipulate a child's unconscious hormonal volatility and naivety for their own sexual gratification is especially sickening. Boys and girls the world over have reported the shame and anguish over their inexplicable responses to it, ranging from arousal, reciprocation and instigation all the way to perceived real love for people they later realised as adults were textbook child sex offenders. By modelling crude language and discreetly erotic behaviours, in addition

to sharing suggestive anecdotes, pop culture and more, perpetrators coercively convince children that they are consenting to – or worse, inviting – an equal sexual relationship.

6. *Maintaining control:* by striking a perfect balance between causing pain and providing relief from it, perpetrators keep their child victims entrapped and exhausted by confusion, self-doubt and fear. They are at once the poison and the antidote; the villain and the saviour. The harm child abusers inflict on their child victims may take the form of increasingly underhanded comments, followed by increasingly sexualised displays of affection. This creates a dynamic wherein the latter becomes physically and psychologically dependent on the former. Once a child has been isolated, their self-esteem is dependent on and dictated by their abuser.

Needless to say, experiencing this complex abuse mechanism during one's formative years is particularly damaging. All trauma permanently alters the brain's neural pathways. By taking a closer look at the direct effect of grooming on a child's reward triggers, we see that it is the ultimate betrayal.

During the grooming and offending, child victims seek most of their validation from their abusers. This is because they have been groomed into isolation and dependence. Abusers in turn take advantage of their vulnerability and trust by exploiting their reliance to make sexual advances, instead of soothing them platonically. This conditions children to associate 'sex' with approval, comfort and self-worth. Perpetrators thereby maintain control long after they are in the picture.

It is common for survivors of child sexual abuse, perversely, to unconsciously seek sexual validation as a coping mechanism because it is what they think they know is supposed to make the hurt stop. Perpetrators and their apologists often frame this behaviour as promiscuity, and wilfully misrepresent other maladaptive strategies in order to discredit their victims and their narratives.

When survivors speak of betrayal, they are not just speaking about the betrayal of their perpetrators; they are speaking of the betrayal of their own conditioned bodies and terrorised minds. To the boys who got erections, to the girls who walked over and sat in the laps of their abusers: it's not your fault. I understand.

A key component of every grooming phase is 'gaslighting'. Gaslighting is an invisible, untraceable form of psychological violence designed to make victims question their own beliefs and behaviour. Perpetrators rarely cease actively menacing their targets even after the physical offending itself stops. Using persistent veiled threats, intimidation and harassment, many offenders will do their best to occupy the minds of their victims; to possess them, forever. It sounds scary, and it is when you are subjected to this kind of obsessive, relentless evil. But think about it like this as well: if it's true that each of us only gets one confirmed human earth-side existence, spending it all day torturing people is pretty fucking sad. Crochet. Scrapbook. Put a knife in a plugged-in toaster. Just spitballing here.

'Give me a girl at an impressionable age and she is mine for life,' is the last line of a 1969 (don't) film my abuser also made me watch. *The Prime of Miss Jean Brodie* it's called, starring

Maggie Smith, and it follows the arc of a schoolteacher in an institution where one of the male staff members has a sexual 'relationship' with a student that is portrayed as being romantic. Another good one, knucklehead.

Mainstream culture has a lot to answer for in the ongoing sexualisation of underage girls (and boys). Nabokov (a man) wrote *Lolita* from the perspective of Humbert Humbert (a man) fantasising about a twelve-year-old girl. It's been adapted for the screen twice; first by Stanley Kubrick (a man) in 1962, then again in 1997 by Adrian Lyne (A MAN). Where is Lolita's right of reply? I'll wait.

Legally, a person isn't an adult until the age of eighteen.

Biologically, the human brain doesn't finish forming until early to mid-twenties, even longer for some. This is what science shows.

And at the end of the day, a seventeen-year-old has more in common with an infant than they do an adult. They have memories of living at twelve, but they have not had one moment's experience of life with a fully developed brain, let alone any time to reflect on it.

It doesn't matter how they *look* to you. It doesn't matter how they *act* to you. A child's life is not yours to decide. It is not yours to live.

I said earlier that the devil is in the details. I mean this in several ways. Firstly, in the sense that it is vital to pay close attention to survivors' stories. If only so that 'The Sound of Silence' was not written in vain, I'm asking now that you hear my words. Where I am about to go might cost me dearly. But it is a price I am willing to pay if it means saving lives; if it means that others do not have to retrace their steps to find their way to where I am now. Only through learning from survivors' lived experience will we break the cycle of abuse.

Devils are also fuelled by the semantic, petty, deliberately cyclical defences made by their apologists and sympathisers.

When the outcomes are the rape, violence towards and death of children, it doesn't matter which angle you're viewing them from. It doesn't matter whether or not you are near or farsighted; whether your glasses are on or off. The privilege of semantics is one only afforded to the living.

I'll say it again: nothing is harmless in the hands of the harmful.

And so I return to the vision that was planted in my brain, that for so long has remained within the sound of silence. Until now.

Allow me to zoom out; to retrace my steps. To a time before I could walk. To a time before I was born, but to one that has informed and shaped my entire life.

The Devil in Disguise

The gaping hole in the picture that you might have noticed is less of a hole than a sharp drop. Literally, Cliff. That's his name – Cliff Wright. Mum's dad.

Reportedly, our grandfather was barely around even before he was actually gone. I believe it. I didn't meet him until I was three. He called Mum after I was born and said he had a gift for me but never showed up.

Mum tells of the hours she and her sisters spent sitting in his car outside the pub while he drank with his mates. Jenny reflects on how she would see him give so much attention to boys who were good at sport, but not her, even though she was a brilliant athlete who could outrun everyone. They'd all try their best to please him, but it would never be enough. That would seem to be a theme.

By the time Nan caught Cliff cheating in 1975, he'd already had another two daughters with his soon-to-be next wife, Maxine. Mum was about nine. Nan told me how it unfolded over the phone.

Before I go on, it must be said that the only thing our family wants is peace. Each of us has found that, in our own way. In our own Wright.

When my mum and her sisters were growing up, their parents owned a small shack at Park Beach, about a 40-minute drive east from their house in Milford Street, Lindisfarne, on Hobart's Eastern Shore. One night, their father went to stay at the shack. He said he needed a break, somewhere quiet. Given his renowned absence, when Nan got to this point in the story, I couldn't help but ask her what exactly he was taking a break from. She just laughed with me. Call me biased, but Nan is far too kind. I have seen her sit next to my grandfather at family Christmases. Voluntarily too.

'You don't believe him, do you?' Shelley asked Nan after Cliff left for Park Beach. Neither of them did, so they hopped in Nanny Beulah's red Mini Minor and headed to find the truth. They got it. All of it: Cliff, Maxine, and confirmation of two children that they'd had together, Amber and baby Jacqui – although they weren't there with them that night.

The girls had, in fact, already met their eldest half-sister by this stage; they just didn't know who she was. Even while Nan was at the house, Cliff used to bring Amber to Milford

Street before anyone was aware of what was going on. The girls would babysit her.

When the judge pointed out Nan's right to both their properties during the divorce proceedings, she politely declined. She gave Cliff the Park Beach shack because she was worried he and his new young family wouldn't have anywhere to live. She took mercy on them. She just wanted peace. And yet, according to Mum, it was always Cliff – the constant Catholic – who was asking the girls if they were good and going to church.

'He has an eye for the ladies,' Mum joked when I called her to clarify the details. 'You could say something like, "He had another four daughters after us . . . *that we know of*."' Amber and Jacqui were followed by Olivia and Tessa.

In 2009, Cliff left Maxine for their neighbour's daughter, Elizabeth, who is the same age as his daughter Wendy. There were allegedly others in between.

None of us will forget the night Maxine found out. I can only imagine what it must have been like for her. After all those decades of loyalty to someone, only to watch them dispose of it like it meant nothing.

It coincided with my stepfather's Dracula-themed fiftieth birthday party, held at his and Mum's old gothic sandstone house in Bellerive. We were all dressed up – fake fangs and all – when Shelley rang from work to say that someone needed to go and help Cliff because Maxine and Jacqui had both lost it and the police had been called to the scene.

Jenny couldn't go because she was at work. Mum refused on the grounds that he'd made his bed, but also because she was in a Morticia Addams costume. Wendy, who'd come as a witch, wouldn't go either. And Denise, whose choice of curly black wig made her look more Greek than vampiric, was even less inclined because she feared it might appear as though she was impersonating Jacqui – who has dark ringlets. In the end Shelley took the liberty of arranging for her partner, Greg, to pick up Cliff and bring him to join us. Very little was said when he suddenly arrived. He's lucky that there are some who feel sorry for him, who fawn and forgive at their own expense. He's lucky that to fit in with a band of bloodsuckers he didn't really need a costume that night.

I was fourteen then. Fourteen, with my mother's 'disease to please' – another condition I told my Maths teacher about seven months later.

Too Close to Home

The last time I saw my grandfather was at my aunt Sue's funeral. He asked me what my name was, but not before telling me he thought I was a pretty girl.

And by only writing the things I have written, I have honestly been quite kind in the scheme of things – a scheme of things that aren't all that grand. I never witnessed the worst of it.

I never heard him call my grandmother names.

I never saw Maxine give birth to her first child alone at nineteen. I never saw her walk down the cobblestone path to the hospital after my grandfather dropped her off outside. She had to be hidden her entire pregnancy. Her parents didn't know their granddaughter existed until six months after she was born. My aunt Olivia, the second youngest of all nine, told me that when Maxine fell pregnant at eighteen, Cliff rented a small flat in Battery Point, and she would only go out at night to get groceries. Today, Battery Point is one of Hobart's most affluent suburbs. In the 1970s, however, it was a working-class industrial area, and a favoured drinking domain of all the local sailors and fishermen who docked nearby. Walking its craggy streets alone as a young woman wasn't an option back then.

After the baby was born, he would visit her every couple of days to bring her food. But she grew tired of being on her own, trying to look after a newborn alone. So after six months, she put herself on a bus back home to her parents' house.

My mum says she was playing by the side of her parents' bed one morning when she was four. Her dad was awake but hadn't got up yet. 'Can I just call you Maxine?' he apparently said.

I'm reminded of one time at my high school, when Mr Bester – yes, that's his name – and I were leaving campus late at night on a weekend. Needless to say, we should not have been there. What exactly we had been doing that night I am not sure. All of the incidents lump together like claggy vomit in my throat. There are too many for me to tease apart in order; trauma doesn't work like that. But each of them stands out distinctly, and the moment he told me to pretend to be his daughter if anyone saw us leaving together is like an acid burn in my brain.

Just like when my cousin Griffin was on a school trip and saw Cliff out in public with Elizabeth, before Maxine had found out about his affair with her. He told Griffin that Elizabeth was his cousin.

Life or Death

Maxine is now seventy years old, and she has only been with one man her whole life. She idolised my grandfather.

There's plenty more that I could add, details or moments that some of my aunts might say I have missed out. My words do not invalidate their truth, but rather honour a story that should be told.

The bittersweetness of realisation is impossible to describe. How can a child understand something they can't even see, let alone explain it to someone else, if they don't have the knowledge? Or even the words? If they are kept in the darkness?

The majority of us have both the vocabulary to communicate exactly what happened should we experience a violent crime, and the knowledge of how to seek appropriate help. If you get stabbed, for example, even should language fail you in a state of shock, you can point to the wound. Blood speaks for itself. Few people would deny the horror of such an obvious attack. The psychological trauma of child sexual abuse is very different.

It is often said that seeing is believing. When Maxine watched an interview of me on television describing my experience of grooming on my own terms, under my own name, for the first time, she turned to Olivia and said, 'Your father groomed me.'

Maxine was sixteen when she and Cliff met. He was 35. She was working as a checkout clerk at a department store, and came from a background of poverty and violence. There was some contention for a while over whether or not she might have been seventeen, but her birth certificate has proved otherwise. There were also some suggestions that my grandfather thought she was seventeen, and that so did Maxine, as if that changes what he did to her, to my nan, to his daughters and to everyone else.

I'll just keep pointing out that the real cost was more than a split hair. It was a fragmented family of his own making. It was a hell we all inherited to some degree, but not one we all survived.

We have been through a lot; there is not really any other way I can put it. And there is so much love, so much happiness, so much strength, and so much fight in all of us. To deny all of this other stuff would be a lie.

As a child I didn't stop to think about how messed up all of this was because Mum shielded me from some of it. For a long time she didn't speak to her father, and I don't remember seeing him much except for at Christmases. But really, we have all always been swimming in this water. I have some fond memories of Maxine and her daughter Jacqui, whose son Clifton is around my age. But when I was younger, I was always shuffling around from place to place, so I wasn't aware of anything being out of place – except me.

Olivia had this to say about Maxine:

'The sad thing is, my mum was used to being treated poorly because of her upbringing. But I can tell you one thing. My mother is so strong and hardworking. You know, I don't think she thinks she was a victim. In fact, somehow I believe she still loves my dad. I actually dread telling her when he passes.'

Three of Maxine's grandchildren are dead.

My grandfather will die soon, too, and when he does I will not go to his funeral.

I say that not out of spite, or bitterness. I say that knowing that even though blood is thicker than water, amid all the broken bonds, the bullshit and the barefaced lies of life, the one moral high ground I will take is that I will not forgive people who do the things he has done. For the love of my grandmother, his second wife, my mother, all of his children, grandchildren and great-grandchildren. For the values of truth. I will not.

Call me callous, call me cold, call me whatever the fuck you like.

Before I was born, when she was in her early twenties, my mum was part of a volunteer debating program at Risdon Prison to build her confidence in public speaking. Cliff worked there. One night he, Mum and some of the prisoners were chatting in the cafeteria. After Mum left, one of the prisoners said he fancied her. He was a convicted murderer. Cliff then gave him Mum's home phone number and address.

Her own father.

Olivia's daughter, Taylor, is incredibly bright. 'It's a pity she's the wrong gender,' he said, right in front of her.

His granddaughter.

My stepfather, Ron, is the fairest man I know, and he is not quick to anger. He lost his temper at my grandfather once because he kept coming over to ours unannounced. But when Ron went over to apologise – not out of necessity, but thinking it was in Mum's best interest – Cliff responded by saying that Ron must have residual anger because of his German heritage, given that they lost the war. Only, Ron's mother grew up in Romania. She was a child of war, a refugee no less, who was displaced and separated from her parents for two years because her family were forced to leave their home because they were German. Cliff had walked right into that one, but Ron was a person of dignity who was there to defend his wife.

What Ron then said to my grandfather is what should have been said to him years ago. Apparently, Cliff had the front to say that Maxine wouldn't let him see my mum and her full sisters, and that she even threatened his life. As if after all this time it was him who was the victim in this tale. As if he were some kept man who did not have the capacity to think for himself. As if he was not the same man who would hold you up for hours – or cut you down – with the words he learned from his days spent in university halls, where none of his wives ever got to go, and only one of his nine daughters ever completed a degree.

'So what if *you* lose *your* life?' Ron said. 'That's a risk you take for your children.'

If society seriously wants to make progress, hard lines must be drawn. Ones that can't be walked over like abusers try to walk over all of us.

Peace is not freedom from pain; it is the acceptance of it. If you make friends with pain, you can be at peace with it. It is not your enemy. Silence is.

I dare to disturb the sound of silence. Are you listening?

Turn that fucking song off.

You have to get rid of something old in order to create something new.

Many things can be true at once. I am in so much pain right now, yet I am hopeful. I am at peace not knowing what is coming next. I am not restless in my unrest. I am still, metaphorically, just clicking in my bassinet.

Chapter 5

Chalk and Cheese and Charcoal

None of These is Like the Other

Standing side by side, my dad, Michael Tame – born January 1956 – and his younger brother Rick (April 1957) could not appear to be less alike. While Dad dresses himself almost exclusively in linen shirts and Italian leather shoes, you'd be hard-pressed to catch Rick in anything other than a flannelette shirt, ripped jeans and Blunnies.

Not long before I started writing this book, Dad came over to visit me at 11 am on a Tuesday wearing a waistcoat and monk-strap shoes on his way to run errands. Before noon. On a Tuesday. It's worth adding that he's retired. From teaching at a public high school in Tasmania. Not from investment banking in Luxembourg. The man has been known to hold socks – SOCKS – of the same colour underneath a lamp to select the right variance in shade. Lest he wear the wrong ones and risk the sudden collapse of civilisation as we know it. All hail the Sultan of Suede; the Conquistador of Cashmere. He's like a (much) older male version of me with better taste, a bigger nose and no hair. Not many people know the story behind the myth of Michael, not even him.

Rick, on the other hand, has a water delivery business and among his most prized possessions would undoubtedly be his son, his angel of a partner, Sue, a digger, a cement mixer and his private, permanent patch of outback paradise far removed from the fickle world of fashion. He's a man of life's simplest, purest pleasures, at home in nature. In silence. His son, my cousin Jarrod, very much takes after him.

Dad's sister Susie (September 1958) is different again. She's a go-getter. An entrepreneur. An explorer. Switched on and ready to sort shit out. She's travelled all round Australia but if there is one thing that Susie doesn't do it's beat around the bush. Her honesty is as raw as our red earth, and I love her for it. She's someone I can always turn to for the unsweetened truth. She named her absolute legend of a daughter Gemma, or 'Gem' for short. It seems she got that right too.

Then there're Dad's parents. Although they lived together for 65 years and only parted at death, my nan and pop were very much chalk and cheese – respectively. Pop, Laurie 'Wally' Tame, was the cheese of the pair, if only by default because Nan, Valda Mae, was unquestionably the chalk; hard, straight, but not without a certain softness that rubbed off on you. 'Love many, trust a few, but always paddle your own canoe,' was one of her mantras, according to Susie. Believe it or not, her maiden name, before she married Pop and became a Tame, was Free. There's a street in Rokeby named after her family, who first came to the area (formerly Clarence Plains) almost 200 years ago among the first settlers.

In contrast, Pop was the gentle, self-effacing – albeit cheeky – handyman. 'He was less blokey,' Dad recalls. 'He wasn't aggressive.' He had 'a lot of skills that people don't have'. A shipwright by trade, he spent most of his days tinkering in his shed, teaching locals to drive or playing sport. Having grown up in Manly, New South Wales, he played a lot of rugby, which he kept up when he moved down to Tasmania. I think he even captained a team down here. He also had a talent for cricket, which he passed on to Dad, who kept most of the talent for himself. I'm just grateful I still have my nose and both kneecaps.

Such is Dad's immediate family of five freestanding Tames; each uniquely capable and decidedly independent.

But put them all in a room together and they got along – dare I say it – like a house on fire.

Of the 1293 homes tragically lost in the devastating fires that ravaged southern Tasmania on 7 February 1967, one was theirs.

Black Tuesday

All the kids were at school. They all went to Lauderdale Primary. Nan sewed every single one of their hockey jumpers by hand.

Dad was eleven years and eleven days old. Numerology would have it that so many ones signified a message of good fortune from the angels. Bullshit.

When the flames tore through Clarence Plains, the two youngest were with a group of students that ended up by the water in Ralphs Bay. As for Nan and Pop, it was a waiting game. They didn't know where any of their children were.

It came to pass that they lost just about everything, except each other. That's the miracle, I suppose. Our most valuable possessions are immaterial. Agnostically speaking, I promise to report back if there was any help from above when I'm gone.

When the five of them were finally reunited outside the house that Pop had almost finished building for them – the house beside 'Preston' – it was all but ash on the inside.

They hadn't even moved in yet. The whole family had been living together in a one-room shed next door while Pop diligently toiled away for months on their new home. They had installed all their belongings, though; their knickknacks, whitegoods, furniture and photo albums. What was left was a burnt-out husk.

'It's just stuff,' people often offer as a feeble condolence to disaster victims. It's never just stuff though, is it? It's memories. Countless hours of labour. Literal blood and sweat. Whole families' tears. Planned futures never lived. Objects of supposed permanence. Parts of a whole real enough to hold, reduced so suddenly to absolute nothingness.

Or might it be
that we
can't bear to see
that every single one us
is just stuff
too.

One of Susie's memories of standing in front of the rubble is particularly symbolic of life's fragility. There was a brand new

Encyclopaedia Britannica set that appeared to be still intact. Alone, among Mother Nature's ruins, was the whole world according to man, catalogued from A to Z. But when Susie went up to touch it, the collection crumbled into white ash.

With the one-room shed now gone too, they all had to go and live with Nan's mother. At 'Preston'. On Princess Buildings Parade.

Being true blue warriors of the working class, Dad said they didn't have much growing up besides each other. Certainly not after Black Tuesday, that's for sure. He told me they didn't even have any clothes after the fires, besides the ones on their backs. 'Maybe that's why I'm a bit of a hoarder now!' (Those are his words, not mine.) It's like Wendy with her pantry full of biscuits or my mum with the toilet rolls. Or me and, well, people who remind me of my mum and dad.

Intergenerational trauma is nothing to be sniffed at. Pain is stored in every cell of our bodies. We can't talk it out of us. We can't think our way around it. We can't deny it or drill it down into some dark corner of dormancy. It's a living thing.

It doesn't turn into ash until we do. It's an unpredictable, inextinguishable ember.

Like love. And the core values we learn as kids too. They're the fire that sustains us. The good kind that overpowers the bad. That kind that warms your soul and lights your way.

Like the idea of not taking everything too seriously, and to be familial but not tribal.

Dad says the kids were taken left, right and centre to every sporting event. 'Mum and Dad always did things for the family.' They were home-grown on home truths without handouts, in a time when if you wanted something done you had to do it yourself.

Every single Tame is a self-made success in their own right. Rick with his own businesses, Susie and her husband Eddie with theirs too, and Dad playing cricket for the Tassie Tigers from '84 to '87, then going to teaching college and working for the Department of Education for over 30 years. They're not high-flying millionaires, but they are three of the most dedicated, hardworking people I know. Just like my grandparents.

The Ghosts Who Walk

It never occurred to me that my experience of grandparental guidance might have been slightly atypical in the same way that my parental setup was. Not to say that there is such a thing as 'normal', or that if there was that it would be a good thing. I loved being looked after by Nan and Pop after school. It was one of the highlights of my bumpy week growing up. It gave it some routine and rhythm.

There is a tattoo under my left collarbone, where one might pin a name tag. It says 'Flossy'. That's what Pop used to call me – he's no longer with us. I broke my left collarbone at the beginning of this year while riding my bicycle along the South Arm Highway. I had started my route just before his and Nan's place. And although my agnostic faith tends more towards science, I have a barrow-full for the man who used to wheel me around; maybe he had a hand in saving me from flying right out into the middle of the highway that day. He built number 28 South Arm Road. 28 is my birthdate.

Nan worked until her late seventies. She used to put catalogues in the newspapers at the old white *Mercury* building when it was in Macquarie Street in Hobart. Three or four in the morning she'd finish up. When I was little, I remember always seeing squished-up orange ear buds next to her oversized acetate bifocals and wondering what they were for. They were to block out the sound of the printing press. And Pop's snoring.

Although Nan and Pop were products of their time in a few obvious ways, in so many others they were not. Pop was a multi-skilled handyman and Nan cooked every meal, but he wasn't a dominant man and she wasn't a subservient woman, as far as I could see. Then again, because of their financial circumstances neither of them were afforded the opportunity to go to university (again, not that institutional education is the be all and end all). Although she never said it, I think that, deep down, a part of Nan always wished that things could have been a bit different. That's not to say that she resented having to look after her family or anything like that – as if women or *anyone* can't have it all – but that she longed for the chance to test the potential of her brilliant mind beyond daily cryptic crosswords and *Letters and Numbers*.

Maybe her strength of character came from somewhere deeper. Nan's mother was apparently very difficult. Nan told of a particular memory she had from when she still lived at home of her mother attacking her bedroom door with an axe.

Perhaps Nan just was the way she was, and she didn't want anything to be different after all. Regardless, she was a fighter who played by nobody else's rules. Until the very end. That much was obvious. Much like the rest of her sporting kin, she was a master of almost everything she tried her hand at. She played table tennis for Tasmania at some point, and in her later life entered a national golf tournament and came third. There were just as many, if not more, trophies with her name on them as Pop's in the living room cabinet at their place. When she wasn't being sedated by the sermons of *Dr Phil*, she was watching the cricket or tennis on mute with the wireless blasting from the kitchen because *the commentators on the telly are bloody useless.*

Every now and then Nan would treat herself to a visit to the casino. I could tell when she'd had a win because she would give me $20 and tell me to behave myself. I wish I knew back then what that really meant. It makes me deeply sad to think about it. I despise the Federal Group for all the ways they have infected my local community. If you don't believe that corruption is normalised, you haven't done a pub crawl in Tasmania and seen that there are pokies in almost every single one. It's a stain on both the major political parties that they don't have the guts to do anything about it. The truth is that they've been bought by the gambling industry and without profiting off its dirty system they wouldn't survive.

Really, though, Nan's whole world was Pop. They were lovers of the simple life. They were everyday heroes without capes. Instead, they wore hand-me-downs, handmade clothes and cheeky grins, proving stereotypes are all made up and true strength comes from within. When Wally Tame passed in April 2015, Val's first words were, 'What am I supposed to do now?' Her soulmate was gone, and part of her soul too.

Nan's health deteriorated after Pop left, but she refused to go and see anyone. She was determined to let nature run its course, and to take her eternal scepticism to the grave. She'd had a few falls in the following years and busted her hip pretty badly, which meant she couldn't really drive and even walking too far inside the house was a challenge. Still, she stayed at South Arm Road, in the lounge room, with the blinds closed. Her brother, Graeme, was living next door, and would sometimes check on her and deliver the paper. Except that pride and aloofness were also in his genes, so a passing wave from the front lawn was usually what that meant.

It was a Saturday night in late October 2019 that Nan fell so badly she was unable to get back up. She was about to get into bed but didn't quite make it. But when Graeme knocked on her door the next day, Nan's ego told him to bugger off. She was on the floor, with no food or water, but being helped was a fate worse than death.

She was there for four days before Graeme eventually let himself in and found her. Bizarrely, he called Susie first, who then called an ambulance. Nan, at 83, miraculously, had survived. She barely had the energy to speak to any of us in the emergency room of the Hobart Royal Hospital, as she lay there, toothless because her dentures were still in a glass in her bathroom, covered only by blankets because she'd been found in her birthday suit, as if starvation alone wasn't bad enough. She had absolutely no problem, however, telling every doctor who came by that she hadn't been to the hospital in 'OVER SIXTY YEARS'. And that was only because she had to *give birth* to her last child.

For the next couple of weeks, Nan clung to life in hospital. Although I would say that it was life that clung to Nan. At the time I was living in Tasmania and working a few blocks away so I was able to visit her often. Unsurprisingly, myriad underlying, undiagnosed health conditions were discovered by the staff while she was there. One of them was diabetes. Physically, her prognosis was not good. Her faculties, on the other hand, remained as sharp as ever. Arguably too sharp. Or too blunt, even. She was telling the nurses to smother her with a pillow, which I had to keep reminding her was illegal in our so-called democracy. 'Well, you just clock me then,' she'd counter. And as much as I am an advocate for voluntary assisted dying, I wasn't quite ready to do an on-the-spot DIY job on my own grandmother. Certainly not in a shared room in a public institution behind a curtain.

I'd spent more time with Pop as a kid growing up, but that time with Nan will stay with me forever. It was brutally sad and confronting, for all the humour and light there is within it. Nan and I are kindred spirits. There's no denying some of her fire found its way to me. Pop was known for his outward warmth, but Nan held hers inside. I doubt that many other 83-year-old diabetics would have survived for four days on the floor without food and water after falling like she did. Nan was a force to be reckoned with. She was the Free who had been Tamed. But at least she was herself in the face of death.

Because she was all gum, I had to feed her. All she wanted was a mandarin. I'd pass her a segment, hold a napkin under her chin, she'd suck out the juice while maintaining eye contact with me, then spit out the pulp. It was a silent bonding of anti-establishmentarians who had felt some unspeakable pain. I made a promise then that I would do my best to do justice to a life walked in her shoes.

'Remember this,' were her parting words of wisdom to me, and may they be mine as well, to you.

*

Pop's selflessness was self-evident. It's something I remember well. Nan was often sleeping during the day after her nightshift, or pumping *Judge Judy* into her veins with the blinds closed, so Pop would pick me up from school. Every Monday. And sometimes other days too. He'd drive us back to theirs along the old Pass Road in his 1990 cobalt-blue Toyota wagon with grey sheepskin seat covers, letting little me control the gears. When we got home, Nan would make me her signature bread and Promite in the kitchen while I took my pick of the lollies from the squat glass jars on the shelf by the front window. I'm not a fan of plain sugar, so I was always on the hunt for something chocolate, like a Clinker or a Malteser or – if Dad hadn't cleaned them all out – a coveted Jaffa.

Between the shelf and the front window was a tanned bamboo Chinese New Year calendar from 1970-something. On its wheel of twelve creatures were a yellow tiger and a blue dragon that presided over a foot-high stack of newspapers on a wicker chair, next to a polished pale-grey table that looked out onto the highway and across to the local Vinnies. Nan used to pride herself on always being the first person to tell the police whenever vandals set the donation bins on fire. When I was really little, before I started school, and Dad would drop me off before his classes started, I would sit on Pop's lap and eat Rice Bubbles while Nan did the crossword, and watch the stream of morning traffic.

Pop said there should be two words removed from the dictionary: 'war' and 'religion'. His top choice of literature was Lee Falk's *Phantom* dailies. It was a rare sight to catch Pop reading anything, though. His natural habitat was a world entirely of his own design. It had silver foil–insulated walls lined with wooden shelves full of tools, varnishes, motor oil, timber and paint. Its raw concrete floor was a canvas of stains. There were wooden horses, but not the kind you could ride. From the ceiling hung a bar held by metal chains that I used to swing from if he picked me up to reach it. Pop told me it was for doing pull-ups. All around were rusted tins stuffed with sandpaper and old ice-cream tubs full of hinges and nails. Running along the north side was a long window that spilled sunlight onto a broad and weathered workbench. It had a big steel vice attached to one end and was always littered with flat, wide carpenter's pencils that Pop used to sharpen with a Stanley knife. The rich smell of sawdust, grease and mower fuel stuck to everything in the room. 'The Shed', it was simply called. And it was his. Any time you stopped by his and Nan's to visit and asked, 'Where's Pop?' Nan would invariably reply, 'The Shed.'

Pop and I spent hours in there, side by side, two toiling Tames, totally lost in each other's company and time. Sometimes we wouldn't even say a word to each other. He would give me scraps of wood, a small hammer, some nails, and just watch over me as I made little houses and other nondescript creations while he chipped away at whatever project he was working on. Other times we worked on projects together. He had a machine that could make circles that we used as wheels for miniature carts or homemade French knitting spools. We were the perfect companions. 'I thought *I* was your best friend,' Pop replied, when I told him one day that Dom was my best friend. I had to correct myself. I have more than one. And he is most definitely among them still. There were very few whose company I felt truly comfortable in as a child. For several reasons, I'm not sure that many people understood me. Pop did. It makes me well up with emotion just thinking about it.

'G'day, Flossy,' he would say as soon as he saw me jogging towards him in the carpark after school had finished. There he'd be, a steady beaming lighthouse over a topsy-turvy sea, ready to take me home, safe and sound – if only for a short while. With his woven worn-out brown leather sandals, grey slacks, dusty Boag's Draught cap and a red check flannel under one of Dad's secondhand cashmere jumpers, his style was effortlessly, authentically sentimental. It reflected a man who lived his entire existence for the people he loved and the work he did.

It just so happens that Pop played rugby for a time against my maternal grandfather. Like my aunt Denise, Pop wouldn't have an enemy in the world. He was neither hated nor did he harbour hate for others. Wally Tame had all the time in the world for my mum, her sisters and their mother, long after my parents split, until the day he died. He never had time for Cliff.

When I think of Pop, our times together play back one after the other, like scenes from a nostalgic arthouse film. Him pushing me around in the wheelbarrow at top speed as I laughed myself stupid. Hitting golf balls together into the high heavens over the back fence and into the churchyard. Dodging swooping plovers aiming for our heads. Playing cricket in the tall grass with Graeme's two unruly dalmatians as fielders. Me sidling up next to him on the couch at dinner time. The two of us with our plastic meal trays with the bean bag bit underneath, as I followed Pop's lead and mixed Nan's mint peas with my mashed potato to dull the flavour. Muffling giggles whenever Nan started snapping, because he'd just give me a sly wink and turn his hearing aid off, and she never figured out he couldn't hear a thing. Watching *Wheel of Fortune*, knowing even back then as a little tacker that there was no fortune in the whole world worth more than the love and friendship of people like Pop. Even though that is hard to see sometimes through the fast-flinging muck of modern life.

Wally Tame was the truest and bluest. The best and fairest. I really do find it hard to believe in something bigger out there. But I do believe in him and Nan – two unsung working-class legends, whose superpowers were their authenticity and integrity. To me they'll always be immortal – simply because of those things. They walk with me wherever I go.

Sock-filled Sea Monsters

Taxidermy. While most eleven-year-old boys aspire to be professional sportsmen or fire-fighters, Michael Tame entertained a dream of stuffing dead animals for a living. A dream that was thankfully fleeting, but one he nevertheless gave a good crack.

After catching a three-foot gummy shark off the local jetty, he brought it home, cut it down the middle, gutted it, filled it with balled-up socks, and replaced its eyes with marbles. In hindsight, he deserves points for creativity and innovation. Fortunately, there is no such thing as hindsmell.

It would seem that when he was younger, my dad was something of a fun-loving, free-spirited, wildly adventurous anarchist – like me. Then again, I never drove the family car through the front room of Pop's second gallant attempt at building a home from scratch. Or straight into the local church when I was eleven. Reportedly Pop reconstructed a chunk of the obliterated picket fence and replaced it in the middle of the night when no one was looking.

An Imperfect Spy

Before male-pattern baldness crept up on Dad's deceptively smooth forehead, he had shoulder-length jet-black ringlets. On top of his deep tan and angular eyebrows that the creators of *Sesame Street* quite possibly referenced for The Count, this meant that in his youth he looked positively Mediterranean. So Mediterranean, in fact, that when he and his friend Steve went to Turkey in the 70s, Steve kept losing him among the actual Turks.

As with Dad and Rick, looking at Dad and me next to each other, you might not be able to tell we are related, aside from the piercing blue eyes, a few elastic facial expressions and our uncontrollable laughter that often turns into tears when you get us good. Start a conversation with us and you might think you're hearing double. Our shared DNA is undeniable.

Neither of us is very good at small talk. For instance, the moment you start telling me you got your eyebrows waxed or something, I'm gone. You've lost me to a two-hour plot of a 90s Ralph Fiennes movie. What's that? Your legs, too? It's too late, I AM *The English Patient.* I'm in the desert, on a stretcher. My burning face – it is covered in gauze. That's not to say that neither Dad nor I will make the effort, and Dad in particular is renowned for being wildly entertaining and gregarious. It's nearly impossible to walk down the street in Hobart without running into one of his ex-students or someone he played cricket with in a past life. He is, however, also renowned for making phone calls but not saying anything when you answer and offer him your name. It's only after you keep saying, 'Hello, Michael?' over and over into nothingness, that he'll eventually say an impatient, 'What?!' as if he is very affronted by the whole situation – which he instigated. It is, hands down, simultaneously one of his most hilariously bizarre and frustrating quirks. In his defence, he's pretty deaf. It's one of many oddities I love him for. I also have a feeling that'll be me in 40 years.

Dad was 39 when I was born, so the generational gap is reasonably wide. The expansive and eclectic pop-culture diet that he fed me on from day one has helped bring us somewhat closer together and bridge an emotional impasse. We have a common language of laughter, lyrics and lines of thought in place of all the ways we're different.

One thing I struggled with as a kid was processing the adult experiences I was absorbing constantly and internalising without knowing how to translate and release. The words I knew back then failed me. What I had was the frustration I felt, and that I was taught.

My father, like his mother, is not one to suffer fools. He is brilliant, kind and decent, like my mother. He is also fiercely witty and at times coldly abrupt. He often operates in a world of his own, not out of malice or choice, just inclination.

His household was an eggshell environment where there was a lot of emphasis put on appearance, and criticism was common currency.

I didn't want to be in anyone's way. I didn't want to cause a fuss. I put on a brave face, but in the end, I used to spend most of my time alone in my room and found solace in schoolwork. All I wanted to do was see my dad. And to be myself.

At three, Dad taught me, via Aretha Franklin, that the only boy who would ever reach me was the son of a pizza man. We listened to all sorts of sounds from the Neville Brothers, Blondie, Dusty Springfield, Jethro Tull, Sade, Robert Cray, Lucinda Williams, Martha Reeves, the Cranberries, Talking Heads, Ry Cooder, Dire Straits, Led Zeppelin, Van Morrison, the Rolling Stones, the Beatles, the Kinks, Bonnie Raitt, the Clash, the Jam to Cold Chisel, Missy Higgins, Crowded House and more. I found my own way to more hardcore punk and the psychedelic side of town. I don't know if Mr Hygiene 2014 could stand the sight of Shane MacGowan, or if the 5 am early riser in him would want to see Les Claypool play a midnight show in downtown San Francisco.

Then again, it was Dad who introduced me to the dank, deadly and dystopian *Delicatessen*, and other way-out-there silver and small screen masterpieces. We doubled over watching the likes of *Fawlty Towers*, *Blackadder*, *The Commitments*, *The Vicar of Dibley*, *The Castle*, *Mother and Son*, *Kath & Kim*, *The Gunston Tapes*, *Life of Brian*, *The Birdcage*, *In Bruges* and all of Peter Sellers' *Pink Panther* capers. These are just the titles I can remember off the top of my overflowing head. We found ourselves short of breath in the audience of Bill Bailey's sell-out absurdist comedy shows and we can riff endlessly reminiscing about them and other bits we love. Folding the washing often involved a recreation of Monty Python's fish-slapping dance, with me running at him with two pairs of my tiny socks and him playfully whacking me with one giant pair of his.

On a more serious note, Dad also introduced me to the thrilling tales of British intelligence operative George Smiley, written by former MI6 agent David Cornwell, known by his more recognisable nom de plume, John le Carré. Anybody who has read le Carré knows his work is as thought-provoking as it is plot driven. I love indulging in implausible Bond blockbusters as much as the next person, but I don't reckon I'd be in the mood for sex after getting my head bashed around on a train.

There's only one Smiley novel that's set outside the world of espionage. The story of *A Murder of Quality* unfolds in and around the grounds of Carne College, a fictional well-to-do English school. As Smiley unravels the mysterious murder of one of its students, his path crosses with characters who offer piercing observations on the stale, empty traditions of stagnated institutions. The killer turns out to be a psychopathic teacher and ex-member of the Royal Air Force, convicted of gross indecency during combat. The story concludes with a chilling note on the nature of evil.

Four days before I reported my experience of child sexual abuse, I confronted the child abuser in his office. I had asked that the contact offending stop in December 2010, at the end of the school year. We maintained a 'friendship' but he continued to surveil and stalk me. Even though he wasn't my teacher in

2011, I would often turn around in class and see Bester standing in the doorway, watching me. The longer we spent apart, the less physical control he had over me, and the more my resentment grew. If grooming was a spell, it had begun to lift.

In April 2011, Bester walked past me in the courtyard one day. I stuck my rude finger up at him. That evening, he sent me a message online, asking me why. I said I didn't want to talk to him, but that I would see him in his office the next day. Throughout the abuse I had submitted to his every will. He terrified me. But when I walked into Bester's office that day, I could not stem all the untempered sadness and molten rage that had been coursing inside me. There was nothing I could've done to make it stop. All I could do was scream and cry. I can't speak for all survivors, but I think it's because a single body isn't designed to contain that much hurt.

I only knew about one other girl at this point. I didn't know about the videos of adults raping children on his computer or what the school was hiding. I didn't even know the word misogyny. But I knew enough. I told him I thought he was a monster. I told him I hoped he died, and that I hated him for what he'd done to me, to my family, and to his. The one lie I told him that day was that I would never tell. And he just sat there in his chair, without moving. His eyes were blank. He was staring at me, watching me writhing in pain. I had scars on my arms from self-harming throughout the abuse. If I wasn't terrified of him before, his reaction would have tipped me into the abyss. He shrugged and said coolly, 'Well, if that's what you think of me.' I left. I never looked back.

By reading the philosophy-drenched pages of Dad's old le Carré books, unconsciously I absorbed tiny morsels of reaffirming, lifesaving knowledge and perspective. Ideas of what it meant to speak truth to power; deconstructions of the hollow myths that often belie institutions; the value of working for the greater good, even if you have to bluff sometimes. The significance of these things is something I would not understand until I was much older. And this is for the best.

I repeat that I am glad I didn't understand the depths of evil I was exposed to in my own life prematurely. Innocence is a shield. Or a double-edged sword. There is much to be said of the power of naivety as a complement to a sense of injustice. In rare moments, fearlessness in place of paralysing doubt can be just the thing that saves us. I didn't know exactly what I was doing, or even the language to articulate it. I didn't know exactly what good and evil were. They aren't exact. What I did have was an immovable foundation of these things, a reinforced innate sense of them, that guides me to this day.

Just off South Arm Road, past Free Street, is a mental health recovery and rehabilitation clinic. I checked myself in there in April 2022, a few days after I tried my own hand at stand-up and had felt right at home on the stage. As I'd absorbed with Dad when I was a kid, comedy is a language that comes easily to me as an autistic person. It might seem odd to you, but to me, telling jokes to a large audience is the opposite of frightening. It frees me from the perplexing realm of neurotypical dialogue and allows me to connect with people in the purest way. Laughter is a force none of us can resist. That to me is so beautiful. We might be on the verge of tears, or try to fight it out of pride, but it is the ultimate overpowering reflex of happiness that literally cracks us up.

I went to the clinic because I knew my sympathetic nervous system was burnt out. Externally I was going through the motions and presenting like everything was fine. At that I'd had a lifetime of practice. But never before had I been so unnaturally overloaded, poked, prodded, co-opted, chewed up and spat out by strangers on all sides. I was holding fast to gratitude and responsibility. To my family, and opportunities. I was also outnumbered, and exhausted. I am human.

For the first week or so, I was quite reclusive and couldn't stop shaking. There is often a disconnect between our minds and our nervous system. I had taken myself there, and I knew that I was safe and shouldn't be ashamed. My body, however, thought that once again I had been abandoned. What I could see, which helped ground me, was a bright blue storage building on the side of South Arm Highway, just in front of 'Preston' and Pop's house, where I grew up. It was right in the centre of the view from the window in my room. So I hardly came outside of it. When I finally did, I went to the common room and sat myself down in a red lounge chair. There was an old man reading a spy novel on the couch opposite me. 'You like spy novels? So do I. Do you like le Carré?' I asked.

'No. He's too soft,' he said bluntly. Which took even blunt me aback.

'Fair enough,' I conceded, 'I can see that. Who do you like to read?'

Once upon a time, I would have scrambled for a book by one of the authors he listed. Once upon a time I would have tried to relate. I would have fawned and mimicked his taste.

But I didn't want to be like him. Nor did I want to be like any of the old men who had tried to shape me throughout my life since I was a young child. My forcibly tangled wires had uncrossed.

I loathe the grooming material that Bester fed to me. As if he were above me and everyone else, flaunting his superior unrivalled taste in culture. Fucking *Little Dorrit*, *Love Story* and *Brideshead Revisited*. Call me unsophisticated, but F. Scott Fitzgerald is not for me. Isn't sophistry just glamourised fakery? If the shoe fits.

I love my trash as much as I love my treasure. There's really no such thing as good art or good taste that's superior to anybody else's. There are only things that move us, move with us, and change the way that we see the world. I adore *my* own personal bad taste. Literally, *Bad Taste* is brilliant. Give me *Videodrome*. Give me Jodorowsky's unholy *Holy Mountain*. Give me Patti Smith, Primus, New York Dolls, Lou Reed, Frank Zappa, Nick Cave, Amyl and the Sniffers, or Iggy and The Stooges.

I love my youth. No one can take that from me. I'm not like old men because I like espionage thrillers or classic rock. I'm like my dad. I'm like my dad because he's my dad. He is a part of me, and I am a part of him. And that will never change, regardless of the clothes we wear, the films we watch or the books we read. We are each other's family. No matter what, I am my father's daughter, if only in the smallest ways.

Chapter 6

A Real Cambridge Education

The German Pruner

A broad-shouldered and barrel-chested six-foot-one, with ageless olive skin and thick brown hair despite being in his sixties, my stepfather Ron Plaschke is built like a Bavarian bear. To look at him, he's not someone you'd want to go up against in a fight. Thankfully, the chances of that happening are slim to none, although he does have his share of hard-earned battle scars. The size of his heart dwarfs even his impressive stature. His mind, too, is remarkably sharp. He is an even-tempered humble man of science and reason; a patient listener and constant learner, with a wealth of knowledge and practical skills in many fields. Ron will only ever raise his voice as a last resort, and when he does he is almost always justified in doing so. On the rare occasions he does cross the line, he's never too proud to apologise.

Although Ron was born in Australia, German was the only language he knew how to speak until he was five. His mother, Erika, comes from a German-speaking enclave in Kronstadt, or Braşov, in Romania's Carpathian Mountains. His late father, Horst, was from a town called Braunau, formerly of Sudetenland, now part of the Czech Republic. Both of their families moved numerous times to avoid conflict during the Second World War. Horst's family ended up in Ochsenfurt in Germany. Erika's family wound up in Austria after she and her brother, Gerri, were separated from their parents at the ages of six and ten respectively. They made their way to Tasmania by boat as refugees when Erika was still a girl. Horst immigrated alone and found work at the local hydropower station.

Ron's parents met as young adults in the 50s and made a home together in West Moonah, where many European refugees settled at the time. The pair spoke fluent English by then but for some reason didn't speak it in front of their firstborn, who got a very rude shock when he found himself in a public primary school in Hobart's northern suburbs with a mouthful of an Eastern Bloc surname, copping earfuls of insults, but unable to understand them or reply. He was, justifiably, pretty put out, and refused to talk to his parents in their native tongue after that. If they spoke to him in German, he would answer with whatever broken English he picked up at school until he was fluent.

Like me, Ron had to wear an eyepatch for a time when he was younger. We both have one lazy eye. Needless to say, it can make one an easy target for bullies. Add to that pervasive prejudice, and it makes sense why Ron would say, 'I became a bit allergic to my heritage.'

Ron has three younger sisters, Lindy, Hilda and Maya. The family grew up in the 60s, and, like my mum and dad, were children of the working class. But their life as children of wartime immigrants sets them miles apart from my parents. Ron's stories of the xenophobia he wore growing up as a white citizen with foreign roots are bad enough. I wonder how much progress Australia has really made since then in our attitudes towards so-called 'others'. I dare you to mention First Nations peoples, people of colour, the transgender or disabled communities, or any other marginalised group in the same breath, though. That would make you a leftist, not just a decent person. As if compassion is a matter for politics.

It was in school that Ron developed a passion for science, and he worked as a lab monitor in his final years before graduating. His first real job was at the local zinc works, and eventually he put himself through night school to become a qualified chemist before marrying his first wife at the ripe old age of twenty. In 1984 he started working as a marine chemical analyst at the CSIRO. 'Don't put too much detail in your book, people will fall over from boredom,' he warns me now. Too bad, he can write his own book, with fewer adjectives, if he likes. I think mapping the behaviour of the ocean out at sea on big research vessels for months sounds quite exciting. Admittedly I did have to translate that from 'we used markers in seawater to characterise waterbodies'.

In his early thirties, Ron found himself as a single dad of two teenage boys, Ben and Sam. About six years later, he met my mother. I was about three or four, I think.

The now Mr and Mrs Plaschke met on the set of an educational video they co-starred in. Oh, yes, that's right:

Switched On, it was called. It was a fictional character-driven short film about hydro-powered electricity, complete with a hero, a villain and a grumpy schoolteacher played by Mum. It is a precious relic of 90s cringe material made on a shoestring budget and I am delighted to tell you that every cheesy minute of it has been immortalised on VHS. Without spoiling the truly shocking – pun definitely intended – ending, I can tell you the villain is just the silhouette of a bald man in a blazer with a broom handle across his back to make his shoulders look pointier.

Mum is quite open about her initial uncertainty about Ron. She maintains this was not personal; she was a young single mother with a blurry background being cautious. This meant that at first she would bring me with her on dates to test his commitment. At the time I was just stoked to have fish and chips at Mures. Here we are, two decades later. They're happily married, and I have a little half-brother, as well as two step-brothers who each have two children of their own.

We call Ron the 'German pruner' because his idea of gardening is to approach everything with the same ruthless efficiency, regardless of whether it is an ageing tree or a rose bush. His favourite tools are a chainsaw and another chainsaw, but smaller. What doesn't kill it, makes it stronger, apparently. He doesn't mince his words and nor does he beat around any literal bushes. His technique has never failed, though. I will never forget the time he warded off an entire mob of pigeons that were attacking his grass seed by covering the front lawn with two kilos of cayenne pepper, which he bought from the discount spice store. Among Ron's few flaws is that he doesn't know his own strength.

From the Cottage to Kaoota

In 2001 or 2002, Mum and I moved in with Ron and his boys to their house on Kaoota Road in Rose Bay. That was a time of big change. That was also when I moved schools.

For my first three years of schooling, I went to a community-based primary school called the Cottage School on Queen Street in Bellerive. When I was there, there were only about 40 students split between four classes from kinder to Year 6. There were no uniforms, teachers were addressed by their first names only, and everyone's food was shared at lunchtime. My gut tightens when I look back on those years. Four, five and six are tough ages, made worse because we can't explain why.

Out of necessity, very early on I had become too adaptable for my own good. My brain could remember numbers and phrases with ease. I can't see properly out of my right eye, but the first time that Mum took me to the ophthalmologist when I was three, I memorised every line on the Snellen alphabet chart and passed all the tests. I didn't get my first pair of glasses until I was four. Object permanence and separation anxiety, on the other hand, were big problems for me for a while. I went to creche and daycare and spent a lot of time alone, but mounting schedule changes meant decreasing consistency where there hadn't really ever been any to begin with.

There were also things I could feel but didn't understand. Things that were happening and ways I was hurting that I couldn't take a picture of. The neurotypical world was rushing at me in hard straight lines, but I was suspended somewhere curvilinear that I couldn't describe. What I was being taught didn't match the language I was living internally. How can you box things neatly inside a rolling sphere?

My mind sees time through the glass door of a front-loading washing machine on a never-ending spin cycle. Past, present and future are indistinguishable. I can pull out specific memories that look as clean as yesterday because at any given moment everything is churning at high speed in colour. There is no beginning. There is no end. There is only the middle. There is only now. I hear most noises as if they're right in my ear. If I don't catch what you say, it's not necessarily because I'm not listening. It might be because I'm constantly sifting through a torrent of sound. It's not that I can't hear anything, it's that I hear everything, all at once. All around me, life's cacophony of stimuli is always buzzing on high.

I've no innate way of ordinating anything into linearity, without descending sharply down a path of ill health. Invariably, every time I've tried, I've found myself subconsciously trying to retrieve the same things I can never get back: my childhood and my child's body. I starve until I can't menstruate. I stop socialising and become a recluse. I run until I lose my curves and my strength. Then I ride, and I ride, until my bones break. I don't want to be thin – I want to be a girl. Just one last time. I don't want to bleed and see my blood on his body, on the floor again, or feel that pain, anywhere. I don't want to be looked at like that. Sometimes, momentarily, I can escape to my own dissociative reveries, but I can't stay in those forever. None of us can, and nor should we. That defeats the purpose of a life connected to the people we love. And the line between privacy and isolation is blurred as it is for survivors of violence. Whenever we're alone, we're rarely alone. Corruption is irreversible. Innocence is irreparable. You can't replace the hard drive of a mind.

Wherever I could assimilate I was a good chameleon, but it took work. Some days I was physically unable to go out to recess until I had finished putting all the Faber-Castell oil pastels back into their boxes in their original colour order. I can still see my little hands grabbing at them, and the sheets of paper strewn across the tables in the room.

In Year 1 I got a lead role in a play that we did. I had a natural talent for doing voices and memorising lines. It would always make Mum laugh, I remember. We used to sit on the floor in her living room at Bellerive to watch Michael Parkinson interviews and do arts and crafts together some nights. I would impersonate the chat-show guests as we worked.

To be accepted, I had to put my whole system in overdrive. Where I didn't fit, I was far adrift. When I was rejected, I had to do the work hard just to get back to base. As such, I could rarely rest. The trouble was that it wasn't obvious I had such gaping deficits, because the skills I had, I mastered to a fine art. I had to overstretch them to compensate for what was missing.

It's also just tough for children in general. Everything is new. Everything is intense. Everything is bigger than you.

Some mornings I would be dropped off long before any other students or staff and feel disoriented. Other mornings I was late and would feel ashamed. I would often find it hard to settle down. I'm embarrassed to say I remember lessons that started with me in tears. The teacher that I had for prep was the same teacher I had in Year 1. It may well have been the case that she got sick of me being distraught, because I have visions of her being sour with me. That is understandable. I can't imagine what it would be like being a teacher tending to all the competing needs of so many little ones at once, week in, week out. Still, I found her quite intimidating. It's been over twenty years and the distress still lives in my body.

There were positive memories too. I would often gravitate towards the teachers because my father was a teacher, and in my mind teachers meant safety. I think my father knew some of the teachers there too, because he had worked with them at some point. Hobart is a bit like that: it's a small community of about 200,000, and the pool of teachers is even smaller. I also made some lovely friends at the Cottage School. Jessica, Jocelyn, Hamish, Hannah, Jacob, Laura, Alex, Eve and her older sister, Mad. It's been a long time since I've seen a lot of them, although thanks to social media, some of us are still in contact.

Not long after we moved in with Ron, we hosted a Halloween party. Mum handmade me a witch's outfit for it, including a hat with a little blue spider on the brim. We covered the walls of the rumpus room with torn black garbage bags and put shredded white felt over the top, which looked like giant cobwebs. Everyone's hot lunch was plated in the shape of a face made from mashed potatoes under a dotted green pea mouth, two carrot wheel eyes and a long sausage nose. There were buckets filled with tinned spaghetti, which was supposed to feel like intestines when we put our little hands inside in search of missing jelly 'eyeballs'. I also remember staying at Orana Camp near Roches Beach on a Cottage School trip. I still sleep in the same blue sleeping bag. It has my name embroidered in red on the hood.

Special events look so rich and vivid on paper. They just aren't enough to cut through the reality of everyday life that swamps them. In the end I told Mum that I didn't want to be there anymore. I told her I wanted to be where my cousins were, at Cambridge Primary. I didn't know the right words to use, though. In the same way that at three I learned that the One Nation Party generally stood for things that were less than ideal without knowing what exactly, at only six I had figured out that to be 'treated like a piece of meat' was bad without knowing why. Allegedly, this was my choice of phrase when I was trying to express my sadness to Mum, who had to try not to laugh. I was a parrot, sorting through tumbling emotions, trying to locate a set of fitting words I'd heard somewhere down the swirling line.

Life at Ron's house on Kaoota Road was quite unlike anything Mum and I had ever experienced before. We were used to eating like sparrows and singing to each other. One day Ben ate an entire loaf of bread. After he'd eaten dinner. They always kept several litres of milk in the fridge. They bought honey in three-kilo buckets. They all ate seconds. And thirds. They ate everything. And fast. Sometimes Mum would be unpacking groceries and reach into a bag to put something away only to look up and see that it was already gone. It was food consumption on an industrial scale. It was a man's world. A big man's world.

Alle Seelen Waren Eins

Once a week all of Ron's family members who still lived in Hobart would go to his mum's house in West Moonah for dinner. Everyone, including him, calls her 'Nana', much like everyone in Mum's family calls our nan 'Nanny Pat'. Nana's cooking was something else. You could smell it from outside, before you crossed the threshold and left Corinda Grove for the warmth of a 1950s rural European homestead. Her doorstep was a portal to a live fairytale. That's how it felt as a kid, anyway. That house is no longer, some of its visitors too, but its magic remains preserved – if nowhere else – in memory, and now in these pages.

Among the usual suspects was late 'uncle' Gerri, the notorious white-haired prankster who used to pretend to bash his arthritic knuckles on the dinner table, making the tips of his thumbs disappear. Then there was his partner, Shirley, who sometimes brought her late son Craig, along with her slice, which we all worshipped, especially Ben – who was always present, with a stubby of Cascade Draught preloaded. Lanky Sam would be there. And big Ron, of course. I turned up on the nights when Mum went and I wasn't with my dad, but was always late because she had to read the six o'clock news bulletin. Ben's wife, Jo, and their kids, Jake and Sharn, would join the family later, followed by Sam's wife Kate and little Elijah and Adele. Many others came along on random nights over the years. Ron's nephew, the guitar prodigy Dan, lived with Nana for a while. His niece Zoë, the Amazonian beauty, did as well. My brother, Oscar, is now a regular guest, and possibly the most devoted of us all.

'Hull-o!' Nana would sing in her accented English, as she heard you enter. If she didn't greet you at the door, her voice would travel from the kitchen down the hallway. In winter, the wood heater would always be burning in the living room. That's where we'd all usually gather, in anticipation of the epic feast we could see being laid out behind us in the dining area, through a panel of frosted glass. On the sandstone mantel above the fireplace, on the timber-panelled walls and on the wood sideboard were neatly arranged old family photographs, some sun-kissed graphite portraits, Bible passages written in blackletter, and folk artworks of birds and flowers. Nana liked to paint in her spare time. There was a mahogany piano, too, on which she played carols at Christmas. Adjacent to that was a low-seated umber wooden lounge that had matching chairs with big taupe velvet cushions covered in orange and brown leaves. All the autumn tones were offset by an evergreen carpet.

West Moonah is close to New Town, where I used to take ballroom dancing. Some days Nana would look after me beforehand and then drop me off. Even now in her mid-eighties, Nana is fighting fit and sharp-witted. Back then, her spirit was certainly as young as mine, and her imagination was just as wild. She would run alongside speedy little me down steep banks at the local park, and pretend to gallop on horseback in her backyard under her giant mulberry tree. She would sing and dance and paint all at once while I did the same. She could play table tennis at top speed in the garage, and she had the patience to teach me German. And no afternoon was complete without time to stop and eat inch-thick cream cheese on her homemade pumpernickel bread.

Her dinners were what drew the crowds. The menu changed from week to week, but the favourites are undisputed to this day. Vienna sausages with homegrown horseradish. *Sauerbraten*: beef marinated overnight in vinegar and spices, then slow-roasted and drowned in tangy, sweet gravy. Potato salad – potato *anything*. *Rouladen*: thinly sliced, tenderised seared steaks rolled up and stuffed with bacon, onion and lemon, then simmered in beef broth or roasted in the oven.

And for dessert, *Vanillekipferl*, which are buttery shortbread cookies shaped like crescent moons covered in icing sugar. Those, and anything smothered in whipped cream.

Life's natural unpredictability meant there were exceptions to it, of course, but there was a well-oiled routine everyone knew by heart. The wooden table had two sizes to accommodate fluctuating numbers, and the smallest among us would sit on stools from the kitchen if there were no chairs left. That usually meant me, which didn't bother me, because I'm small and a wriggly worm. Nana would say Grace, bless the already blessed food, and we'd all say 'Amen' in return. Our starting signal was the honk of wood on lino as Nana then got up from her seat to serve the first course of soup. Pumpkin, goulash or maybe minestrone. There was always fresh bread, butter and dip ready for the taking. And thus, the wholesome, homely orchestra began. Soles unsticking and knives clanging china. Arms and voices reaching across the table. Drinks being offered and poured for one another. Hot steaming bowls of broth making their way from the kitchen, moving in a circle like pass-the-parcel.

It was as joyful to watch as it was to be a part of. There were very few moments of silence, but plenty of laughter. Nobody ever went without food, nor the natural medicine that is simply sharing a meal with others under a roof.

Nana wasn't one to complain. Nor was she one to talk about herself. On the rare occasions that she did speak about her time in the camps in Germany with her brother Gerri, we all sat in quiet awe. I think we all shared an unspoken belief that to be as we were, eating as a family with two children of war who were separated from their parents and lived on rations, was an honour. It was a gift. Like my dad's parents did, and my mum's mother does, Erika Plaschke lives simply, for the people she loves. She gives back for every minute of life she's been given, without much obvious resentment for its painful parts.

Connection. Community. Solidarity. Family. Love. However you want to term it, it's a remarkable force. I can understand why people wouldn't want to die thinking there is nothing beyond this life. 'Those who have a "why" to live can bear with almost any "how",' was how Holocaust survivor Viktor Frankl put it.

It's no surprise that agents of evil try to isolate their victims, whether from others, themselves or both. I reflect on these pictures of pure happiness, and then on those who would have them cut out, cut up and destroyed. Those who seek to dehumanise and destruct.

In trying to bond and build, humans often perversely default to an adversarial model. It's woven throughout the fabric of our society. Sport. Politics. Religion. War. It seems we are driven by what we understand to be the basic principles of reality: that in life we cannot all be winners. That there is not enough of everything for everyone to have in equal measure. This idea of power as a pie – more for me means less for you. It's sad that some people think of love and friendship in the same way.

All of our experiences will stir emotions in us beyond our control, but ultimately it's the ones grounded in connection with others that move us and stay with us. As far as I understand it, the purpose of life is to share it, in the here and now, while it lasts.

For all the places I've been and wonders I've seen, grand heights and powerful people will never compare to simply being among family – both chosen and biological – here on earth. There's no need to reimagine it, prolong it, or outdo it. It just is. What is heaven if not that?

Chapter 7

Free to be with Dom

On my last day at Cambridge Primary, the thing that finally brought me to tears was standing alone in the parking lot, watching Dom's face looking back at me through the window of the school bus as he left the grounds for good. After that, I turned around, sprinted into the building, past the toilets, up the stairs, through the foyer, into my Year 6 classroom, got down on my hands and knees with arms outstretched, and buried my face in the carpet. I wanted to take the whole place with me, forever.

It sounds pathetic, but it's true.

After I finally got the courage to explain to Mum why I needed to leave the Cottage School, my five years at Cambridge Primary were five of the best years of my life. There were definite bumps along the way, but I found a home there. I found a home in lifelong friendship.

Dominic Abela knew me before I did. We met in Mrs Palfreyman's Year 2 class. He was best friends with another boy named Kristian Vines. All three of us lived in Seven Mile Beach at that time and often caught the bus home together after school. Dom's family were on Lewis Avenue, around the corner from my dad, and Kristian lived a few blocks away, a couple of houses down from where Wendy, Tony and Eloise had built their new home.

My friends Matt Burgess, Jacob Cooper and Jacob Walker all lived nearby as well. We used to ride our bikes around to each other's houses. Abbie Weidinger too. She was the only person who could outrun me in cross country. Granted, for every step she took, I had to take two. She was an incredible athlete and an even better friend. We would run out ahead of the pack and be side by side the whole way, then she would bolt to the finish line. There was no point trying to beat her. I remember clapping as I was still running behind her in Year 6. She was the undisputed champion. Abbie visited Los Angeles on holiday while I was living there. There we were after a whole decade apart, eating diner food on Highland Avenue in the murky depths of hellish downtown Hollywood. It's funny, though, how comfort food and comfort people will transport you right back home to safety. We slipped into our old friendship so easily we might as well have been back at Cambridge Primary. The same was true of Dom.

Dom and I were in the same class every year. His birthday is in December, thirteen days before mine – the same date as my mother's. He still looks exactly the same to me now as he did when we were in primary school: fine black hair, bright blue eyes, and pale porcelain skin like a doll's with the faintest freckles. He wore glasses like me, except his frames were metallic blue rectangles and mine were metallic pink ovals. Many aspects of our friendship are like that. We are a truly symbiotic match. In some ways we appear to be polar opposites, and in others we're one and the same. He is computer literate and I am a Luddite. He taught himself to drive a manual car and play the piano, while I trained myself to run a sub-three-hour marathon. Dom is shyer than I am – at times. His imaginative, high-brow humour can catch me off guard. I remember being bowled over at seven when he got up in front of our Year 2 class and out of nowhere started reading the most obscurely funny words I had ever heard. They were his very own, inspired by one of the Tashi books. He hadn't just written some standard seven-year-old silliness; this was something uniquely, brilliantly weird. I'll never forget it. It was in that moment, being knocked about by my own uncontrollable laughter, that I saw someone I understood among all the unknown. And I felt like he saw me, too.

Trying to condense twenty years of friendship into a few paragraphs is an impossible task. It doesn't shrink down, it only expands, the more I think about it. It has become so much more than a friendship. Dom and his family are my family too. I was with Dom and his sister Anna when the story of what happened at my high school broke in Tasmania. We were all sitting together on Anna's bed. 'Teacher admits to affair with student,' the headline read, on the front page of the local newspaper. With a big picture of his face. The article inside had a romanticised description of the first time he showed himself naked to me. The time he took me to a storeroom with a supply closet and told me to take off my clothes. Just like I had told him someone else had done, before molesting me, when I was six.

Dad had to work that day. So did Anna and Dom's parents. It was just us three. I think we were on school holidays. We were just kids. Anna had been writing articles for the *Mercury* newspaper's youth section at the time. She managed to get hold of a phone number to call, and I dialled it. When it was answered I didn't say who was calling, I just said I wanted to speak to David Killick, the man who'd written the front-page story. 'Do you have children?' I asked, as soon as I heard him ask who was speaking. Anna was crying. I was crying. To realise you have been groomed is one thing, to be able to explain it is another. I didn't know the concept. I didn't know the half of it. I just had this gut feeling that everything was around the wrong way. I knew that I had been played, and that everyone else was being played too. The account I was reading was the account of the child abuser. How were things so broken? There were too many things to say all at once. The conversation ended with Killick saying that he would publish anything I wanted to say. I told him that was not the point, that it was not why I had called. The damage had already been done. I just wanted him to hear me. To hear the truth. He had written this story and he had never even heard my voice before. He had no idea what I looked like. How could he not see the injustice? Survivors just want you to listen to them, in the same way that you listen to perpetrators. Is that too much to ask?

I never had to explain to Dom what happened. He never asked a single question. He didn't have to. When everyone else around me was talking at me, over, around and about me, he held still in the crossfire of confusing words. He knew then we were still too young to understand, and that that was all that needed to be said, but not with words. He knew that what I needed was belief, support, solidarity and love. He said nothing. He just wrapped his arms around me like the brother he's always been. The brother who sat next to me every single day, and plucked hairs out of my head. The brother who knew as many *Little Britain* quotes as I did at the age of eight, and still does. Sometimes all you could get out of us was 'Ya, I know', or 'A-yeeees' à la Ray McCooney the Scottish riddler.

I didn't know that Dom was autistic then. Not that that would have made a difference. I do remember seeing diagrams of faces expressing different emotions in a book on the floor at their house in Lewis Avenue once. I was too young at the time to make the connection.

The stereotype of people with autism being emotionless or unempathetic – at least in my experience – couldn't be further from the truth. I think about those simplistic faces, and then I think about the complex and gentle individual that is Dom, and all the other giant-hearted individuals that I know with autism and it makes me sad. Sad face.

I think about the TV show *Love on the Spectrum*, and I wince. Wince face. (There is still no taking-the-piss face, as far as I'm aware.) Whatever educational benefit that show brings in offering a glimpse of different representations of people with autism, it doesn't outweigh the ultimate, inevitable cost of selling those people's differences – their struggles – as a commercial product; as entertainment. As long as there are shows like this, no matter how sensitive the approach, we will continue to be othered, pitied and infantilised. Just because people are different doesn't mean they are separate or less than anyone else. The show is widely enjoyed by neurotypical audiences. Why? Because its subject is a novelty. Yuck. I'm reminded of films designed for the male gaze.

The creator of *Love on the Spectrum*, who isn't autistic, has made a show about the lives of autistic people, from which he reaps the bulk of the financial and commercial benefits. The majority of the perspectives deferred to throughout are those of the autistic people's parents. Add to that the fact that the autistic people are counselled by a non-autistic therapist who gives them patronising advice, and ultimately it's the autistic people – who I am not criticising at all, to be clear – who are the subliminal punchline with a downtrodden, compromised voice. If the truth is not told on your terms, it is not your truth. It might not be obvious at first glance but the show is not empowering to the main characters. It may be more representative of autism than many shows. It may be moving, relatable, and quaint. However, it still reinforces the conditioning that people who are different should have to make an effort to conform. How does that actually advance anything? C'mon. I'm seeing the naked emperor again. What if people who are different could just be? What if we all did the work?

There's this issue of political correctness that seems to grant certain sensitive topics immunity from criticism. Bullshit. I am autistic, and I'm not a protected species. Just because some well-intentioned abled man makes a documentary series – on his terms – that spotlights autistic people dating, doesn't make him a protected species. Has the world gone mad? We all have the right to constructively analyse these things, abled and disabled people alike.

Reality television is a lie in any case. I know, I've done my fair share of it through gritted teeth. Some of it was well worth it. Some of it was borderline exploitative. Hindsight is 20/20. There's a family I can't keep up with, or slow down for, more like. I'm loath to mention their name, because to acknowledge them in any capacity whatsoever is to legitimise them, and that is not my intention here. Such is their vacuous brand of incurable self-indulgence that even to critique them is to feed them. It is effectively impossible to say anything about them without becoming a part of the same hollow system that sustains them. What a ghoulishly toxic business model: hijacking every culture for their own personal gain while the world burns beneath them, and repackaging it all as self-empowerment. It would almost be clever, if it didn't come at the expense of nearly everything on the planet. It is pure, unadulterated, glorified greed.

'Feminists don't tear other women down.' I mean, am I tearing down the Great and Powerful Wizard of Oz? Or just the curtain he's hiding behind? Whisper face: I reckon their emerald empire will survive, regardless. The truth is visible to those who are willing to see it. And an exorbitantly wealthy capitalist dynasty have chosen how they wish to tell their truth, and how they wish for the world to consume, mimic and fetishise every ounce of their material excess in their never-ending quest for more, more, more. That is their right; that is their wish. Just don't forget that there are many others who have not yet won the right to even be heard, let alone worshipped, no matter their brains, heart and courage. There's no place like home. Didn't the cast members of that film die from the toxic make-up they wore? I digress.

*

In Year 3, the Abela family moved from Seven Mile Beach to a property on an acre of land in the neighbouring semi-rural suburb of Acton Park. It linked up to what are locally known as the 'Tangara Trails', and over the back fence were empty paddocks. When I was staying with my dad, I would often catch the bus home to the Abelas' after school and we'd all walk back to their house through the bush.

Our universe was a self-generated, self-contained imaginarium of spontaneous play. It was bacon and eggs cooked on the grill after school. It was making diabolical messes on the kitchen bench, as we concocted laborious and often inedible cooking disasters. Filling the whole bathroom up with bubble bath, sculpting foam hats and beards, and staging soap wars. Putting on every single item of clothing we could find in the house and attempting to walk. Watching *Titanic* on repeat and remaking the film clip to 'My Heart Will Go On' by Celine Dion. Double bouncing each other on their oversized trampoline, as we giggled at Pedro their miniature horse eating the washing. It was birthday lunches for their giant salt and pepper groodle, Toby, who sat upright at the dining table like a human and got his own cake, and whose special tricks weren't sit or roll over, but the arm gestures from the evening gameshow *Deal or No Deal*, which he'd make by crossing or uncrossing his paws on command. It was laughing and laughing and laughing until I pissed myself.

Dom is the third youngest of four Abela siblings. Aside from him and Anna, who is about two years older but only one grade ahead, there is their little brother Sam (born in 1997) and the eldest, Kahryn. Kahryn is about five-and-a-half years older than Dom and me. She was in the same year as my cousin Ryan at Cambridge.

I spoke to Anna while I was writing this. 'You were a staple in our household,' she said, offhand. 'You just fit in.' There aren't words you could say to an unstable child that would mean much more than those. Theirs was certainly an understated but implicitly unbreakable kind of acceptance. Anna's memories of that time line up pretty well with mine, notably that we were 'free-range children' who took care of each other, for the most part. Kahryn was our ringleader. Their dear parents, Mark and Nadine, who sadly split in 2009, are two highly skilled and driven people. I remember them working late, and almost always being on the go. How could they not be, with so many mouths to feed?

The Abelas had a shack, down south past Port Arthur on the Tasman Peninsula, in a place called Saltwater River, about two hours' drive from Hobart. There are some old convict ruins and coalmines nearby, but its grim human history is belied by a raw landscape of lush green fields that roll into ice-blue seas. The shack was a classic 70s cream vertical weatherboard number with a side sliding-door entrance and a timber verandah that looked out into a small, flat grassy yard on Coal Mine Road. That's where the whole family would often take time out to slow down and relax. That is, except for one now infamously stressful evening in 2006, just before our Year 6 leavers' dinner.

Mark had lit a small bonfire by the water tank. It was dark. There were a few of us kids there that night, although the only faces I can remember are Dom's, Sam's, Mark's, Anna's and her best friend Jaclyn's. Everyone and everything else is distorted in flashing pictures.

If it's not your first rodeo, then you'd already know you don't just toast a marshmallow. You torch it until it's a flaming cannonball, carefully extract it, blow on it, wait for it to cool off, remove its obliterated charcoal shell, eat that, then stick the goo back into the open flame for round two.

That's how I've always done it, anyway. And despite what I'm about to tell you, it's how I continue to do it.

I can recall I was standing in front of the fire next to Sam. I was overseeing the first phase of a molten masterpiece, alight on the end of an unwieldy gumtree branch. At the exact moment I decided to retrieve it from the inferno, a perfect storm of miscues struck as quickly and brightly as a bolt of lightning. The angle of my giant makeshift toasting fork was too high and too sharp. All around, bodies and shadows were dancing. The mass of pink sugar, still ablaze, was fast becoming liquid that now hung above me. In a split second, the sound of children's laughter turned to blood-curdling screams as it fell and landed on the bare skin of my right hand.

The bubbling, oozing marshmallow began to spread. It burned, and it stuck to my flesh. The next thing I remember was the bright white of the bathroom, as Mark held my raw wrist in the sink under cold running water. I could see Anna and Jaclyn's faces in the doorway, and heard them ask me if I was all right. I was looking at them, but was unable to answer. I was eleven and I was in shock. At least, that was part of it.

It wasn't the first or last time I would be nonverbal, that I would seize in a state of autistic overwhelm. It still happens today.

*

Many people know me as being loud. It's widely assumed that I am naturally confident. I've even been told that I am intimidating. At five-foot-three, and as someone who works overtime just to function socially, is prone to shame and secondary embarrassment, and who's always seen themselves as goofy and awkward, that seems implausible.

Yet I have watched in bemusement, from a distance, as a version of a person who is supposedly me has been haphazardly crafted by a portion of the nation's media. And I don't know her. Mind you, not all versions are bad. It's that very few are even accurate. That there are so many conflicting versions is, in and of itself, very telling.

The critical commentariat have done a great job of fabricating their own Frankenstein's monster, stitched together with unflattering photographs, hyperbolic headlines, disinformation, conjecture and blatant conspiracy. Their initial ingredients may well have included the bare bones of truth, but those have long been buried beneath relentlessly ugly reworked flesh. With every new scrap of widely disseminated 'content', with every new projection, the kaleidoscope takes another slight turn. There's very little unbiased reality that makes it into accounts of your actions as told by others – others who've never even met you. Especially those whose agendas were well and truly fixed long before your time. Whose job it is to sell papers for someone else, whose career is centred around making a name for themselves.

As for the vocally hateful among the consumers, it's a particularly bizarre kind of hypocrisy, to judge another through the eyes of someone else. All the naysayers who are so confident they have made an accurate assessment of me based on my actions can't possibly have done so. They have made one based on a removed, distorted, technicolour version.

There is, as well, of course, the uncomfortable fact that anyone who actively helps expose and work towards ending grooming and sexual violence is a natural target for those who may have something to hide. It's certainly not the case that minds are incapable of changing. It's that many people deliberately, actively resist because their power is under threat. In the absence of silence, denial, deflection, distraction and disinformation are the last refuges for the abusers who live among us.

I'm aware of some of the stuff that's been said about 'me' in the media. It's there and sometimes it crosses my path. To follow it all, however, would be senseless. I have a life, but it barely resembles the one that's been portrayed. That is because it is real and because it is mine.

In life we may find ourselves at junctions. However, it's only upon arrival that we realise that choosing the right path is not always a simple task. For it may be that some paths are not as they appear. It may be that others are pulling you in several different directions at once. It may be that you're blindfolded and everything is spinning too fast. It may be all of the above. You may have to walk down some paths to learn the hard way that, in the end, you have to forge your own. Max and I did, with our values as our compass.

There are plenty of things I could do to earn a living that wouldn't expose me to the abuse I cop. I've been offered several big opportunities that would've put me on the world stage and launched me into a different financial bracket. I've declined offers of large corporate sponsorship deals.

Instead, my partner, Max, and I have set up a not-for-profit foundation that works with government, legal experts, educators and other not-for-profits towards a future free from the sexual abuse of children and others. Our approach is multi-dimensional. While prioritising the need to centre and support victim-survivors, we also seek to help drive structural reform and shift the core focus of the national discourse to prevention and understanding of the behavioural precipitating factors of physical abuse as opposed to reactive and responsive measures. In July 2022, we received an update from officials at the Commonwealth Attorney-General's Department informing us of a proposed National Review of Child Sexual Abuse and Sexual Assault Legislation to be conducted in conjunction with the Australian Institute of Criminology (AIC). The update stated:

> this review has been proposed in response to Ms Grace Tame's address to the Meeting of Attorneys-General (MAG) on 12 of November 2021. At this meeting, Ms Tame noted the importance of national consistency of wording relating to the 'persistent sexual abuse of a child', legislation relating to the age of consent, and the definition of 'sexual intercourse', and presented a paper by Marque Lawyers, outlining legislation in relation to these terms. The AIC review would consider this legislation, as well as a number of other additional definitions, offences, aggravating circumstances, defences, and maximum and (where applicable) minimum penalties in relation to sexual assault and child sexual abuse (including online conduct and preparatory behaviour,

such as grooming). This would include legislation with respect to consent and stealthing, which has been the subject of recent calls for reform from victim-survivor advocates.

I have no legal expertise beyond what my decidedly sassy lawyer, dear friend and fellow wannabe Spice Girl, Michael Bradley, teaches me, but I am told this is unprecedented. This is the product of a team – not a big team of champions, but of a champion team of big-hearted, tireless workers.

If you ask me what drives me, it's achieving things like this. Awards, accolades, symbols – these things may enable change, but they are a step on the journey, not the end result.

Apparently, the foundation is a Labor slush fund. I like that, it's good material – maybe I'll work it into my stand-up, which I'd love to do again. Not for the money. It doesn't pay. Comedy is a wonderful source of healing and connection, and it is a personal passion.

And the most gratifying joke of all is that my best friends don't recognise me in the media either. We don't live there. We live outside in the untouchable glory of peaceful privacy. The greatest days of our lives are hidden gems, never to be seen by prying eyes.

There is no freedom like friendship. Nothing could ever come too close to Dom and me. He is a diamond. A diamond in a coalmine.

Chapter 8

Spread Your Wings

The Cambridge Primary School emblem is a cartoon plane, with a rounded nose and a welcoming smile – the campus is just up the road from the Cambridge aerodrome, and Hobart Airport is also nearby. When I attended, there were about 400 students from kindergarten through to Year 6. It was big enough to feel established, but small enough to feel like a family. 'Valuing the past . . . creating the future' is the school motto, which suits it to a T.

The uniforms are still much the same: navy blue shorts and matching rugby jumpers with a pale blue horizontal stripe broken up by thin white lines, a white collar and buttons, with the happy logo embroidered high on the right side. Girls also had the option of wearing a light blue checked dress, but I seldom wore mine. It didn't suit my lust for climbing and running amok, nor my tomboy style. In winter we wore zip-up polar fleeces. Dom and I would obsess over the softness of brand-new ones. We both love fluffy things.

I was never all that keen on Barbie dolls, but I had teddy bears, and I adored animals. In Year 3, Mum caught me trying to smuggle my pet rabbit into my schoolbag so I could take her to class with me. She used to sleep on my pillow and sit and watch morning shows with me in the living room before everyone woke up, on the blue corduroy couch that Mum had upholstered. Her name was Tennessee – I was already a big fan of the King by the time I was eight. I had another two rabbits around the same time whose names were Elvis and Memphis, and when Mum and Ron got married that year, I briefly joined Ron's sister, Hilda, and her husband, Mark, for a cover of 'The Wonder of You' in my little flower girl outfit.

That was a very special day. Mum and Ron's wedding was the perfect expression of the simple kind of love they share: it felt effortless and pure. All of us cousins were sat at our own round table, and by the end of the night my belly was sore from laughing. The venue was not far from Cambridge Primary, about four kilometres along Richmond Road, at a vineyard formerly called Meadow Bank, now Frogmore Creek. I've only been back there once, but I've got enough memories of it to last me a lifetime. Rolling on the grass with Griff and Ryan. Playing Pass It On and dancing barefoot. Standing beside Mum and her bridesmaids, Karen and my unofficial godmother, Jane.

When you're a kid, you don't understand the full significance of moments like that. You don't understand what it means to be in love. You can feel the resounding joy and warmth of the celebrations, though. You can feel alive and free in the company of family and friends.

For someone like me, who is very receptive to routine but who is also independent and doesn't always learn the same way as the rest of the crowd, there was the right amount of structure at a rural public school like Cambridge. It struck a neat balance between direction and freedom; between community and fostering individual growth. At Cambridge, with the support of nurturing staff and friendships with people like Dom, I was able to work through some of my social struggles and explore hidden passions that I still pursue now. I owe a lot to my teachers, especially Mrs Dow, Ms Brown and Mr 'Wat' Watkins.

Dom and I did Art Extension and choir together. In Year 6, Mr Wat held a table tennis tournament and Mik Mosley and I won the doubles championship. Abbie Weidinger, Samantha Dobby, Katie Kube and I won the 4 × 25 metre freestyle relay every year at the inter-school and champions swimming carnivals. In 2005, all the Year 5s and 6s joined together for a musical production of *Alice in Wonderland* called *Wonder in Aliceland*. Knowing I wouldn't be cast as Alice, but also hoping for something more comedic, I put my hand up for the Queen of Hearts and lucked out. In the end they let me ad lib. Ten-year-old me had an absolute ball of a time putting on a ridiculous voice and breaking the fourth wall in character. Mum made my dress for that too. Diamond Dom was the tree-iest tree. His sister Anna played 'big' Alice and my cousin Maddie was a divine Daisy. What videotape? I've said too much.

'I threw myself at life with every fibre of my tiny but mighty being' is a line I've used before in a few public talks. That much is true. It's the following part about being 'unafraid of falling' that must be corrected. There are some details that are too complex to address in certain contexts. More to the point, there are just too many. They are messy. It was painful enough for me and for those close to me to step out of obscurity onto a national stage and begin sharing unheard parts of a story about child sexual abuse, let alone to simultaneously provide a life's worth of background right off the bat. I did my best to explain that mine was a coloured past, while also protecting people around me and helping to educate the public about the reality of grooming and abuse being a perpetual, multilayered system. Of course, there was so much more to my truth, but where does one start, and how does one end? How does a whole person survive it, all by themselves, all at once?

The more that people dug around and put me on the spot, the harder it became to shoulder the entirety of the compressed, unspoken hurt I'd felt and witnessed since birth.

Get over it. Move on. Shut up. I don't buy her for a second. Crocodile tears. Feral skank. Cunt. She's so privileged. She's so rich. Money bags. Her dad's a famous cricketer. Her mum's famous too. She read the news on TV. As if in life one can only be rich or poor, and money is proof against human suffering. As if my own parents' pasts weren't painful too. Dare I defend them, though, because there's always someone worse off.

People think 'fame' and they see 'money'. Mum's salary was less than my father's, who was a public school teacher. She was also a single mum who didn't receive or ask for any child support until the last year. 'It wasn't worth it,' she told me.

Dad played the game he loved, but at 50 bucks a pop, he played at a loss. The time he had to take off from teaching cost him more in wages than what he earned playing cricket. It's not worth explaining. It's not the done thing to tell someone how much money your mum made, or didn't make. Or what she had to go through to get to that place. What a strange world this is, that puts people's jaws in tight locks. Unless your trauma is the worst, your pain is supposed to stop.

You've said enough, I kept telling myself. That, or *it's not bad enough*. So goes my own internal monologue of shame, humming to the beat with all the other voices in my ear. The strangers, the friends, the family out there. The truth is, I flogged my guts out because I was not only never sure of my next move, but I was born of two people who flogged their guts out too. Even back in primary school some of my passions teetered towards unhealthy obsessions. In Year 6 I was doing 'too much' homework. Matt Young and I ended up being the joint winners of the award for academic excellence. I wanted to impress my dad so badly. That was a huge part of it – I'd be a liar if I didn't admit that. It wasn't his way to show an obvious display of affection but few things felt worse than letting him down. For an only child of divorce, success is also one of the few forms of validation and security. When you're in trouble, you don't know which way to turn. Achieving, I thought, was the gateway to acceptance. Only, it never lasted. The harder I tried, the harder I had to try to sustain it. I couldn't keep outdoing myself. I never felt like I was good enough just as I was.

Somebody posted a picture of my maternal grandfather online recently, praising his achievements and comparing me to him. There he was in all his protected glory, smiling in a newspaper clipping from days of sporting fame. I see that photo and I want to be nothing like him.

In July 2022, Victorian Liberal MP Tim Smith bemoaned Australian rules football for its lack of 'biffo' – or casual violence, in other words. Rugby, in comparison, he said is 'a quintessentially Australian sporting contest that's physically brutal'. Its 'old-fashioned masculinity' is something he finds 'reassuring', apparently.

His comments made me think. I don't know Tim. The following words aren't for anyone in particular.

I kidney-punched a man once. He was the bouncer of a bar called Harvard and Stone in Los Feliz, Los Angeles. It was the night of the Super Bowl in 2016. Some men were picking on a woman on the street outside, where my friends and I were waiting for a ride home. I told them what they were saying was disrespectful. Then the bouncer chimed in and started picking on both of us. I'd never hit anyone before in my life, and I've never hit anyone since.

I've been in arguments, tussled and the like. But I'll never do what I did then ever again. 'I told you once,' I said, all high and mighty. Or maybe it was my Heather Graham in *Boogie Nights* moment and I had every right. I don't remember the rest. I just remember my friend Jason laughing in the car, like it was a triumph. 'You just hit him! It was awesome,' he was saying. He is a great guy. But even though what I thought I had done was speak to those men in their language, the truth is they learned nothing from me, and I just got banned from a bar for life.

Both of my grandfathers played rugby. In the same team, in fact, in the 1960s. Wally was the captain. This was well before my time, of course. But I know those men. They're my blood. They've shaped my life.

One went to university and made history with another man when he kayaked from Sydney to Hobart across the Bass Strait. He also left Nan and five daughters, including my mum, for a sixteen-year-old when he was 35. He never picked me up from school. Not once.

My other grandfather was a working-class gentleman who captained his team. He had some trophies, but I never even bothered to look at what they were all for. What do they matter? He showed up. He was there for everyone. He was a great man, because he was a great person.

Sportsmanship, as far as I understand it, is about camaraderie. Glory in solitude is meaningless. As for masculinity, that's another malleable myth.

Whole lifetimes of violent abuse can be hidden behind a fake veil of accolades.

I see that picture of my grandfather in the newspaper clipping and all I see is pain. His awards and successes mean nothing. He is a coward who doesn't know his grandchildren.

When I look back at my Cambridge days, the best memories I have are with someone by my side doing something we both love, or in a team. They are the ones that mean the most to me. Not because they came with trophies, but because they were triumphs of the heart. Individual awards are a bit of a catch-22. You sound like an arsehole when you bring those things up. There's nothing better than a shared moment everyone can look back on and laugh about together, though. So when I see pictures of my paternal pop, Wally, who is always flanked by family, I'm reminded that it's him I want to take after. I want to die happy with my grandkids, having lived with purpose, with a cheeky sense of humour, and a bold, sentimental style. That's it; that's all. I hope my funeral is electric.

While I could not be prouder, more honoured or more grateful to be the first public survivor of child sexual abuse to have been named an Australian of the Year, there is something I must tell you. It was a beautiful moment in history, that night. One that was shared with so many. A necessary moment at that, which above all was symbolic, empowering, and hopeful of what is to come.

It was simultaneously one of the loneliest moments of my life. Because the one person who couldn't be there to share it with me was me when I was a child. She was hidden from everyone's view.

My cousin Millie had handwritten me a letter. I read it in my hotel room while Max was fast asleep. It was two o'clock in the morning. My phone was aglow and flashing on the bedside table beside me, messages coming thick and fast. I had two hours, they said, until I had to be downstairs in the lobby. Until my life wasn't mine again. I didn't know what was going on. I couldn't see the end of the day ahead.

In those final moments of silence, I found myself. The fifteen-year-old girl in her uniform. And I sat with her. I held her. I cried.

I was 26 then, still fighting my womanhood, without a period and terrified. I didn't sleep or do my hair. I just changed my clothes. And put my mask back on before I made my way to reception, onto the press bus, to Parliament House and into your living rooms.

*

The good and the bad. It's all enmeshed. They say time heals all, but that's impossible. Oxygen both sustains life and causes decay. And so we must live, and die one day. There is no moving past, there is only moving with. You can't hold secrets at bay forever. They'll consume you one way or another.

From Years 3 to 6 I played soccer, and was the only girl on the team. I was never any good. I think I scored one goal in four years. It was endurance that was my strength. The coach usually put me on the right wing because I never seemed to tire. That was something else I learned to love at Cambridge: running. Running wild, and running long. I carried that love with me into high school, and retain it now. Its raw, transportive power; a moving meditation that sets me free. I did lose touch with it for a time. Quite suddenly, unexpectedly, in one fell cold and brutal swoop.

I was in my sports uniform the day I lost my virginity, on the afternoon of the school athletics carnival in early August 2010. The first time he attempted to penetrate me he had failed. He'd stupefied me with Amarula beforehand, but still my vagina froze up, so he'd given up and left me legless on the side of the road next to the local cinema. I was so drunk I had to crawl through the entrance. My cousin Millie came to meet me and had to pick me up off the bathroom floor. I remember clinging to the sink.

This time, on the floor of his office again, he just forced himself in, despite my whole body's resistance. I tore and I bled. Inside and out. I still had my rugby jumper on. 'I didn't think we would get that far,' he said. And he told me he couldn't believe how much cellulite he'd seen that day on all of the legs of the girls in my grade as they were running up at the track. He was laughing. I could only mumble. I was there, but I had already left.

'You wanted it,' they say. 'It' covering all manner of sins. 'Isn't this a sin?' I dared ask one day, on my back, as usual, the crown of my head almost touching the bookshelf where his statue of Jesus peered down from above. He reassured me it wasn't, not realising any words he said could never reassure me.

My childhood was no longer mine. I could no longer identify with so much of it, because if I did, what was happening to me would become real. The laughing child with her hands in the air that I knew in my memory would be in pain. I tuned out as much of myself as I could. I didn't want to do anything that I loved anymore. I didn't want anymore. I didn't love anymore.

Such are the sacrifices that survivors of child sexual abuse make to cope with what happens to them during and after. We are robbed of ourselves. What feels natural and innate are the very things we lose. Everything becomes stained. Even when I slowly began to rediscover and reconnect with parts of my past, it was often during times when I was escaping from other traumas.

You see, people don't shatter all at once. We don't fall to pieces. We fall in pieces. And piece by piece, we pick ourselves up over the course of time. If it were a clean break, it might be a clean fix. It's not. It's death by a thousand cuts. Or a thousand micro-tears. Such as those caused by a bone slowly splintering inside a body.

That's what happened to me when I came off my bike and broke my shoulder. I'd been to visit my old English teacher,

Janet, who lives in Opossum Bay. It was a blistering summer's day, 1 February 2022. I was ignoring all of the advice from everyone around me to slow down. I had already ridden 100 kilometres that week and it was only Tuesday. I was riding for exercise because I'd fractured my foot running two months before, and my pelvis six months before that.

I hadn't eaten much that day. Not enough to compensate for the energy I was burning, at least. It was all in the name of self-care, I insisted. I was taking time for myself amid all the chaos of public life. I knew what I was doing. I was on home turf. I'd ridden this route before. The worst part, I thought, was already behind me, when I had made it safely across the Speaks Bay neck and out of the midday crosswind. Anticipating the steep climb that awaited me, I shifted into high gear and descended the hill just before the turn-off to Gellibrand Drive at top speed in the hopes of building some momentum. The road was smooth and hot under my thin tyres. The turn was a sharp dogleg dotted with loose gravel where the highway met the backroad.

As soon as my bike tipped, I could feel time begin to stretch. Adrenaline screamed before I did. I knew I was going to hit the ground. I couldn't fight. I let myself fall. 'Ah' and 'fuck' were the only two words I could say out loud. I repeated them a few times, still underneath and attached to the metal frame of Eloise's seventeen-year-old triathlon bike, lying on the highway. 'You're all right,' I told myself privately, 'if something was broken, you'd be crying.' After a minute or so of inertia, I freed my feet, moved the bike, and sat myself down on a slab of concrete on the corner. I'd ridden in just my shorts and crop because of the heat and my left side was now a mess of dirt and running blood from gravel rash. On my way up, before the descent, I'd passed an old man on a pushbike who stopped briefly when he reached me to see if I was okay and kindly check my chain. I told him I only had about 30 kilometres to go. I was planning to ride home. I just needed to collect myself. The ripping feeling inside my chest would surely subside soon enough. I would just have to be mindful not to turn my head that way. Or breathe too deeply. Or lift my arm like that. Or move too suddenly.

Not long after the other rider left, an orange and yellow-panelled dune buggy pulled up. The driver was a white-haired, beach-swept man in a short-sleeved button-down. He offered me a lift. He seemed harmless but I was keen to keep moving. I told the man I was planning to make my own way back to Rokeby. 'You can't ride like that,' he said. 'No way.'

The adrenaline in my system was starting to wane. I'd carried my phone in a pocket between my shoulder blades, but we were out of range in the bush. I'd sent some messages to Max and tried to call him but nothing was going through. My upper left side was giving me grief and messing with my thinking. It was starting to sink in that I might not be able to get back on the bike, let alone ride it. I could hardly make a fist. The man was very kind and kept insisting that he take me home. In the end, I accepted. I asked what his name was, and he guessed mine. When we were in the car, he told me he had seen me on the news, but that he also knew my grandfather, Cliff.

There it was. Right there. A perfect example of the endlessly cycling slow burn of life, still taking bumps on the highway and breaking inside. The driver was lovely, and he meant well, so I kept on talking. I may well have smiled. I was in pain of a different kind.

Later that day at the ER, a scan revealed my clavicle was broken but not displaced, so they put me in a sling and sent me home with a week's worth of Endone. With the health-care system under strain from the pandemic, there was no attending orthopaedic surgeon there to see me at the time. I was told someone would ring me in the coming days to book an appointment at the hospital's fracture clinic. The call never came.

On 9 February I had to give an address at the National Press Club in Canberra, with Brittany Higgins. By then, the opioids had run out, and the ripping sensation I'd been feeling inside me was getting worse and more frequent. The swelling had gone down but only slightly. Max's mum, Andrea, kindly gave me some of her leftover ibuprofen and Comfarol Forte to see if that might help. It made me a bit groggy but the sharpness of the pain remained. Sleeping was nearly impossible. The sling was as irritating as all get-out and I kept taking it off to get relief. On the morning of the speech, I took some ibuprofen, knowing I could handle that without slurring my words, and hoped the sling wouldn't bother me.

After we got back to Hobart, Max noticed a white bump on my collarbone. I took myself back to the ER on 13 February and asked for another scan. As I suspected, my collarbone was now no longer intact. I don't have seven years of medical school under my belt, but I have two eyes, albeit not 20/20 ones. The orthopaedic surgeon told me there was an 83 per cent chance my shoulder would heal on its own, so I decided not to bother with surgery. I would wait it out instead. So long as I could eventually get back to running, riding and swimming, I was content. Yes, the doctor reassured me, I would be able to. I clearly needed a rest and this might have been the only way my stubborn self was going to be forced to take one. 'You're not a shotputter, though?' he asked, which was almost funny enough to make me want to take it up.

How fitting, after the year I had in 2021, that I wound up quite literally shattered. Of all the injuries I could have got, that was perhaps the most powerfully symbolic of them all.

First off, the clavicle – unlike most other bones in the human body – can't simply be set in a cast to heal without disturbance. Much like child sexual abuse, it's a trauma you can't isolate. There's nothing that can be done to stop it from being re-aggravated and worsening while you attempt to recover. It connects to so many other parts of your whole being. It's a total disruption to and of the self.

Secondly, when I first had the accident, the bone did not actually completely break upon impact, much like a person at the onset of an emotional trauma. Instead, over those thirteen days, in a way I couldn't control, it slowly but surely snapped, splintering and splitting into two pieces inside me, leaving a half-centimetre gap between them.

And then there's the fact that there is now a part of me that will always be misaligned, misshapen, out of place. There'll always be a bump; there'll always be something there that wasn't there before. Not something that defines me, but something that will inevitably affect most of the things I do from here on out, for the rest of my life, even if only in ways so small

I don't notice. Nonetheless, I will never be the same as I was before. For worse. And for better. To create a bright future we must value the lessons of our past.

For the most part of the past twelve months – for the past twelve years, in fact – I have been carrying immense pain, only now there are also signs of it beginning to show physically. Of course, my past isn't to blame for my busted shoulder, but the two stresses aren't entirely unrelated. That said, if I were to visually translate the complex trauma of child sexual abuse and all its other resulting, compounding, re-traumatising manifestations – it would look a lot worse than just one snapped collarbone and some patches of gravel rash.

More to the point, it would be impossible to capture all of it in just one single image. Every incarnation of trauma; every reinvention of the vulnerable, hanging-by-a-thread survivor unconsciously stuck in the cycle of self-destruct, bottom out, rebuild and repeat. There is simply no way to show all the cumulative layers of hurt, sandwiched between happiness and unspoiled childhood memories.

There is just so much that we don't see. Beneath the surface.

Riding on the Horses

Growing up, I had two friends named Alex who owned horses that I used to ride. One Alex was the daughter of a friend of Mum's, Toni, who lived in Lindisfarne, which is the suburb next to Rose Bay. The other Alex was the daughter of a family who owned a trail-riding place in Sandford where I used to go on weekends before they sadly had to close down in the mid to late 2000s.

I wasn't into showjumping. I never did any equestrian competitions. My parents didn't have that kind of money anyway. It was my love of animals, adventure, nature, dirt and the thrill of running wild through the wilderness that drew me. I've always been pretty light, unafraid of speed, and empathetic with animals of all shapes and sizes, so the horses seemed drawn to me too.

The second Alex and I used to stay at each other's houses a bit. Her family's place had a small sand arena with some jumps, although I preferred the rugged terrain of the bush tracks and galloping on the flats. Regardless, riding with Alex was one of my favourite things to do. I was at peace just being with her and the horses. We were both playful and carefree. I usually rode the same horse, a small bay called Lady. She was patient, but still quick. Sometimes I would forgo her, though, because she was a trusted ride for first-timers or tourists on the trails.

One time I rode a big grey called Kimberley, who was notoriously slow. We took a group down to the beach. In my mind's eye I can still see the endless low tide of Mortimer Bay. I could be wrong, because that would mean a whole group of us would have had to cross the highway on horseback, and I don't remember that. I am sure I remember the shock on the faces of Alex's mother, Kathy, and her sister, Lucy, as I raced past them on the sand.

'What's got into Kimberley?' I heard Lucy ask.

'Grace has got into Kimberley,' Kathy replied.

Being the free spirit I was, I had my fair share of falls – backwards into a ditch, up and over the neck tearing down a steep paddock. They were harmless – for the most part.

When I was ten I was thrown off a seventeen-hand retired racehorse. My stepbrother Ben's wife Jo had grown up with horses. She'd even broken a few in. Before they built the house they live in now, they were renting a property on top of a hill that sloped downward to a main highway in a place called Mornington. Their place used to be one of the last in a row that backed onto empty paddocks that joined up with the Pass Road in Cambridge, but now nearly the whole area has been developed. For a brief time, though, Jo kept a horse over the back fence. Construction was already starting then – that was the reason for the accident. It was before the workday had ended, one afternoon after school. The horse, Tango, whose race name was 'The Devil's Tattoo', got spooked by the sound of machinery. Jo had just led us under a tree, then all of a sudden I went flying in the air as Tango jumped explosively with all four legs. 'Pigroot' is the delightful term for when an animal does that. After that, I blacked out. Thankfully, I was wearing a helmet, as apparently, my head hit a rock when I landed. I don't remember the ambulance ride. I don't remember asking the paramedics questions. I just remember sitting on the bed in the emergency room hours later. And that was that.

It didn't stop me from getting back in the saddle. And it wasn't the last time I danced with a devil and lived to tell the tale.

Chapter 9

Bidgood Boys and Big Goodbyes

Over the back fence and not so far away lived two boys named Michael and Austin Bidgood. Theirs was the house behind Ron's in Rose Bay. The three of us became instant friends.

When Mum and I moved in with Ron, I brought my weather-beaten trampoline with me and put it out in Ron's yard, up against the craggy, saggy, peeling red-painted wooden fence, which reached with the hill towards the house facing the River Derwent. Its companion was Ben and Sam's senior version, whose springs were losing tension and whose fraying mat had a human-sized hole near the centre, which made perfect jumping target practice from the alternative launch pad. On the weekends I was with Mum, if I wasn't out playing soccer, it was customary for me to climb up onto the fence's middle rail or bounce myself as high as I could and yell, '*Mi–chael*,

Au–stin' over and over until two strawberry-redheads came running onto the grass on the other side. That, or I would be summoned from inside by their familiar unified calls of '*Gra–ace*' ringing through the house.

Michael is about six months older than me and Austin is a year younger. For the five years that we lived next door to each other, we were like three little musketeers. We built Lego; played cricket, footy, chasings and hide and seek; watched *Star Wars*; had sleepless sleepovers and full-scale water fights in their pool.

One of the hardest things about a fragmented life is all the moves you have to make, and all the people you wish you could take with you, but can't. Sometimes it's the best ones you're forced to leave behind.

In 2005, we bade goodbye to that house and the Bidgoods when Mum and Ron bought an old Gothic-style property in Bellerive that needed to be rewired and looked so fancy it really should have had permanent staff. By then, both Ben and Sam were gone. Sam and his lemon-yellow Datson wagon, which he sold for a grand total of $14.50 to a man on the side of the Cambridge highway. He was expecting $100 for it, but settled for all the buyer had in his pocket on arrival. It was honestly a pretty good deal, considering Ben had pimped it with his own DIY budget paint job, which included two fat black wonky racing stripes up and over the hood and some black flames on both front doors accompanied by the initials 'SS' in his own wobbly handwriting. Supposedly that stood for 'Super Sam' but those aren't the kind of letters you want to leave open for interpretation while parked on the front lawn. Add to that, all of the car's doors were broken, so the only way

Sam could get in was through the boot – and he was a pizza delivery man.

Before we moved, we renovated Ron's house ourselves. We had done a bit of work on Mum's Bellerive house before that too. My memory bank contains ample scenes of us painting and sanding and stripping wallpaper.

At one point, Mum thought she would get ahead with some of it to surprise Ron while he was away on a work trip. Inside the red-brick exterior of the house were salmon-pink walls with olive-green skirting boards. This 'getting ahead' involved putting fourteen-year-old Eloise and ten-year-old me in charge of painting a tiny, elaborately detailed spice rack. Mum's plan was to make everything white. We did as we were told and completely covered the spice rack, but not without also covering each other, from head to toe. The paint she had chosen was an oil-based one so we would later have to be scrubbed with turpentine. Still, Mum achieved her goal. Except that when Ron got home, he didn't even notice that his previously putrid pastel walls were gone. He is nothing if not a man of depth.

On that note, there is one last character, another man of depth, who I'd like to mention. He went to Montague Primary School, which sits right on the edge of the river, in the shadow of the Tasman Bridge. His parents' house was just along the esplanade and down the road from Ron's. His name was Felix. He was my dancing partner. More importantly, he was my friend.

We met when I was eight or so, which would have made him nine at the time. I don't have any significant memories of us on the dance floor. Dancing ballroom wasn't my thing. It's too rehearsed and stiff for me, and there are too many Trump lookalikes, if you know what I mean. What I do remember is Felix and I hanging out together, messing around and laughing out the back of the old Polish Club, eating handfuls of mints that we'd snuck out of the jar that sat on a little table by the front door.

His mother is a wonderful artist who used to hold art classes at her house. Sometimes we would practise there, or just play in their big yard. I stopped dancing when I was twelve, just before I started high school. Nevertheless, Felix and I kept in touch.

As soon as I was old enough to work at fourteen, I got a job at the Cornelian Bay Boathouse, in the restaurant's kiosk. That's where Anna Abela worked too. We served ice-cream and fish and chips, and made coffees for visitors who came to the waterfront park area. There's also a grass hockey field, and the place would be buzzing with life on Saturdays during the winter. Bester would come and visit me there. It took all my energy every time I was around him to be in gear. But such is the paradox of fear that I also became paranoid and anxious when he wasn't around – I was waiting for the other shoe to drop. It was a tiring game that I played as much as I could behind closed doors. Anna recalls the owners asking her one day if she had any idea why I might have been crying in the coolroom.

What is more frightening than spotting a spider on the wall? Knowing there's a spider nearby, but not being able to see it. That analogy only works if you have a fear of spiders, though, I suppose. I've overcome mine. Exposure therapy works for some. Max and I saw Bester by chance at Max's gym in early January 2021. My whole body turned to quicksilver as I stood at reception, waiting for Max who'd gone in to use the bathroom. On his way back out he paused in the middle of the room and started beckoning me to come out from behind the counter. I shook my head, turned and bolted. 'He's just a pathetic old man,' Max said in the car afterwards. Max is right – he is. But not one that I have to learn to tolerate. If I ever find that spider in the corner of my ceiling our whole house is toast.

Felix also used to come and visit me when I worked at the Boathouse kiosk. Although instead of driving there and sitting outside in his car, he would walk over the bridge from his house, along the path that hugs the river until it reaches Cornelian Bay. It's a beautiful track; I've run it quite a few times at sunrise on still days. The whole Derwent becomes an oil-slick mirror of candy pink and lavender. From the shoreline you can see a neat row of multicoloured boatsheds on the right-hand side, raised above the water. Hence the restaurant's name. The beach itself is almost directly opposite Rose Bay, facing the river, crowned by the famous arch that joins the east with the west.

Felix and I hung out a bit during my high school years. He introduced me to Prince. I remember one night I was in my room crying to all eight minutes of 'Purple Rain' like a fucking cliché, wearing a giant sombrero and my Collegiate uniform, trying to kill insomnia with a tall glass of straight vodka from Ron's booze cabinet. And when I went to school the next day, one of my classmates, Megan, told me I had sent her a message about having fuzzy ears. I had blacked out eventually. In my uniform. On the floor.

Traumatised people, without realising it, become cemented in narrative tropes which mimic their past experiences. They also feel shamefully bound to the stereotypes of victims subliminally marketed to them by society. As people we often engage in behaviours that are superficially suitable to the category or identity we find ourselves in, despite how constructed those myths are.

There is no other way to put it than to say, in the years immediately following the abuse, and during the abuse itself, I was a mess. I was still a child, and I was in uncharted territory without a guide or any information about how to deal with any of it. My family has always been remarkably supportive in that they have always backed everything I have done and never doubted me for a second. They have always been there. However, beyond my initial statement and a couple of speeches, the trauma is not something I have talked about at length with my mother and father. And certainly not back then. After I disclosed at sixteen to the school, and then to Dad because he picked me up that day, both my parents heard my story via a television screen at the Hobart Police Station. Beyond that – if you think I'm going to make my parents sit through the worst of what happened to me, you're out of your mind.

There'd never even been any sex talks before. There was none of that. A lot's changed in twelve years. There's a growing wealth of accessible resources out there now. There's solidarity, and less stigma too. I didn't know a single other person I could relate to back then. It would be seven years before I met another survivor of child sexual abuse. As far as I was concerned, I was a freak. Until then, in my town, I just felt like I was *that girl*. I got a Facebook message one day that said,

'Is she that girl who fucked the teacher?' I shut my account down after that. I wished I didn't exist.

Between disclosing the abuse in April 2011, and leaving the country in July 2013, I had one boyfriend, from January to March of 2012. It would be another three years before I dated another man, and that lasted all of a month. My next two relationships were with women. I had occasional one-night stands and short-lived flings, but I could not seem to fully release my body from the wreck. There were glimpses and flashes of hope, but I was stuck.

It must be said that my first boyfriend will always be more to me than just that. He remains one of my greatest friends to this day. I have self-worth because of him. We met at a cafe in town where he worked as a barista. I used to sit and read on their leather couch by the window. One afternoon I returned my empty cup to the counter, and he handed me back a scrap of paper with his phone number on it. We both went bright red and could hardly speak, but I remember skipping down the street on my way to the bus. He's a gorgeous man – Mum says he looks like George Clooney. On our first date, we met for a coffee and ended up spending the whole day just sitting together, talking on the lawn outside Parliament House.

After our second date, he drove me all the way home to my dad's house in Seven Mile Beach. We had been to see a screening of *Tinker Tailor Soldier Spy* at the boutique State Cinema in North Hobart. He was very conscious of the fact that he was older than me. I was seventeen and he was 23, although he'd had only one girlfriend before and was quite shy. We were both very nervous and liked each other a lot. He had a medical condition which made him less confident physically, especially when it came to intimacy. Without invalidating what has affected him every day of his life since birth, he needn't have been. He was, and is, nothing but a gentleman. And that is all that matters.

I had no idea how to tell him, or anyone for that matter, at that point. On the drive back from the movies, we were talking about sex and relationships and I didn't know what to say. I felt very ashamed and alien. 'It's okay,' I said, 'I've had sex before,' and then the tears rose with the words, 'but the man was older than my father,' and he pulled over onto the side of the road.

The first time I truly had sex was about two weeks after that, in a bed, with him. I knew it was sex, because it didn't hurt like it did before. It wasn't tearing. It wasn't resistance. It wasn't the force that jolted my insides. He showed me his vulnerability, I think, because he knew my story. And despite his own pain and insecurity, he still put me first.

The exact date escapes me, but I have a distinct and impactful memory from sometime after the court case in 2011, of a night I spent with Felix. What makes this particular memory so significant among all our others is not when it took place; it was what happened, and what he did. Good acts mean more than bad ones, even if they seem smaller at the time.

We were at his house. I had come over in the early afternoon. His parents weren't there, I don't think. We had planned to have a sleepover, watch some movies and have a few drinks. He had told me he liked me long before that. Nothing had ever happened between us, though. We'd known each other for nearly a decade. He was like a brother to me; he was protective without being overbearing. And his kindness was genuine. There was no trade-off or hidden agenda. He was always honest and understanding.

By then I had already taken to using alcohol as a crutch. I hid behind the newcomer-bingeing-on-previously-forbidden-fruit culture that typified my age group. As soon as I turned eighteen, there was always an excuse to go out. Every Wednesday it was cheap drinks night with my friend Georgie, Fridays were the end of the week, and Saturdays were an extension of Fridays.

On that particular night, Felix and I were drinking clear spirits. I remember getting quite emotional. There was a lot that was irreconcilable and tangled close to the surface. For instance, I didn't understand why boys were expressing interest in me, when in my mind I was worthless. I was looking for an answer to why I was to blame for being abused.

'Go on and fuck me!' I was screaming at Felix on his parents' front lawn. I was drunk, hysterically sobbing my way through iterations of 'Just do it!' and all kinds of inebriated nonsense that I had never said out loud before. In the company of strangers this would never happen. It was the kind of melodrama that was all front and no meaning. The ultimate mimicry, behind a mask. I loved Felix, but not in that way.

Sometimes when we are our most vulnerable selves, we say the exact opposite of what we want to say. That, and when we let out our anger not at specific people, but in specific moments; at the times we feel we are safe to do so. I wasn't angry at Felix. I knew he liked me, but I didn't want to sacrifice our friendship for something I associated with hurt. I just wanted to be held without being trapped. I needed a release, and I trusted him, even if he of all people didn't deserve a spray. In that moment, all I could do was scream. All I saw was rage.

It is at once validating and incredibly confronting to realise another layer of your own past like that. It has taken so long for it all to unfold, piece by piece. No wonder I can sit and chat in a moving car, unfazed by my freshly broken collarbone, or give a speech while it cracks inside me. No wonder I can run 72 kilometres in one go with a shoe full of blood and feel like I didn't run fast enough. No wonder I was numb to the burns that tore through every layer of skin on my calves the night I fell over a fire pit at Max's parents' place just after we first met, and he was baffled that I didn't cry. The man who tattooed my sternum and ribs when I was nineteen in California remarked how quiet I was. He knew. He knew that I'd been raped when I was younger. If I could smile through that, I could smile through anything.

Conventional intimacy was a language I didn't speak. Even what I had with my boyfriend was unconventional. It was profoundly special, but it was also atypical. Growing up, I skipped over a lot of the hands-on (haha) experience I needed to form healthy, consistent ideas about relationships. I'd always struggled socially as it was, and still didn't know why. I had nothing to fall back on. My toolkit was a mess. It was heavy and cumbersome. And then, completely and unintentionally, I lost a crucial stage of my development, and had it replaced with something harmful and destructive.

I wasn't someone who took any real interest in boys romantically at school. I think I was 'on the tune', as it was called, with a boy I met at the inter-school cross country carnival in

Year 8 who I texted a few times. The first phones I had were Nokia bricks back in the days of sending credit and playing snake on colourless screens. And there was no way my parents were letting me get a flip Motorola or a Blackberry. In Year 11 I went on a date with a student from Hutchins, a local all-boys school, who was in our English class. That was about it, though. While a lot of my peers were writing their own rites of passage, I had little if any control, understanding or even want of mine. The shark cage analogy springs to mind. Better yet, the idea of being taught water safety by a fucking great white.

I remember one Friday while I was still at Collegiate, before I disclosed the abuse, my friend Megan and I had a sleepover at her house. She lived in a place called Glebe, which overlooks the city, near the Queens Domain athletics track. It's quite an eerie part of town, especially late at night. The residences are suddenly gobbled by dense bushland at the top of the hill. A couple of her friends from Hutchins came and met up with us at a neighbourhood playground. One of them was Matt, who I went to primary school with. The four of us just sat there and chatted, before the boys left and Megan and I went back to her place to sleep. I suspect Bester was stalking me that night; he often drove to my house after dark and sat in his car. Somehow he knew, when I saw him at school the following week, that I had been hanging out with some Hutchins students the night I'd stayed with Megan. His version of events was that he had overheard boys gossiping about me. '"Tame by name but not by nature," that's what they were calling you,' went his unforgettable jingle of shame.

I've since repurposed it because it's a good rhyme. He wasn't the first person to say it to me, nor was he the only genius to ever point out the irony of my surname, but I've reclaimed it mainly because he is a geriatric fruitcake and he doesn't own my name.

Felix just listened. He knew I had to cry. He knew I wasn't angry at him. He just allowed me to be. To be whatever I needed to be. He made up a bed, and we watched *Dogma*. He gave me water and talked me back down to earth. He let me sleep alone. To this day he has never laid a hand on me.

'You were asking for it' might just be more insulting to everyday people than it is to survivors of abuse. For it relies upon the logic that every person, when presented with the opportunity to have sex with a vulnerable person, will not be able to help themselves.

When it came down to it, it didn't matter what I did, how I behaved, or what I said. The people who understood me, and who knew the right thing to do, did not 'take advantage' of my confusion and vulnerability. There was nothing I could do that could provoke them into being a bad person. And they weren't about to let me believe that I was a bad person either.

I've moved around a lot in life and in love. I have had to leave people and places, but the lessons they taught me will never leave me. Test the boundaries all you want. The only thing that causes abuse is an abuser.

With Dad.

With Mum.

Standing in my light.

Above left: Painting the spice rack (and ourselves) with Eloise.

Right: I've always loved the outdoors.

Below: Swimming with friends Rosie (far left) and Lucy MacDonald (far right), and Eloise (to my right).

Left: Hanging around with Dom.

Below: I've always loved athletics.

With Mum and Ron at their wedding.

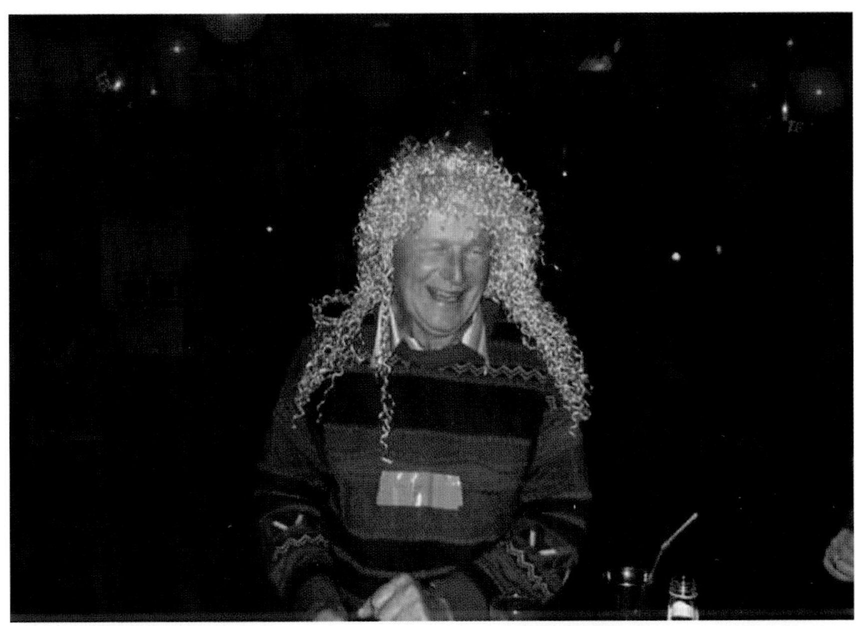

My wonderful pop, Wally, and (below) a portrait of him I created.

Left: Fourteen-year-old me in Mexico. And (above) more comfortable in formalwear at Eloise's wedding, with Dylan, Millie and Max.

Below: With my not-so-baby brother, Oscar.

Left: Sparkling in the sun with Christian.

Below: At Park Beach, Tasmania.

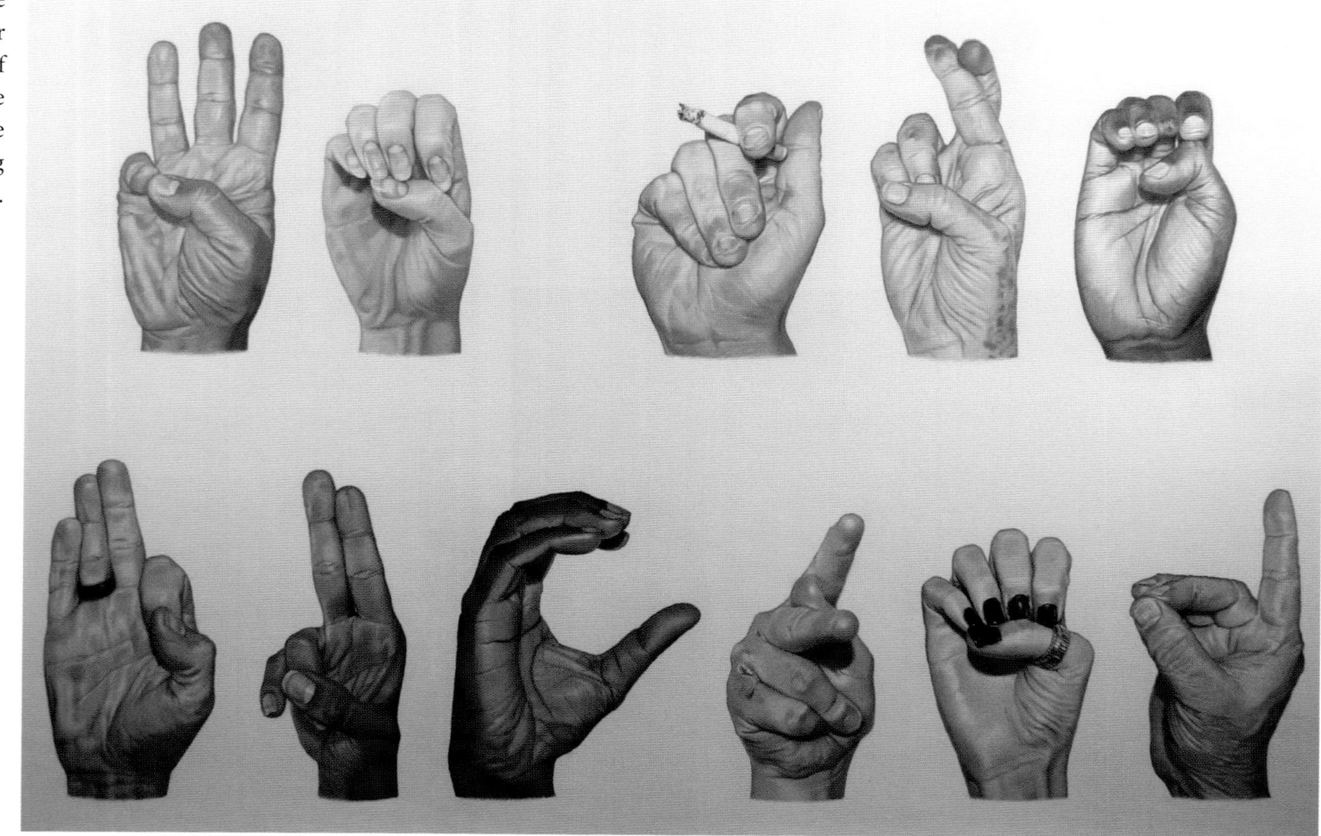

The picture I created for Martin Gore of Depeche Mode – eleven diverse hands signing 'We are Fucked'.

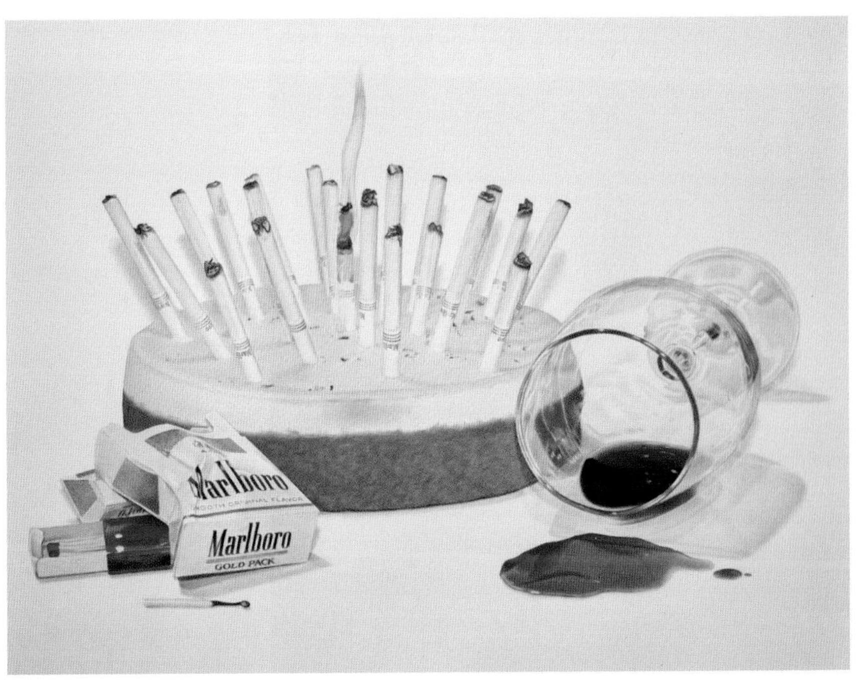

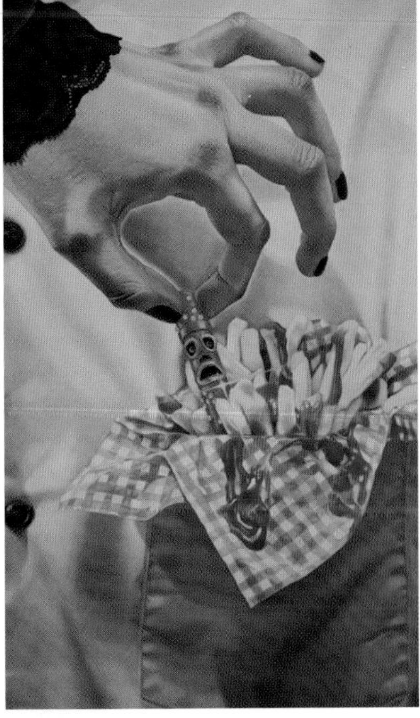

Some of my illustrations from my time in the USA.

Left: In my wedding dress created by my cousin Morgan.

Below: With Spencer.

Right: Dad visiting me in the USA.

Below: Standing proudly in awe of my mum.

Above: Yoga: a habit and then a career.

Left: Celebrating with Eloise after the Ross Marathon.

Above: My illustration of *The Last Supper.*

Left: With my surrogate big sister, Camilla.

Below left: Signing prints with John Cleese.

PHOTO CREDIT: KARLEEN MINNEY © *CANBERRA TIMES*/ACM

Left: My first press club address.

Below middle: And my second, complete with broken collarbone.

PHOTO CREDIT: AAP IMAGE/MICK TSIKAS

PHOTO CREDIT: AAP IMAGE/MICK TSIKAS

Above middle: The photo that launched endless projections.

Right: Standing in solidarity at the Tasmanian March 4 Justice.

PHOTO CREDIT: NIKKI DAVIS JONES / NEWSPIX

PHOTO CREDIT: ALEX ELLINGHAUSEN / *THE SYDNEY MORNING HERALD*

Above: My gravitational pull with Max on the night of the 2021 Australian of the Year Awards.

Below: My newest family members, Zappa and Iggy.

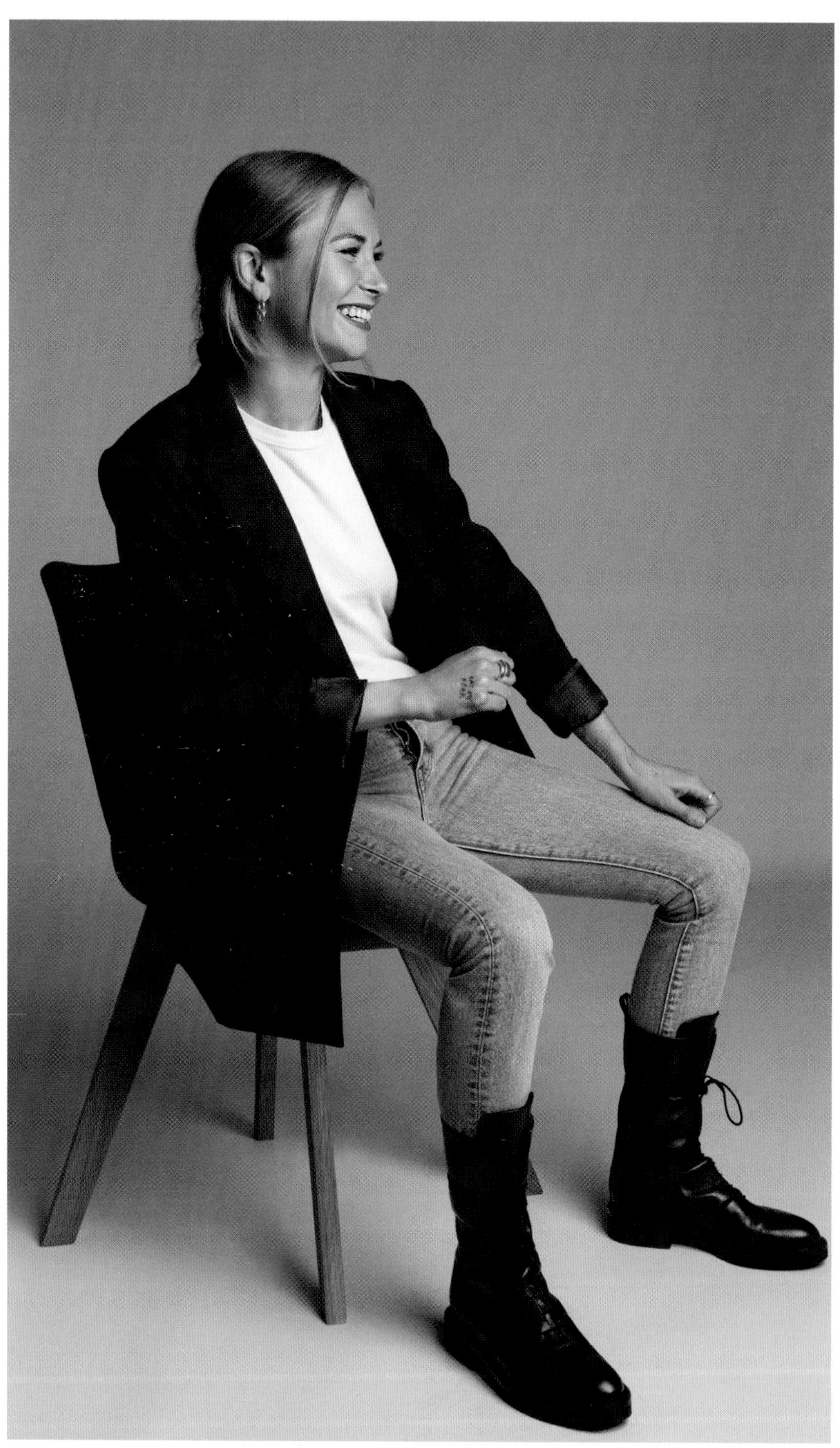

PHOTO CREDIT: KISHKA JENSEN

Still smiling.

Chapter 10

I Do Voices

Once upon a time, I might have called myself a cinephile. And I do like going to the movies every now and then, although I don't go as much as I used to. I'm a creature of habit and comforts. My stubbornness is such that I tend to want to watch the same flicks over and over again, ones I know I like. I'm already tutting the era of Marvel superhero blockbusters and subtle war propaganda with curmudgeonly catch-cries like 'They don't make 'em like they used to!' followed by cartoonish fist-shakes.

All throughout my childhood and following the abuse, film and television were my favoured self-medications for my neuroses. When my reality became better, I stopped craving escape.

French director and one of the founding figures of the French New Wave, François Truffaut, reckoned that 'film lovers are sick people'. I wouldn't go that far. That's a bit harsh. Not everyone who enjoys films is 'sick'. However, I think he had a point when he said, 'When life doesn't give you satisfaction, you go to the movies.' I believe that is true of many people, and certainly of the lonely among us.

St Michael's Collegiate is located in Hobart's city centre. It's a private, all-girls Anglican school whose motto is 'Set for Life'.

I got in there on a scholarship to study drama at their School of Performing Arts. I memorised a piece of dialogue that Mum randomly found while sifting through books, which included several phone conversations between the main character and different callers. For each of them I put on a different accent, one being Scottish, I think. It was probably 'muddled', like Mrs Doubtfire's Irish according to Pierce Brosnan.

(Sucked in, Andrew. That Pierce Brosnan reference will well and truly cement my position on the leaderboard in a long-running game called 'Piercing' that I was unwittingly drawn into by my friend and fellow anti–child sexual abuse advocate Andrew Carpenter, of Webster Lawyers in South Australia. He and his boss sneak Pierce Brosnan's name and face into everything. Well, now Pierce Brosnan's name is written four times in my memoir. Which is a lot for someone who went from 007 to singing fucking ABBA in lycra!)

As I was saying, I got into Collegiate's Performing Arts School. I rode in on a one-off reduced fee. Mum remembers that discounts weren't usually part of the deal for being accepted into the program, but they were impressed with me so they offered 25 per cent off. (What a wanker I am, flexing like this. I wonder if that's just what they said to everyone.)

To be honest, I didn't really want to go there. I had never heard of the place before Mum told me about it. I wanted to go to MacKillop College with Dom, or Taroona High, where Dad taught. Collegiate's Open Day certainly opened my eyes to a culture that was foreign to me, one that perplexed and daunted me. My instinct was that I didn't belong there. The autistic female brain is supposedly wired more like a neurotypical male brain. Perhaps that is why I find it easier to socialise with boys, and didn't relish the idea of attending an all-girls school. I was still eleven then, and I remember feeling like I was on another planet. The sheer size of the place dwarfed me. Its history too, which hovered in the air of the common rooms and the high-ceilinged Linmor Hall.

After an awkward day of activities, I didn't have much hope. That is, until I went to the afternoon assembly and saw, to my surprise, that among the showcased performers was a fellow misfit offbeat comedian from the School of Performing Arts: a whacky and wild tomboy whose name was also Grace. She was only one grade above me, and had seen as much *Mork & Mindy* as I had. There was another, among the crowd.

I've heard actors say they feel more at home on the stage than they do elsewhere, and oddballs and neurodivergent people often find themselves there. This may well be because performing is essentially just a form of masking and mimicry that is celebrated and unmitigated. It is an opportunity for the out-of-place to *be* – to connect, communicate and express themselves in ways they're unable to day to day. While masking and mimicry in everyday situations are typically fear-based and protective, in theatre these things are validated, interactive, free-flowing and empowering.

In Year 2 we had to do a worksheet in which we nominated the career we imagined our older selves undertaking in twenty years' time. Twenty years from then is now, as it happens. I said I wanted to be a comedian, because my favourite thing to do was laugh. It was how I reached my father. It was where I felt at home. It was the moment I connected with Dom. It was the spark that lit up my mother's eyes. It was a language I knew how to speak in a world that felt foreign to me.

There's a distinction between pre-recorded footage and live shows. The magic of the latter is impossible to capture. It can't be recreated. You are either there or you are not. The same goes for people.

But the difference between real and fake is not always clear. In the modern world, especially, we are often misled, or misinformed, deliberately. It's taken me a long time to separate the two; for the scales to fall from my eyes. It's as difficult as trying to discern between gold and fool's gold. Moreover, you can't necessarily strategise while flying by the seat of your pants. All you can do is present well, and do your best to not let others down, and make the most of opportunities that might dry up at any moment. My parents met on set making a commercial. My mum met my stepfather making a promotional video. My mother worked in television. Me? Well, I can smile through anything, remember?

Last year in March I took part in a documentary that I'd agreed to amid the initial maelstrom of requests following the Australian of the Year Awards. It was pitched as an inspirational piece about finding hope during dark times, and I was told that I would be one of many included in it. In my view, however, it was, in the end, an unethical, disingenuous gathering of vulnerable people for the purpose of entertainment. It was trauma pornography in disguise. Before arriving on set, I hadn't met the other participants, who I must say are some of the loveliest people. Among them was a sixteen-year-old recovering from anorexia, and the mother of a boy who had died by suicide not six months prior to filming. There was also an eleven-year-old present, whose parents weren't there. Yet not a single trauma-informed counsellor was on site to debrief anyone after the long hours of naturally exhausting work.

I should have known better. There were so many red flags, one being that I kept being pulled to the front of the pack, to lead people I barely knew. Another was that when I was asked to chat one on one with the host I heard the words '. . . and Grace is funny too. Grace, be funny.'

On the first of the two days I was there to shoot, I had to give a keynote address to the Real Estate Institute of New South Wales at around three in the afternoon (another commitment I'd agreed to in the whirlwind). Only, we were on location filming a nature walk an hour and a half south of Sydney in the hills above Austinmer. The producer had arranged for his wife to drop off a blazer and white T-shirt at our destination so I could give the speech via Zoom from a small local cafe, a hidden gem in the bush about fifteen kilometres from our starting point. He assured me we would make it with plenty of time to spare.

As the production schedule lagged more and more, I realised I was going to have to make my own way. Thankfully Max and my cousin Eloise were with me, and all of us were in our trail-running gear. The producer pointed us in the direction of the path, and off we went; three Tasmanians in outback New South Wales. For six kilometres we ran through steep scrub, only to be spat out on the side of a highway with a few grass cuts and muddy legs. We must have taken a wrong turn at some point. Thankfully, we knew the name of where we were headed and were in phone range, because we were still almost four clicks off the mark and in unfamiliar territory. The shortest route meant we just had to suck it up and run alongside the road. Max recalls the truckies honking at Eloise and me as we powered on in the heat. Ten kilometres later, I gave an off-the-cuff speech on the designated theme of 'relaunching' and 'rethinking' life at a makeshift lectern from a rest stop restaurant storeroom in country New South Wales in my shorts, covered in dried sweat.

I told my story to a roomful of people I couldn't see while I didn't know where the fuck I was – both literally and figuratively speaking – in a world I had to run to keep up with. You really have to laugh.

Then, without any consultation or prior warning, the documentary was promoted under the title *Walking with Grace*. You cannot make this shit up. The icing on the cake is that this – this is what they call 'reality television'. If Max hadn't got on the blower and given Foxtel – oh yes, you guessed it – a bloody earful, they wouldn't have even let any of the interviewees watch the thing before it aired. And no, they didn't yield easily to that request. At first we were met with the defence that no director 'worth their salt' would ever allow such a thing as a preview. They weren't going to let me watch the project that they were selling as though I'd had some kind of editorial control. They weren't going to let the grieving, underage and traumatised people who featured on the show see how their own sensitive stories were going to be portrayed to the nation. My personal objections aside, I believe the mistreatment of the others involved was beyond the pale.

Everything is a balancing act – advocacy and raising awareness especially. You can't know what the behaviour or the goodwill of others will be like until after the fact in a lot of cases. You also don't necessarily know how much power you have in any given situation. In addition, every individual has varying expectations, wants and needs.

It took a threat of legal action before we were all finally sent a copy of the final edit. Within the first three minutes, Max and I were alarmed to hear the narrator refer to the group of interviewees as one that I'd supposedly gathered together myself. On top of that, the sixteen-year-old anorexia survivor (whose parents weren't there, mind you) was introduced with the line, 'Looking at her now, you wouldn't be able to tell she was anorexic.' Call me a fusspot all you want, but anyone who's suffered from an eating disorder knows that is just a shocker of a thing to say. Say anything, anything the fuck you want, but for the love of all that's fluffy and soft don't comment on the way they look – rule number one. Rule number two: don't put it on the telly!

After much huffing and puffing it ended up being called *A Walk with Hope*, and they made the changes that were requested by those of us involved.

The shoot took place, I might add, mere days after I gave a speech at the National Press Club on 3 March 2021, in which I talked about how the media retraumatises survivors by not listening closely to the boundaries they set. I was there to share my story. It was a golden opportunity to amplify the issues of grooming and child sexual abuse, which still remain shrouded in layers of mystery much to the benefit of perpetrators. The emcee asked reporters not to ask questions about the then-recent politically charged rape allegations, but almost every gallery journalist ignored this and asked about them anyway. This resulted in a provoked adversarial comment that was assumed to be about the then-prime minister, who had said he needed his wife to remind him to contextualise the act of rape as if it had happened to one of his own daughters.

I was already deep in my past, having spilled my guts to a pack of hungry wolves, and in that moment I saw the face of the man who abused me, who had a wife and two children who were twice my age at the time of the offending. 'It shouldn't take having children to have a conscience,' I said with a burning chest, and as the young man who'd asked the question went to sit down, I realised I wasn't done yet. '. . . Actually, having children doesn't guarantee a conscience.'

I'd stopped talking to anybody in the room. Their 'gotcha' was not my 'gotcha'. I was fighting a ghost only I could see.

A chance to spotlight the complex crime of child abuse was overshadowed that day by a confected feud that then spiralled and became an ongoing convenient media distraction used to dilute the work I did. The press were baiting me to talk about the prime minister and they succeeded, although they got more than they bargained for. While I didn't like the man's disingenuous politicking, out of hundreds of events I did in 2021, and the thousands of words I spoke about grooming and sexual violence, he was to me a minor character. Let me be clear: that comment did apply to Scott's words, but it was bigger than that. I own their original context, but it must be known that they run so much deeper. And gee, it felt good – nah, I'm not that petty. (Yes, I fucken am.)

As for the side eye – what more is there to say? An entire nation projected onto my face. What's done is done. The man showed his true colours long before I frowned at him. And being responsible, and loyal to your cause and friends, is not about being liked. It sure as fuck is not about being polite.

It's funny that the little people, who have the most to lose and who gain the least, are the ones put on display. They are the ones who bare their wounds and bear the brunt, for the benefit of the media-industrial complex. So much of reporting exists inside a vacuum. Those who wish to tell stories seem to have lost interest in simply helping them be told. They want to create them, but without taking responsibility for them or sharing the load of the suffering. Sensation has replaced education. There's little space for nuance on the main stage.

I am weighed down by a feeling that I should defend the fact that I went to a private school, the fees of which Mum paid all by herself. Without disclosing every financial detail, all I can say is, appearances aren't always as they seem. People project things from both sides, don't forget. Especially people who've had to fight for security, or feel as though they have to prove themselves.

Five weeks before Mum and Ron got married, she was in the newsroom, inquiring about a story. On this particular occasion she needed her dad's expertise. For what, I don't know.

Something about bigotry, maybe? When he answered the phone he said, 'Are you calling for money?' She assured him she wasn't. 'You must be pregnant then.' That wasn't it either, she told him. Having just received her wedding invitation in the mail he insisted, 'You must be, that would be the only reason a man like Ron would marry someone like you.'

There will always be detractors. I know, I've had a few too.

A big part of me wishes I hadn't gone to Collegiate, for obvious reasons. And I feel embarrassed about having even gone there in the first place, in a way. Not because I am not grateful for the opportunity or some of the lasting friendships and great memories I did make, but because it really wasn't somewhere that I felt suited who I was.

I feel embarrassed by a part of myself that tried to become what I thought I had to in order to fit in there. To be slender. To dress a particular way. To wear too-nice clothes. It has taken me a long time to work through the outward expression of perfectionism that was always bubbling inside me but which really boiled over in such an environment. The illusion that certain fashions were representative of coolness.

Clothing for me has always been more than that. It has served as another mask. Or, at least, I thought it did. In hindsight, I look back at the times when I flaunted certain styles, thinking that my well-put-together exterior was a perfect disguise which served the dual purpose of helping me present like everything was okay and deterring anyone from messing with me. Instead, I just looked like I was trying too hard, which made me all the more vulnerable in the end.

I'm ashamed to say I spent a decent portion of my tenure as Australian of the Year suppressing parts of my inner and outer self-expression. Despite authenticity and integrity being among my highest values, there were sacrifices I thought I had to make in order to prioritise my message.

In February 2021, I appeared for the first time on ABC TV's *Q&A*, alongside a panel of talking heads in my first ever long-form live national television broadcast. Beforehand I was told that I wouldn't have to share my story, and that the only related content might be an analytical discussion about the stages of child grooming. I was also told to familiarise myself with other issues, like the controversy surrounding former Collingwood Football Club President Eddie McGuire's racially inappropriate comments. Finally, I thought, here was an opportunity to demonstrate that survivors of abuse are not defined by their past trauma; that we can speak intellectually about any number of complex topics.

Instead, the host introduced me by asking me to 'catch everyone up' on why I was there. I had to qualify myself. I felt like a fool. Thankfully, I have a sense of humour. 'Does this show go for eleven years?' I asked, before stumbling my way through a gut-punched regurgitation of my trauma, and I swallowed my disappointment and humiliation. Only, then I was asked to show my tattoos. I was the pitiable, one-dimensional, sensational cartoon. I got it. I definitely got it. I was *it*.

Without warning, they played a disclosure from a 73-year-old woman who had never shared her story before, not even to her own children. Live, on national television. Before the program, there was no warning that the content of the episode might distress viewers, or indeed anyone with even a shred of empathy. If my awareness of the microphone pinned to my shirt hadn't held me back, the censorship team would've been working overtime.

By the time the show wrapped, after a touch-and-go tense hour – which included Alexander Downer saying, 'we don't see a lot of racism in Australia' as he sat beside powerhouse First Nations woman Tanya Hosch – I'd cut right off. Any performative energy had been used. Used.

In the green room I found Max and could barely speak. I just wanted space. I was shaken and a bit pissed off to tell the truth. Although I must express my gratitude to Tanya and to Shane Fitzsimmons, who had my back that night, all the way. People could tell that something was up and kept coming over to check in on me, while Max did his best gentle-but-firm Berlin nightclub bouncer impression. The optimist in me doesn't want to assume ill will in people, but when I explained that I felt upset because I was blindsided and heartbroken for a woman I had never met and who I had no way of contacting, whose story had just been broadcast nationally, it wasn't a comfort to be told, 'It's okay, you're a Twitter sensation.'

I learned something about the commodification of trauma that day, which is that you have to take things into your own hands. If you don't speak, people will put words in your mouth.

My Pork Soda Primus T-shirt, studded belt and safety pin earrings had been kept aside in favour of blazers and crisp shirts. Only to be called a 'boss bitch' in a 'power' suit by the woman who nominated me for Australian of the Year. On Twitter, of all places. What a sensation.

It was when I ditched the stiff jackets for my lived-in Rolling Stones cactus tongue jumper (which my friend Maddison always takes the piss out of me for never taking off) that I realised it didn't matter. I could wear my Iggy and The Stooges *Year of the Iguana* shirt during interviews and still be heard. If people took issue with it, that would be more of a reflection on them than on me. You might not believe it, especially considering what the media portrays, and indeed what I often do myself, but of all the voices I listen to, I'm only just learning to prioritise my own.

By the time I finished Year 12, I was down for the count. I graduated only eighteen months after I'd disclosed the abuse. The very thought of staying on the education treadmill was exhausting. My ATAR gave me some options, and after taking Economics and German I'd considered moving into International Relations, Global Studies and Law at different stages in high school. I remember Dad asking me if I had thought about becoming a lawyer, and Mum too. It's a common and wholeheartedly good instinct to want to give your child opportunities that you didn't have yourself.

Still, I felt the pressure. I felt it all. And the real world had usurped the classroom at that point in time. Not to mention the fact that the trauma I was processing had occurred at an elite school at the hands of a highly qualified and once well-respected teacher. All I wanted to do was get out. Get out and make new. And although when I left I enrolled in a community college in a foreign country with the intention of continuing my institutional education, all that I had come to know and trust about learning had been torn down.

My faith in the system was all but gone. In my first semester at Santa Barbara City College, I took English 101. I was eighteen. The very first text we studied was *Disgrace* by J. M. Coetzee, a book written from the perspective of a self-aggrandising ageing white South African teacher who sexually abuses one of his students and doesn't think he has done anything wrong. Hello darkness, my old and twisted fucking friend. The universe's sense of humour is as bleak as mine, apparently. It wasn't all that funny back then, though – comedy is tragedy plus time, as they say.

I couldn't actually bring myself to read the whole thing and there was no way in freshly frozen hell I was going to be able to write an essay about it. Thankfully, the English professor wasn't marking my syntax while he and I stood outside the classroom and I attempted to explain to him why I was willing to do any other project, just not *that*. I couldn't form full sentences. It was the epitome of disbelief and dysfunction, but also distrust. Who was this man standing before me in this distant land, teaching lessons from this of all titles? This story of all stories? What were the odds?!

Still, I showed up, and while the rest of the class viewed the larger-than-life film adaptation on the projector screen, I sat nonchalantly with headphones on watching a documentary on a laptop about the corruption that belies the privatised prison system and the war on drugs in the United States, called *The House I Live In*. Some metaphors just write themselves.

In school, I honestly didn't ever really have a strong idea of who I was or what I wanted to do with my life. It's the 'why' that's led me, above the how. I didn't follow a clear career path. I blew with the wind while holding on to what I knew where and when I could.

Whether it's been spontaneously making art in the eastern suburbs of Los Angeles, lending my story to grassroots law reform campaigns, or even running – it's a sense of injustice, seeking truth and wanting to help others that's shone through. It's my friends and family. It's fellow survivors.

I've made mistakes and some thoughtless choices along the way, no doubt. At times I've been selfish and rigid in my outspoken opinions. I've been foolhardy and determined to the point of impatience. I've fallen. I've broken. And I've had to learn to pull myself back up. Over and over. And over again. That's part of the play that tests your limits and builds your character.

Qualified or unqualified, voiced or voiceless, I think people's biggest actions speak for themselves.

Chapter 11

The Misfits

Wherever I go, I seem to be drawn to square pegs in round holes. Not that any of the friends I've made are people I would call square, I must say.

My first friend at Collegiate was a girl named Jess who lived around the corner from Mum and Ron's Bellerive house. We are still really close. Like me, she was somewhat of an outsider who ended up finishing school in the public system, at the school where my dad taught, in fact.

Jess is a hilarious, sharp, self-determined firecracker who takes no prisoners and has seen things that many of us have not. Her mother, Jenny, a former psychiatric nurse, is much the same. They are both brilliant women, who have always been very dear and very good to me.

When she was only five, Jess lost her father, and her mother took on both parental roles. The pair looked after each other, through good times and bad.

There are lots of things I could write about Jess. She was there for me back then, and she is here for me now. Of all the people who have come and gone, there was only one Collegiate student in my year group who sat in Linmor Hall the day I went back there, ten years after disclosing, to give a speech to the staff and senior students about the abuse that happened on those very grounds. It was Jess.

We both cried. For many reasons. Her loyalty, heart and courage don't need context beyond this. I love her and always will.

In Year 8, I became close with an impressively multitalented and fiercely witty girl named Gillian.

The circumstances of our initial meeting escape me. They have long been saturated by the joy and laughter of the wave of fully formed memories we've since created. Like the time we strapped my bulbous plush toy hamster to the top of Gillian's head in Faith and Life class, and pretended with deadpan nonchalance for the entire lesson that there was nothing awry. Or the time I snuck into the classroom before one Maths Applied lesson in Year 9 and adjusted Mr I's prewritten heading on the whiteboard from 'General Quadratic Equations' to '*Genital* Quadratic Equations'. Yes, I'm a dag. It was worth it for the smothered sporadic giggles from students.

Good old Mr I. He was a legend of a teacher, with a wicked sense of humour and the patience of a saint, although I can understand why he eventually moved on and became a craft beer brewer. Teenage girls would do that.

When the global internet sensation of en masse public statuesque 'freezing' was at its peak, Gillian attempted to lead our Maths class in its own coordinated effort without Mr I's knowledge. The cue was supposed to be Gillian grabbing herself a tissue. The plan would've worked if a blissfully unaware Mr I hadn't foiled it by saying, 'Why are you all staring at Gillian? She's just getting a tissue. Leave her be!' At which point I howled with contagious laughter which set the whole room off.

In 2008, Gillian and I filmed a sketch video in which the two of us played a cast of thousands. The highlight might have been a staged political debate held from opposite sides of her parents' polished wooden dining table. Shot before the era of Obama, it featured a decidedly frustrated Kevin Rudd, played by a thirteen-year-old Gillian, and an unhinged George Dubya, brought to you by yours truly at the ripe old age of twelve in full Texas drawl. Both of us wore oversized black blazers we borrowed from Gillian's six-foot-one father, our long ponytails tucked down the back.

The two of us were diehard fans of Eddie Izzard, Monty Python, *Absolutely Fabulous* and *Black Books*. When absurdist comedian and classically trained musician Bill Bailey announced a tour of Australia in 2009, our excitement was akin to Beatlemania. He was as good as a Spice Girl to us. Such was our nerdy fandom that we even made signs. I can still see us sitting on the black leather stools in her parents' kitchen, hunched over big sheets of cartridge paper, boldening the lines of our permanent-marker lettering. We went hardcore too. Went *niche*, baby. We wanted to show the depth of our passion. In the 2001 recorded special of his *Bewilderness* tour,

Bill jokes, 'At parties, sometimes, for a laugh, I introduce myself . . . People say "What do you do?" And I say, "I'm Aled Jones, it's all gone wrong for me. No, look, I've still got it."' Then, after a feigned drunken cry, he launches into an off-pitch send-up of 'Walking in the Air' by the Welsh teenage prodigy. When Gillian and I held up our obliquely referenced 'We love you, Aled' masterpiece in the audience at Wrest Point Casino and Bill himself read it out loud on stage to the crowd with an everlasting 'nice touch' to boot, we were about ready to burst.

We were cheeky, we were subversive, but we did our work, and we meant well. For all our class-clowning antics, we handed in our assignments on time, and studied hard. For Mr Simon's Year 10 English class, Gillian and I performed a sock puppet version of *Romeo and Juliet* behind the back of Mum's couch that we got Dom to film and Photoshop grass into. Gillian was a star, a straight-A student, who could achieve anything. She *can* achieve anything. Alongside our friend Gabby, she followed her heart and talents to VCA, and she is now a thriving filmmaker. She was the quintessential Quince to my punk-ish Puck in the School of Performing Arts' production of *A Midsummer Night's Dream*. We could move and shake to Shakespeare, but surprisingly our rap duo, 'G-Force', never made the big time.

Both Gillian and I had a great rapport with our teachers. We spent many recesses and lunchtimes with our friends Caitlin, Jess, Rachael and the two Emilys in Mrs Ride's office because she had to supervise my meals. So did Mr Bester. For Christmas in 2009, Gillian made personalised gingerbread houses for all of her teachers, complete with pi to fourteen decimal places on Mr I's. Comedy nerd me gifted my teachers discount DVDs from the since-closed down ABC shop in Centrepoint in town. Mr I and my German teacher Frau Roach got Bill Bailey specials, as they'd both attended the Hobart live show. They'd run out of copies of *Monty Python Sings*, which I'd been quoting from in Mr Bester's Maths Extended class, so I burnt him a copy of mine instead.

The love, support and friendship of Gillian and her adoring family make up another example of a lifetime connection that has withstood the tests of time and trauma. It is one of a handful of bonds that has held fast through the storms and one I've been able to rely on without a second thought or fear of judgement. Her brothers Max and Harry, and her grandfather, David, are another three good eggs. Max, in particular, is someone I have a special bond with. His way of thinking and seeing the world parallels my own in many ways. His artistic style is as distinct as it is mesmerising to watch, in both real and sped-up time. It's a prismatic fusion of the left brain and right brain and the result is synergistic harmony. He combines his command of geometry with unrestrained freehand flare. It's mathematics meets creativity, brightened by 80s neon. It's funk. It's punk. I love it, like I love him and all our psychedelic, decimated but somehow always nourishing and tessellated times.

In 2009, while I was still an outpatient in anorexia recovery on a monitored exercise and food program, Gillian's mother, Sally, introduced me to yoga. She and Gillian and I used to take Bikram together. This proved to be the gift of a lifetime. I had been a keen athlete from the moment I could tumble, and being sidelined had broken more than my spirit. Moving my body while also practising stillness became not only a habit but eventually a career: I'm now a qualified teacher. More importantly, it became a practice that enabled me to reconnect with myself and the world around me.

Sally was a beacon of steadfast maternal love who epitomised commitment to the very art of being. She lit up every room, each and every corner of it. Her very presence was like drawing in a deep breath. The world sadly lost Sally in May 2020. To have known her is a great privilege.

Paul, her life partner, was her perfectly matched yin. His whole world is his family, and his heartfelt hugs speak to a man of sincere depth. His humour is black, but his home is warm and his cooking will knock your socks off. I often found myself not wanting to leave their household. After Dom's parents split up, it became a new stronghold of safety and consistency for me.

I am very grateful to Sally, and to Paul. Sally is missed by so many, but she will be forgotten by none. Paul has been like another father to me at times, and those times will never be forgotten either.

Chapter 12

Beatniks and Refried Beans

When Mum was in her twenties, she went over to Detroit for a year and worked in a boutique clothing store. Busted, what a crook.

While she was there, she befriended a customer named Sigrid, who is ten years Mum's senior, and Sigrid's husband, Richard. The pair own a sandstone house that backs onto a Detroit golf course and is a few doors down from one of the late great Aretha Franklin's properties. When I was three, Sigrid flew Mum and me over to stay with her and Richard. The first live concert I ever witnessed, albeit at a distance, was on the green outside Aretha Franklin's birthday party in the American summer of 1998. Mum, Sigrid and I had been out walking in the neighbourhood, and some of the houses didn't have fences. We'd stopped because we could hear music. 'It's okay if you want to stand and listen,' the security guard kindly told us. Behind him were people seated in Aretha's yard, watching Wilson Pickett and his band of musicians swinging their instruments in time with the beat and each other as if they were extensions of their effortlessly rhythmic bodies. 'And then Aretha grabbed the mic,' Mum recalls, 'and her voice . . .' Her voice. I was three, and even I remember that. I can't explain it. Respect. We didn't hang around for long, not wanting to intrude. It was a moment of serendipity we would savour.

Mum and Sigrid stayed quite close. Sigrid also came out to visit us when I was little. Then during back-to-back Australian summers, at the end of 2006 and 2007, Sigrid came to stay with us for extended periods to avoid the harsh Detroit winters because she wasn't fond of the cold. Like Mum, Sigrid is very petite and active, and is more at home making music in the sun than trudging through the snow.

On one of her visits, I floated the idea of an exchange. I wanted to visit her for a change. To my surprise, neither Sigrid nor my family were opposed to the idea, on the condition that I paid my way to and from America. So, throughout Year 8, I saved up all of my pocket money for a ticket to the United States. I washed and cleaned my parents' cars, did extra chores, and Mum agreed to buy a 1.5 × 1.5 metre painting of mine for $300. That was a pretty good deal for me, I reckon; it was probably worth about $30.

With a top-up from Mum – after Dad, who received my bank statements in the mail, kept making me pay for lunches – I had the dough come adventure time. Sigrid had said that she and Richard would look after me for the Christmas break of 2008–09. Only, they were not going to be in Detroit; they intended to spend their winter holidays in the central highlands of Mexico. At the time their eldest son, Eben, was living in San Miguel de Allende. He is a brilliant academic whose interests lie in Latin American and Indigenous history.

The plan was for me to fly to Los Angeles where Sigrid and Richard would meet me at the airport. We would stay in the city for a few days before heading north to Santa Barbara. Being Midwesterners, the couple wanted to make the most of being on the West Coast. However, their next stop did not include me. While they went to San Francisco, I was to spend a week at a boarding school in Santa Barbara county's Carpinteria, as per Richard's arrangements. He and Sigrid would then pick me up on their way back down the coast to Los Angeles, where we'd board a flight to Leon, an hour's drive from our temporary home.

The first time I flew by myself on a plane I was five. It was only from Melbourne to Hobart, though. I had been on a trip with Dad and his wife and left at the end so they could have time together. The leg to the States when I was thirteen was certainly much longer. I didn't mind it, to be honest. At least not on the way there. I was small enough that I managed to get some shut-eye and was taken by the novelty of being able to order endless free bottles of Schweppes tonic water. (That's my Coca-Cola – my go-to soft drink.) However, on the way back I was seated between an American couple who were in the midst of an argument. I volunteered to move seats so they could be next to each other, only to be told by the wife, 'NO, Jack likes the aisle and I like the window.'

*

Los Angeles is nothing like the curated version of the city we see in films. The City of Angels – long ago, perhaps. Once upon a distant time. What we're shown of it is a handful of polished fingernails amid a graveyard of decaying bodies. When they catch the sun, they glimmer and sparkle, casting shafts of light that hide the waste. But the truth of the dog-eat-dog land of the not-so-free is that it is built on the back of cruelty, under the shade of the Hollywood Tower of Terrorism.

It took me literally being hit in the head to wake up one day. I was living in LA. I thought that was the pinnacle. I thought I was where I had to be, doing what I had to do, to prove myself. I was where I thought I belonged. Walking down filthy streets that don't get any rain. Spending most of my day inside a car, then most of the rest of it complaining about that. The art supplies store I worked at, Blue Rooster, was in the L. Ron Hubbard neighbourhood. There were two gigantic Scientology 'churches' nearby – if you can call them that – each extending for blocks and towering like prisons, with heavy security gates.

I stayed with Sigrid and Richard at a hotel in downtown LA. I remember walking from there with Richard through the streets to the Walt Disney Concert Hall. He wanted to marvel at the architecture, its silver sails reminiscent of the Sydney Opera House. Less than a mile away is Skid Row. Central City East is its official name.

It really is la-la land. There's no turning a blind eye; the extremes of poverty and wealth are side by side.

*

When I worked at Blue Rooster when I was nineteen, I met fellow artist Chris Slaymaker. He also worked there. When he found out I needed a place to stay in September 2015, he invited me to move into his one-bedroom apartment near Dodger Stadium in Echo Park. There was room behind the kitchen, he said, and he had a Japanese divider we could use as a door. We would make it work. And we did. Chris is a phenomenal surrealist, otherworldly muralist and painter. His studio was in a building just around the corner from Skid Row. It is hard to believe that only 28 kilometres from the absolute opulence of Bel Air are homeless communities whole streets long. Fifty blocks, to be exact. Around 8000 homeless Los Angeleans live there. You can hardly see the pavement for all the people and tents in some parts.

There have been countless takes on the United States Supreme Court decision to overturn Roe v. Wade, which saw immediate abortion bans in thirteen states. A point that I believe has been undervalued in this debate is that this assault on democracy is not so much a cause as a symptom of chaos.

Such is the effect of global media and conditioning that people who have never been to America may not realise the horrific reality that is: large parts of the US have been living in third-world poverty for a very long time, and it's only getting worse. There's no social safety net there, in terms of health-care, employment, housing. I could go on, but there's really no need. Those three factors alone – and combined – are killers, literally. This recent decision is a catastrophe in a disaster. 'Meanwhile in the Middle East,' I keep reading, as if America is simply an extension of Disneyland. It's no comparison to an occupied warzone, of course, but significant urban areas of the United States have been completely economically and socially destroyed.

In the aftermath of the Second World War, and in parallel with the burgeoning dominance of Hollywood, America formulated an idealistic narrative of itself as a self-actualising paradise. To the world, through fantastical fiction media, they catapulted capitalism, this idea that *you* can achieve anything if *you* just try hard enough. This idea that your big break will come; it's just around the corner. What was branded and bandied as 'the American dream' is really just toxic individualism. It may just be the cleverest advertisement of all time. It is full of hope, and sheds the system of all responsibility. It is the ultimate moth to flame, victim-blame, cure your pain with attention and fame. It's as if the United States has tried to freeze-frame the whitewashed glossy image of itself and keep selling it to everyone overseas through a rose-tinted lens. That makes red, white and blue.

Beneath their glorious, star-spangled banner, gun violence and organised crime is built into the fabric of their culture. You cannot go near the place without being directly or indirectly affected by it. Google Maps now displays the locations of active shootings. In the immediate aftermath of the 2014 Isla Vista tragedy, which occurred while I was living nearby, no one could leave the town that night. We all just had to stay put where we were, with no idea what was going on. I remember the marshal knocking on the door of our friend's house, and looking out at the caution tape in the streets. All those innocent young students. They were there to start their lives. And just like that, their families, an entire school and the whole town was in mourning. There are constant mass shootings – I know you know this at least, but so much remains conveniently hidden by their media. I don't see the States I remember being broadcast on TV: the ghettos and truck stops that I saw driving through the south. And Hollywood? Nobody hangs around in the heart of that place except tourists in the daytime who are none the wiser. It's a red-light district. Los Feliz is right next door. At Blue Rooster, we worked solo shifts, with a two-hour crossover at lunchtime. Days finished at 8 pm. One night, right before closing, a scammer robbed me at the till and I remember chasing him down the street before my senses kicked in and I realised I'd left the store unmanned.

There is so much destroyed property in Detroit, it equates to the size of San Francisco. There's an entire dead city within another. The decades-long tradition of 'Devil's Night' vandalism, which took off in the 1940s and escalated through to the 90s, saw at times hundreds of simultaneous incidents of arson and other crimes in Rust Belt capital cities like Detroit and Philadelphia on the night before Halloween, resulting in widespread, lasting and compounding urban destruction in those areas. In 2011, I went back to visit Sigrid and Richard in Detroit, with Mum, Ron and Oscar. The scars of this history indeed remain.

From 2002 to 2008, Kwame Kilpatrick served as mayor and led Detroit to near economic collapse, despite maintaining an image of extravagance over the course of his back-to-back terms. As a result, there was a mass exodus of residents. The 'Hip-Hop Mayor', Kilpatrick was called, flaunting diamond studs and trilby hats, taking large cash donations and travelling regularly interstate, while Detroit's finances dwindled. He was convicted on 24 felony counts and sentenced to 28 years in federal prison. Fraud, corruption, extortion, conspiracy and tax crimes were among the findings. Add to that a text-messaging sex scandal between him and his former chief of staff. Just a few small mistakes that one can sympathise with. It's no wonder that one of Donald Trump's final acts as president was to commute Kilpatrick's sentence, despite him only having served just over a quarter of it and still owing the city of Detroit US$1.5 million. How selectively, electively democratic.

The United States has been broken for a long time. Unchecked capitalism is eroding the place. Its pervasive all-or-nothingness has erased too much of the middle ground, and perspective and proportion along with it, it would seem. People identify more with what they're not than with what they are. The American experiment has long been over. How you return the power to the people in these conditions, I really don't know. The Democrats could have prevented what transpired with Roe v. Wade and chose not to. Joe Biden has previously voted against abortion access, even in exceptional circumstances. Hillary Clinton opened her campaign for the presidency by saying, 'Of course you can be a feminist and be pro-life.' Nancy Pelosi has called the abortion issue a distraction in the past.

My distrust in Hillary matches my distrust in Bill. Not because I think she ate babies behind a pizza shop, but for reasons including her unforgivably awful on-the-record behaviour towards Monica Lewinsky. Have you ever been a young woman in her twenties, alone inside a room with the president of the United States? What's that? No?

Forget about Monica Lewinsky the person, just for a moment. Let's talk logic. Let's talk biological science. I'm not defending Monica Lewinsky. I'm defending a little thing called fear. I'm defending nature. And yes, Monica too, because at least I can do a right sight more than imagine what it would be like to walk in her shoes.

The sad and disenfranchising truth is, issues of human rights in the United States are vital political fodder, without which the otherwise indistinguishable, corrupted, intelligence-infected political elite would have few things around which to rally their bases. Regardless of which side of the fence you sit on, those at the apex of society are prepared to toy with the lives of the little people because they are removed from the consequences.

It is such that even in the devastating case of a ten-year-old girl being raped in Ohio, what was more important to the public was choosing which side of the ledger to fight on. Moreover, Fox News not only attempted to claim the case was false, they used their platform to reveal the identity of the doctor to vilify her. A backwards and corrupted society is one in which a mainstream media outlet, which has enough power to open the eyes of the entire world to the harmful effects of child sexual abuse – and help fight it – chooses instead to use it as a weapon of shame to hunt down those who do.

The utter disparity in the United States means that those at the top of its empire, with the most access to wealth and power – and I don't necessarily mean presidents – are so far from their opposites that I don't know if there will ever be a way back. Greed and control for the sake of greed and control has long reached a state of absolute, nihilistic extremism.

Australia's been heading the same way since Gough. We all know what I mean. God save the 'Queen'. See, I . . . Never mind.

And here is perhaps the one thing that pro-lifers don't get: there is nothing natural about a ten-year-old being raped. That's not life. What kind of God would want that?

The saddest part is that the United States is bursting with breathtaking, redeeming people and places. The soul-stopping Grand Canyon. The purple ridges of the Sierra Nevadas behind the Santa Barbara courthouse at sunset. The endless miles of towering Redwoods in Northern California. The whole forests that turn golden in autumn in North Carolina. The rapidly running whitewater in Whitefish, Montana. The Colorado Rockies. Yellowstone. Yosemite. The Florida Keys. Joshua Tree.

Indeed, there is so much wonder to be shared there. The natural beauty is bountiful and boundless. But the smallest few in control of a land which belongs to so many seem intent on burying it.

The United States was and will always be my second home. I spent six years of my life there. Many of my dearest friends are there. And I plan to go back to visit, and explore more of its stunning landscape.

I married an American actor, who had one of the cruelest, most unforgiving, unrelenting childhoods as a result of being a working actor. We may have gone our separate ways, but I will always have empathy and compassion for him. He is a good person who bad things happened to. Nobody deserves what he went through.

It is one of my policies to not engage with online 'trolls', but one day when I saw that someone was not only having a potshot at my family, they were launching into Spencer's supposed millionaire status, I cracked and had to correct the record. 'No way, that's great news,' he said, when I told him about it afterwards. 'Where's my money though? Are they going to send me my money?'

This sort of deliberate obfuscatory bullshit is right up there with the people Photoshopping my face onto fake WEF website pages. It is true that I was invited to participate in their Young Global Leaders program. I even did an interview with someone to suss it out. But it wasn't for me. The Grace Tame Foundation doesn't accept political donations. And as rigid and vocal as I am, I am prepared to work with all sides in good faith. My principles are darn firm, and I wear my heart on my . . . face.

Even if those lies were true, there is no amount of money that could make up for what people like Spencer and his sister, Abigail, suffered as child actors. Theirs were unnatural upbringings in a cut-throat business. Both were subjected to abuse and criticism from strangers on a global scale, from an early age, and it was often about their physical appearance. There are some child actors who survive into adulthood unscathed and continue to work in the industry. Many don't. Do you know why? They are traumatised. Burnt out. Used up. Some don't survive at all. They overdose on drugs, or die by suicide. I was heartbroken by the number of friends Spencer had with stories like these. He'd lost one too, and each anniversary of the premature passing brought him premature grief.

When I met Spencer, he was out of work, and hopping between his grandmother's old flat in New York and his mother's place in LA's Studio City. We would eventually move in together in the latter residence about six months later.

It was a one-bedroom apartment with a balcony that barely fit two chairs.

What bonded Spencer and I was our love of music, art, humour, spontaneous fun and wild adventure. It was also, honestly, our deep-seated trauma, that we'd both experienced too young and too often. Trauma that we were still a long way from understanding, let alone moving through in a way that would allow us to see beyond it. At only 21 and 23, we were just kids when we first met.

We were the right people, at the wrong time. But what is true and special is not impatient. The joy, laughter and vivid memories are what have survived. Those are the things I choose to carry with me now. We were great friends, and we always will be. Since we broke up in 2018, we have kept in touch and made our peace. We've had many long talks and both know that the trials in, and indeed the end of, our relationship actually had very little to do with the other person. In our own time we both came to the realisation that neither of us had the capacity to even look after ourselves, let alone someone else, when we were together. It was a dynamic that produced inevitable pain, but it was of the projected kind, not the premeditated. We sparked each other's trauma, albeit unintentionally. Nevertheless, ours is a connection preserved in eternal respect, appreciation and love. It is impossible not to feel that way for someone you have walked through fire with. Spencer is a good and decent man, who is by all accounts now in a much better place, just like I am. He is also brilliantly talented, and side-splittingly funny too.

Spencer told me that if I had hopes of reaching a broader US audience, for marketing purposes I should change my name on the cover of my memoir to Tucker Carlson or Donald Trump and title it *Drain the Swamp: Every Woman I've Had From the Mississippi to the Colorado.* If we went with Trump, we actually wouldn't need to change much. The typeface is already gold, and we can keep the artwork as is. That man has fucked himself at least twice.

'Not sure about the Trump part,' Spencer second-guessed after I read his own advice back to him. I told him it had to stay because I wanted Donald to try to sue me. Then he'd have read two books.

Spencer and I have a great highlight reel. It was one of our best mutual friends, actress Gracie Gillam, who introduced us at a sadly now-closed bar in New York, called the Gilroy. He was wearing a New York Rangers jersey, and I was dressed head to toe in one of my go-to punk palettes: 'black and red 'til I'm dead'. I even had a copy of le Carré's *A Most Wanted Man* that matched my outfit. Spencer's version of the event would have it that the bartender was cock-blocking him by distracting me and taking the piss out of Australia, deliberately confusing Tasmania with Tanzania. My version of events is that I can see through that sort of thing, and don't remember it anyway. I'd become quite accustomed to it at that point after years of, 'Do you ride kangaroos?' The best I had was, 'You're from Australia? Your English is very good.' What I do remember from that night is hanging out on the scaffolding-like iron balcony of Gracie's Manhattan apartment, listening to Lou Reed, at three in the morning. It was a balmy September night. The air was at once heavy and humid, and heavenly human, because we were at home in each other's company.

We could listen to music for hours. We had a record player at the apartment, or sometimes we would just drive around the valley in Spencer's purple 1970s Chevy Nova that he'd bought for a steal off the director of the film he met Gracie working on. It had a little Hawaiian girl bobblehead on the dash, two racing stripes and the paint was peeling, but that just made it even cooler. It was Spencer who got me into Johnny Thunders and Warren Zevon. He had 'Lawyers, Guns, Money' tattooed on his arm. When I was talking to Mum one day on the phone about him when we first started dating, she said, 'I know who that is, that's the *naughty boy* from *The Cat in the Hat*!' After that, Spencer got 'naughty boy' tattooed on his arm too. My friend Reuben gave us both stick and pokes one night at his old place in West Hobart. Mine was 'Cassie-D', a tiny bottle of beer underneath.

For six weeks over the summer of 2016–17, Spencer stayed in Australia with me. He even bought himself a mullet headband to wear to the local Falls Festival. He embraced his inner bogan with pride. I just wasn't expecting him to say 'this guy's a bit of a wet blanket' when Powderfinger's Bernard Fanning was playing. I could have married him right then and there. (No disrespect, Bernard, 'My Happiness' was part of the soundtrack to my youth.)

It was only another seven months before we did eventually tie the knot, at a ranch in Glendale. Our wedding theme: Elvis. Spencer was The King himself and I was Priscilla. Our friend Trevor officiated the ceremony in aviators, a wig and a bedazzled satin jumpsuit. The aisle was a red carpet, and we asked all the guests to come as their favourite 60s or 70s celebrity. Dad gave me away to 'Wild West End' by

Dire Straits and Spencer entered to Shawn Michael's WWE theme song. I will forgive him because it brought everyone in the house down, including me. Twenty of my family members flew in for the big day. Dad dressed himself like Jack Nicholson in *Chinatown* (notably a pre-controversy Polanski film), minus the busted nose, of course.

I don't know how else to put it other than to say I'm not the bridezilla type. We simply had fun. At the eleventh hour, our friend Michal organised some themed decorations on a shoestring budget. And we got our favourite local taqueria to cater. Everyone served themselves. Instead of centrepieces, we had poker chips with our initials on the tables, and people could take photos with a life-size cutout of Elvis in the ranch courtyard. Although midway into the evening's celebrations, Michal came to report that 'Alice Cooper has just ripped Elvis's head off'. My friend may have had too many beers.

My bridesmaids were Josue, Mahea, Abbie, Audrey, Miranda and Camilla. Needless to say, there was nothing traditional about the day. My dear friend Jason Wisch, a location scout, who'd come as Willie Nelson, carried around a guitar that he got all the guests to sign. My other friend Jason Spencer-Galsworthy, an ex-pat animator from Bristol, came as one of the Sex Pistols and breakdanced in the middle of the floor.

The night before the wedding, Spencer's mother hosted a party at her house and invited my whole family. The chef who catered was a friend of hers who was living in her guesthouse. His creations included a table full of marijuana-laced desserts. Even my mother, who had never smoked pot in her life, ate one. Some of my uncles weren't so restrained. My stoic father ate four, and then went to stand with folded hands beside a tree in the yard. Denise's six-foot husband, Bob, ate at least five, and Wendy's husband Tony – who we now all call 'Stony' – ate something like nine. I wasn't there to see what became of them after the party ended, but none of our family will ever hear the end of the infamous self-inflicted zombification of Stony Tony. He fell asleep on the toilet in his hotel, and Wendy had to softly punch his legs because he could no longer feel them. My father came to life in the Uber on the way home, making very loud riddled jokes that were barely decipherable, but very funny nonetheless.

It was a wild time. But one that I remember not because I was high. I wasn't high that night. I was with my family.

I've written at length about drugs, and their dangers. I've used and abused them. I'm not here to condone or shame their use. As much as there is harm in glorifying them, as someone who has lived the life I have, I also know that there is serious harm – immense harm – in looking down on people who are at difficult points in their life. It is not as simple as saying 'drugs are bad'. Yes, they have harmful effects. I'm not here to argue with that. But there are many people, who, through no fault of their own, have been shown no other means of getting by.

I have come to the point in my life where drugs do not mean the same thing they once did. I will be very frank with you: there have been times in my life where I have sincerely enjoyed myself while being high on drugs. That was not because of the drugs, though, but because of the people I was with, and the circumstances that allowed for connection and reconnection.

The effects of trauma on a brain's neural pathways are such that its response mechanisms become dysregulated. For a time directly after the abuse especially, it seemed like there was nothing I could do to connect with the world and with myself. Trauma puts you in a constant state of fear and stress at a physiological level. However, in controlled moments, with safe people, the misfiring I was experiencing internally was corrected with the help of certain substances. There is a reason there are clinics where drugs such as MDMA, ketamine and mushrooms are given to patients to help with trauma. This is not a blanket endorsement for them; I have personally never been to one, and I don't intend to. Recovery is as personal as life itself. What worked for me, worked at the time. And some of its 'working', to be honest, entailed more trauma that I learned from upon reflection.

The definition of insanity, it is said, is doing the same thing over and over, and expecting a different result. Every now and then, I drink, but I can't drink like I used to. No, I don't own a two-foot bong. I've learned to sit with my trauma. And I know that if I go sky high, it goes sky high with me too. When I was younger, the comedown came later. Now it starts before I even hit the top. I have learned my lesson.

Spencer and I connected because of this as well. We bonded over booze at our local bar. We soothed each other's insomnia. We held each other's hand through the passage of numbness. We watched films together into the early hours. We stared blankly into the abyss. In lieu of closure, people in pain who only know pain medicate with overexposure to more pain.

I have more than one David Lynch–inspired tattoo. There's 'eat my fear' on my red right hand, and 'fire walk with me' on my right rib cage. If you can't fight the fire you walk with it.

We drove up Mulholland Drive and we watched the film too. Just like we watched *Repo Man*, and both of us had our cars repossessed in the end. Was life imitating art, or vice versa? Or was it just a hall of mirrors? It's hard to say. As much as it sounds cinematic, it was plain raw footage.

We also saw Billy Joel at Dodger Stadium together. If only then we had realised that we needed to slow down. We were just children. Ambitious juveniles. We were smart, but still so afraid.

Unlike Los Angeles, the idyllic heritage-listed county of Santa Barbara is slow-paced, community-spirited and decidedly less driven by capitalist impulses. For all its miles that stretch along the California coastline from the quaint town of Carpinteria through Summerland, Montecito past downtown and to Goleta, there are no high-rises, only high palms, high mountains, high bluffs and high seas as far as the eye can see. The locals call it 'Santa Bubble', and many of them have 'keep LA 100 miles away' bumper stickers on their cars. Every Tuesday the city's centre hosts a farmers' market that brings people and produce together, and on regular 'Nite Moves' nights, anybody who wishes to join in rides their bike through the streets in a giant pack.

When Richard and Sigrid dropped me off at the Cate School on their way to San Francisco when I was thirteen, I saw it as a paradise on a plateau. It was exotic meets historic meets outback, in a secluded Spanish-American dream. Tucked away, out of sight, high above the world, up on the top of the hill in Carpinteria, overlooking the Pacific Ocean, it is a small campus that was built in 1910, complete with stables, an outdoor pool and an athletics track ringed by faculty homes, which house its resident teachers.

I fell in love with it instantly. The Monterey Colonial (not *that* kind of colonial) architecture and every other detail of its surrounding environment was a novelty to me. At the bottom of the Cate mesa in the valley are avocado groves, and lining the wide campus footpaths are gum trees that made me feel at home, even though I was on the other side of the world.

I never imagined I would be going from telling you this to sharing that I learned, just as I was writing this very chapter, that in 2020 the Cate School launched an independent investigation into decades of child sexual abuse dating back to the 1960s. However, my loyalty above anything else is not to the school, and it is not to my happy memories of it. It is to every student survivor who was failed by an institution that was supposed to nurture and protect them. My heart goes out to these people. I hope they get the support and justice they deserve.

After having read and sat with the details of the investigation, I have chosen to not write any more about Cate, beyond a select few connections with people I made in its periphery. My memories of that place have now been discoloured. It also does not feel ethical to describe a place I previously associated with safety – to the extent that I would be sent back there alone at sixteen in the aftermath of my own child sexual abuse disclosure, to escape the stress of the court case – when for so many others it was anything but.

*

Ned Bowler was Cate's former Head of Outdoor Education. He is the embodiment of California in one man; as tanned as a leather boot, although he rarely wore any actual footwear bar mismatched sandals he found in the dunes on his post-lesson surfs. It was his home I stayed in, and his then-partner, Julienne, who mothered me. She mothered me then in 2008, she mothered me when I returned in 2011 during the trial, then again in 2013 when I officially moved to the US, knew no one else and needed to find a place to live. She was my Santa Barbara saint who took me under her wing. I can still hear her soothing soft Oregon accent. She is about the same height as me, but twice as strong. Her occupation is physical therapy, and her emotional services were indispensable. Her and Ned's daughter, Nora, takes after her in that regard. She was a budding writer and even at the age of twelve, her perception was well beyond her years. They had a grey cat whom little Nora had named Salinger, after her favourite author.

During the week I stayed at the Bowler residence when I was thirteen, I became attached to Santa Barbara; to La Super-Rica Taqueria, to the fresh avocados you could split open with your hands. To the eternal summer, in eternal calm. To a humble town of vibrant colours and gentle people, content with what they had in their natural surrounds. Even then I knew I would live there one day. Somehow, some way. The moment I left, I felt its pull like a magnet. I still do. Part of me will always be there.

San Miguel de Allende is no Mexico City, but in hindsight, the four weeks that I spent there over the Christmas and New

Year holidays of 2008–09 with Sigrid and Richard might just make up the PG-rated William S. Burroughs vignette of my life. There was no heroin – Christ, I was all of thirteen and fourteen – but it was during that month that my eating disorder crystallised, among other things.

It was also the height of the Global Financial Crisis, which saw a palpably tense Sigrid and Richard cataloguing their assets in the office of the villa while we were there. This meant I had a lot of time to myself, and I took to exploring the town alone some afternoons. It must be said that San Miguel, named after Saint Michael – just like my high school, curiously – is a quaint and quiet place, and not once did I ever *feel* unsafe. Retired ex-pats account for something like 10 per cent of the population, crime rates are low and the precinct is comparatively gentrified. Looking back, however, I'd be lying if I said that I'm not a little bit surprised that a petite thirteen-year-old girl was allowed to wander the streets of a third-world country unsupervised. Poverty was still apparent everywhere, and the culture was foreign to me. Besides, anything can happen anywhere.

Back then, though, I was simply awestruck by the somehow soothing sensory chaos of the central Jardín, dotted with street-food carts and seasonal decorations, lit up at night by the glowing spires of La Parroquia. I spoke minimal, pidgin Spanish but store owners were always very friendly. I tried on dresses just for fun, and did language practice over gift purchases of miniature velvet sombreros – Griff put his blue one on his cat Trixie for a photo once. I was perfectly happy just to sit at cafes in a daze, drinking bottled tonic water, admiring the tiled, soft-edged, peach-painted buildings all huddled together on the narrow cobbled streets.

Aside from myself, Sigrid and Richard, there were some other passing guests who coloured San Miguel. Tristan, their youngest son, arrived just before Christmas, which also happened to be his 21st birthday. Richard is Jewish, so the latter event was what we celebrated on 25 December, although I did get given a Pez dispenser, as per Richard's tradition. Jonah, Richard's son from his first marriage, and his wife Pheung, joined us briefly too, as well as Eben's now-wife Sarah, and finally, Doug and Tracy, who are friends of Sigrid and Richard.

It was an odd bunch in strange circumstances. I can't speak for the others, but I felt like quiet angst was the mood of at least some of the trip. The GFC was an unexpected thunderbolt and from where I was sitting, everyone seemed to be internalising a degree of distress. Although I was too young to fully comprehend it, I could sense the pervasive unease that had descended not only upon the visitors to the homestay, but upon the whole world. My own disorder and dysfunction grew simultaneously, and I defaulted to isolation. All I would eat at the time, between mouthfuls at breakfast and dinner, was over-salted cashews. I bought them by the bag at the local food store.

When I wasn't off wandering, I spent a lot of my time drawing, or helping the live-in chef prepare food in the kitchen. I had no trouble cooking it, I just didn't want to eat large portions of it. I was taught how to make authentic guacamole, refried beans and tortilla chips from scratch, and to shred whole cooked chickens for enchiladas and tacos. The flesh of the chickens was bright marigold yellow because they were fed on the petals of the plant. I noticed them hanging in the street, it's quite a trip.

There were memorable group activities as well, such as morning rooftop yoga with Sigrid and choice film screenings in the lounge room. *Frida* was a must, of course, as was *Once Upon a Time in Mexico*, which was filmed on location in San Miguel. We also did a day trip to Guanajuato and visited Diego Rivera's first home, which is now a museum that exhibits some of his early sketches. Not that I'm fond of that adulterous prick. We rode horses through the dry cactus-filled desert, and relished the richly saturated details in the bellies of churches. We dined out and ate whole jalapeños, and encountered an ice-cream cart whose flavours included octopus and beer.

On the night of my fourteenth birthday, after dinner, I went with Tristan and Eben to an Irish-themed pub. How *that* was allowed, I really have no idea. This would be the second time in my life I got drunk. The first was at my club soccer dinner earlier in the year when I'd been introduced to UDLs by my teammates. Suffice it to say, Mum was unimpressed when she picked me up. Since that time, Wendy had let me have a taste of a Midori splice that she'd made for Eloise, but otherwise I was in untested waters.

Shockingly, I cannot recall every detail of what happened that evening. I remember the brothers had a friend visiting, who was tall and very good-looking. I knew I liked Malibu and pineapple juice, so that is what I asked for. There was tequila, and there was dancing. When I came to on my bed the next day, I still had the rubber-band resilience of youth such that the hangover I probably deserved didn't actually eventuate. I was certainly more pensive than usual, though. I was wearing a long-sleeve grey jersey that I'd bought at

Cate. Eben would approach me in the coming days to ask why I only ate cashews; whatever escape the drinking brought, it didn't last.

'Can you pass me the rubber?' I asked Tristan one morning while I was drawing, not expecting his reply to be, 'The last time I heard that was during sex.' I was out of my depth in a world too old for me. Still, I coasted along, albeit maladaptively. I consumed a culture while an addiction to restriction consumed me. I will forever be grateful for the learning experience of a lifetime, though, because it has taught me the power of travel, both geographically and emotionally.

I used to think that pub story was funny when I was younger. Just like I used to tell myself I loved Mr Bester when I was younger, too. When you're a child, you do lots of things to protect yourself. In saying this, I have no ill will whatsoever. I cannot understate the love, respect and appreciation I have for Sigrid and Richard. I was very unwell when I was away with them; more unwell than anyone realised at the time. Such is addiction's disguise. And thanks to Wall Street's crash, their world had been rocked too.

As always, what remains is the goodness, the teachings, the triumphs and the bright colours.

Chapter 13

The Rock Spider

Before it occurred to me to actually look up the origin of the prison slang term, I'd always assumed child abusers were called 'rock spiders' because they are objectively creepy and, by way of deceptive camouflage, are experts at hiding in plain sight. In reality, its derivation is cruder. They're so called, it turns out, because, like eight-legged predators, they have a particular proclivity for *getting into small cracks*. Darkly funny at best, this analogy is no doubt deeply offensive to many survivors. It is pretty sick and twisted – therefore it's also arguably fitting. Personally, I've become desensitised to this shit. These words are nothing but that to me: words. As far as I'm concerned there's nothing sicker and more twisted than the criminal act of deliberately harming a minor and gaslighting them into believing they brought the trauma upon themselves. Vulgarity is vulgar for a reason. Softening sounds doesn't soften their blow. If you're more upset by the language used to describe a crime than the crime itself, it's up to you to ask yourself why.

Of further fascination is the term's alternative use as a colloquial label for Dutch 'Boer' colonists of South Africa and their white descendants. It's also a name given to soldiers of the Anglo–Boer War, which was fought between October 1899 and May 1902 by two independent Boer states against the British Empire in protest of their rule. Historians allege the conflict began following attempts made by British forces to exploit mineral wealth in the Boer regions. To seize their gold. And their *diamonds.*

He was both a South African soldier *and* a prolific child sex offender. An inveterate veteran. But I knew him first as a teacher. With a sticky accent. That still rings in my ears.

The earliest distinct memory I have of him is from the end of Year 8. I would've been thirteen. He had come over to the middle school from the main campus to talk to my then-Maths and Science teacher, Mr Carmichael, during a lesson. I can't recall why. At the time, to me, he was just a name I'd heard. He only taught Years 9 to 12, but he knew Gillian already because he had substituted one of her classes. They were bantering – I think he was stirring her about her braces. Or, at least, he made a joke at her expense and Gillian, being the quick wit that she is, responded sharply. My first impression, sadly, was that he reminded me of my father. In that seemingly innocuous but pivotal moment, I naively mistook arrogance for charisma and bullying for playful irreverence.

That's not a reflection on my father, by the way. My father and Mr Bester are nothing alike. One is a true man; the latter is a sadist.

Maybe it wasn't entirely the fault of naivety. The man I misinterpreted was the man we were all sold. In the Year 12 Revue that year, a phone rang as part of the performance: 'It's for you, Mr Bester,' a student actor joked, 'it's God, she says she's black.' Everyone laughed, including the staff. Not only were his bigoted views well known, they were also part of the school's fabric because he wore them so boldly. They were part of what allowed him to work for so long in plain sight. He had engineered a tradition of desensitisation that permeated the atmosphere. No doubt he would have laughed at the godforsaken God gag too. He would have laughed, knowing he had fooled everyone in the room.

Through innocent, permissive laughter, we became acquainted with a supposedly harmless man, as if there should be any other kind of character in a school. He just pushed the boundaries, that was all. He meant well. He was a man of faith, after all. The Head of Maths and Science, too, for nearly twenty years. His recycled racy comments were just part of his schtick, and they didn't alarm our young, inexperienced minds in the same way they might have adults'. In the event he did cross the line and anyone dared speak up, it was the accuser who would pay. As the sixteen-page police statement from the former school principal who was there during my time revealed, he was fond of threatening grievances, should others take issue with him.

Indeed, that document was, perversely, almost as damning of the school as it was of him. They had allowed him to continue working despite regular and consistent complaints from students, staff, parents and visitors to the institution, whose resources he'd also brazenly used to conduct his own Amway 'business'. 'She was as easy as McDonald's drive-through,' he said about a former Year 11 student, to a classroom full of her peers, after she left the school because she fell pregnant. This comment is among the incidents listed in the aforementioned statement – he was given a warning but remained in his role.

Year 8, both for me personally and for our entire grade, was very disjointed. We started 2008 on the senior school campus, then partway through were moved to the newly built middle school building across the road. All us were destabilised in the process, and I was getting increasingly sick. Flashbacks of sexual trauma from being molested by an older child when I was six were becoming more vivid and unpredictable, to the point of disrupting my schoolwork. Mr Carmichael was our grade coordinator and had taught me for two years. When I told him, he immediately reported the disclosure, as per mandatory requirements. He also contacted my mother, who did already know to some extent. When we were camping when I was ten, I had apparently alarmed Eloise one night in our tent because I'd started recalling shards of memory in front of her. I made a police statement, but not one that could go anywhere. Regardless, my mind was adrift. Loneliness had set in, and was pulling me under.

*

Such is grooming that it is nearly impossible to draw a line in the sand to mark the beginning of the abuse. Grooming's success relies heavily on the perversely protective mechanisms of human doubt and ignorance. To be groomed is to be unwittingly led into and trapped in aporia. It is a fever dream lived in real time. The more I think about it, the more I am left wondering. And it's not my wish to dwell on it any longer than I have to. All I can do is tell you how it was. There are pages of documents, witness statements, his own partial admission, medical records, seized child abuse material, other accusers, a recorded history of inappropriate workplace behaviour, and more. Since the episode of *Australian Story* about me and my partner, Max, aired at the end of 2021, the current Collegiate principal, Adam Forsyth, has been approached by another five former students who allege they were abused by Nicolaas Bester.

When I asked Gillian what her first memory of Mr Bester was, she recounted the day in Year 8 that he subbed in for one of her teachers during a Science lesson. Gillian remembers him making inappropriate jokes about one of our peers, a thirteen-year-old girl, being 'obsessed with tubular objects', as they were using test tubes.

I've always thought that the grooming started the day he invited me into his office in April 2010, when I was a Year 10 student. That was the day he started asking me direct personal questions, feigning innocence about anorexia and my experience of it. But there's no way he could not have already known that I was sick. He was my Maths teacher for an entire year before that. And we were a very small class. Intimate, as they say. I can't remember the exact number, maybe there were eight or nine of us all up. We'd often goof off; I remember lots of laughter. It was a class I looked forward to.

There were definitely moments that stand out to me from Year 9, though. Whether they constitute grooming or not, I'm unsure, although I think they are worth mentioning.

There's a part of me that feels protective of my fourteen-year-old self, I must admit. In writing this book, I have sat with parts of my life that were previously too unbearable to face. I've gone deeper into the past than I'd ever thought possible. I've barely seen a soul besides my own in the process. It's made me realise that some people may never uncover certain memories, if only for self-preservation's sake. There's certainly no shame in that. Self-preservation is a brave state.

By now you understand that anorexia was a symptom. I wasn't vulnerable because I had an eating disorder; I had anorexia because I was already vulnerable. I wasn't comfortable in my skin, but when I made people laugh I came alive. I remember making Mr Bester laugh when I was mucking around with a calculator and called it 'a weapon of Maths distraction'. People like Mr Bester, who validated my sense of humour, which had always been central to my identity, made me feel seen. He became one of a handful of teachers I looked up to.

I was also half-decent at sports until I lost too much weight and couldn't play. In the swathe of memories, I can see Mr Bester's face at the Rokeby Police Academy where we ran cross country. I can see him supervising at water polo practice. I remember pulling myself out of the pool after winning a race at the swimming carnival in Year 9 and Mr Bester, who happened to be the timekeeper at the end of my lane, said, 'I always knew you were a fast woman.' In the rush of the moment, a bashful and off-guard me just kept moving in my clinging wet bathers. I imagine it was something he said to a lot of girls. Perhaps part of his technique was to throw out bait and see who took it. What a gronk.

He told Gillian, 'Your legs are too long, I can see them sticking out of your skirt.' She was surer of herself than I was at that age, and probably less inwardly fearful of men. She was already equipped with the attitude and language I've had to spend years cultivating. When she and I were reflecting on those days, she guessed she heard him make that particular remark 'at least ten times over the years', and at the time she had no trouble telling him to 'get some new material'.

For the first half of the year or so in 2009, our Maths Extended classroom was right near Mr Bester's office in the old Science block, before we were relocated to the newly renovated rooms downstairs. My memories of Year 9 are divided between those spaces. Before we moved, there was the time in April, right before I went into hospital, when he was giving out chocolates, and hovered when I didn't take one. After that I was gone for about six weeks, and from then, what I can see is in the new room.

I remember one day I was wearing my hair in a French braid, and he was staring down the end of his nose. Why he was close enough to ask, 'Are you going grey?', and to a fourteen-year-old, I don't know. The remark has stayed with me – I always thought that was because it was just off. It was only in the final stages of editing that someone flagged the concept of 'negging' with me. I'd never heard the term.

Pegging, yes. Although that's a different genre. (If I don't laugh, I'll punch a hole in the wall. Now that's a good pun.)

After all this time I'm still peeling back the layers, and the discoveries I'm making are much bigger than I'd expect at this point in time. I think a lot of people assume my knowledge is deeper than it is, in the same way they can assume my strength. I didn't anticipate the precision of the definition that my friend read out loud. Negging, I learned, is a tactic of emotional manipulation whereby a person uses negative comments, often about another's appearance, in order to deliberately undermine their self-confidence. The aim is to assert dominance, engender a craving for approval, generate dependence and ultimately even seduction. I had to get up and have a bit of walk around after hearing that.

I was fourteen.

When I gave all the other teachers their gifts at the end of Year 9, they thanked me on the spot. I don't remember what Mr Bester said in the moment. I do remember that he came and found me days later, all the way over on the other side of campus, while I was in the middle of a drama lesson, to start another conversation about it. Back then, the idea that he must have worked out my timetable, or that he couldn't just wait until he bumped into me, didn't cross my good-faith Aspergic mind. I was just happy to talk about Monty Python, as anyone who knows me would attest. Their surreal humour was second nature, but the sexual innuendo washed over me. So when Mr Bester made a comment about the one song that mentioned the word 'penis', I was a bit taken aback. But at the time, that washed over me too.

*

It would be another five months before I had another interaction with Mr Bester that I can recall. Privately, life's woes and wonders continued to bubble. My then-45-year-old mother was pregnant with my baby brother. Over the Christmas holidays of 2009–10, Mum took Griff, Maddie and me camping up the east coast of Tassie to the Bay of Fires. We had a blissful time, but anorexia and the demons that underpinned it were still nagging at me.

One school day in April 2010, I arrived late after a doctor's appointment to discover the rest of my Year 10 classmates were attending a driving lesson off campus that I'd completely forgotten about. Lapses like this weren't uncommon back then – I was detached and dissociative. My house common area and my locker were just near the entrance to the Science block. As I walked through the courtyard towards the entrance, Mr Bester crossed my path and asked why I wasn't with the rest of my peers. He said he had a free period, and invited me into his office to chat. In that moment, I saw no harm in this.

For over an hour, he asked me questions about my illness, feigning ignorance of eating disorders. I talked. He listened. He promised to support me and offered his office as a safe space for me to retreat to if I needed. He insisted that I could beat anorexia on my own. After school that day, I told both Mum and Dad about the conversation. Mum picked me up from school, and Dad met us in the paediatrician's waiting room.

In the coming days, I remember Mr Cross, who was the Head of the Senior School at the time, came and found me to tell me that Mr Bester had been chatting with him. 'Mr Bester told me he learned more from you than any student in all his years of teaching,' were his words. To a lonely, troubled person with low self-esteem, it's a no-brainer that this meant a lot. You can also start to see here how others (like Mr Cross) were unwittingly doing his bidding, and unknowingly reinforcing his impression of harmlessness.

As the tensions rose in my family life, true to anorexic form, positive reinforcement had become particularly scarce. 'I have the disease to please,' I told Mr Bester during that first chat in his office in April, sharing details about my parents upon request. He quietly filed away all this information and presented the perfect solution. He offered respite and validation. He even gave me a key to his office. I believed I'd found another trusted, well-respected mentor. Just like Mrs Ride, Frau Roach and Mr Carmichael.

If ever they suspected that I was upset, other teachers asked if I would like to see Mr Bester. I didn't always go to him, but there were more conversations that followed, which I continued to share with my increasingly disturbed mother and father. While I saw no issues, they were already reading between the lines. Sadly, this disconnect between my parents and I would work in his favour. I simply saw it as another way in which I was being misunderstood. Mr Bester, of course, agreed with me.

It was known among the staff that I loved art. I had made the poster for the production of *A Midsummer Night's Dream* that was displayed across campus, inspired by The Stones' famous logo, only I drew a donkey's open mouth with a forest full of nymphs pouring down its exaggerated tongue.

(Random donkey story: when I was three, I was bitten by a donkey at the East Coast Natureworld at Bicheno on a family day trip with my aunts and cousins. It grabbed hold of my open hand while I was feeding it and wouldn't let go, even after my mother tried to prise its mouth open. It was only when Wendy thought to cut off its air supply and twisted its nose that it released me.) A children's book about a giraffe with lung cancer complete with a hand-painted cover was the most dedication I'd ever shown in Science class. Mr (now Dr, I should say!) Simon told me he kept one of my sketches on the wall in his classroom for six years after I left. (Incidentally, Dr Simon would like it known that if there's ever a film made about all of this, Meryl Streep should play his part.)

My lifelong passion for art meant I amassed a collection of several books about it over the years, and I had sketched all manner of subjects with various media on all kinds of surfaces. I'd even drawn a nude, while watching the infamous 'draw me like one of your French girls' scene from *Titanic* at the Abelas' shack down at Saltwater River. I remember Dom's mum Nadine, who is a brilliant artist herself, helping me correct my form and proportions. So when Mr Bester asked if I had ever drawn myself naked to help with my body image issues, a possible ulterior motive didn't stick out to me. I'm autistic and literal. I take things at face value, especially in flowing conversation. Beyond that, the man had masterfully cushioned an escalation within a world that was second nature to me. I had books with nude figures in them. I'd watched *The Meaning of Life* maybe fifteen times. The way Mr Bester introduced the idea of sex to me was at once so invisible and so personal. It was not explicit, but it tapped into pre-existing elements of me. No, I told him simply, I hadn't ever drawn myself. It hadn't ever crossed my mind. And the conversation rolled on smoothly, as though his question had the same weight as any other. This was tactical too, for it reinforced the air of normalcy that he designed with such aplomb.

What's more, my mother always told me to 'give people the benefit of the doubt'. When I was ten, we went to Magnetic Island for a holiday, and when we arrived at the motel, the receptionist was in a foul mood. Taking a leaf out of Nanny Pat's book that day, Mum's way of explaining that it isn't fair to assume what drives people's behaviour was to tell me, 'Her cat might have died recently.'

When you're desperate for connection, you make exceptions. These trade-offs we make to have our needs met are often unconscious. Or they are the product of conditioning. I've seen Nan sit next to Cliff at Christmas. It kills me.

Even the way Mr Bester was able to slip in comments like, 'You don't wear make-up do you? No, you don't need it,' into conversations that he paced and balanced so well with anecdotes about his own life, just made my head spin.

Two things started to happen at once. Any addict knows the curse of addiction. The love and the hate. The dependence is toxic. He was starting to scare me, and yet, I *needed* to see him.

Right before I went into hospital the second time, my History class watched the film *Iron Jawed Angels* during a lesson one day. We had been learning about the suffragettes. In it there is a graphic scene during which hunger strikers are force-fed in prison.

I'd never had such an intense, irrepressible visceral reaction to something before. The only way I can describe it is to say that I started vomiting tears, and I immediately left the room.

It had been exactly one year since I'd been admitted to the Hobart Royal Hospital for eating disorder treatment after what I thought was just a doctor's appointment. Mum and Dad had taken me to see a specialist one afternoon after school, who weighed and assessed me, then decreed that I was 'more likely to suffer a heart attack in the next two weeks' than he was, and he was obese. I assume this was a scare tactic, designed to shock some sense into my then-fourteen-year-old self. That night my bags were packed and I was checked into hospital, where I would spend over a month living according to the rules of the Maudsley program.

For the first two weeks I was in the High Dependency Unit on level 1 restrictions, which meant I couldn't get out of bed. Such was my astronomical pulse deficit that I was told there were concerns that I might collapse if I stood up too quickly. Personally, I believe this was another scare tactic. On day one, it was explained that all eating disorder patients had a 30-minute window to eat everything that was put in front of them at every meal or else any unconsumed calories would have to be accounted for via a feeding tube. This seemed both cruel and impossible to me. The first tray of food I was served at breakfast had more on it than I'd eaten in the week before that. I barely touched it. The image of the well-built male nurse hovering over me, shoving the foot-long nasogastric tube down my nose, telling me to 'just breathe in' as it went down my throat while another nurse held me down, will never leave me. It was indeed like a scene from a film. And not a pleasant one. The tube stayed in for the rest of the week, just in case I defied orders again.

You'd assume anorexics would be fond of salads, only the public hospital's offerings were full of bean shoots. I did my best to race the clock, only those pesky buggers kept wrapping themselves around the tube and tugging it down. When I was finally allowed to remove it, I had a red mark under my nostril where its opening had sat, and I tasted everything I'd eaten as it made its way back out again.

Not being able to get out of bed also meant no showering. Of course, after two weeks of no movement, my muscles had atrophied. I could hardly walk. I remember being wheeled to a meeting in a wheelchair, which was more than a little bit confronting for a tree-climbing, horse-riding, soccer-playing long-distance runner. At first I wasn't even able to shower by myself when the time came. The first time my hair was washed in the hospital was over a sink, by a nurse, and for health and safety reasons, they wore latex gloves. Any person with long hair who's ever used bare rubber bands to hold it up, knows that this texture and movement don't mix well.

It wasn't all bad. Between being a shithead who attempted to flush one of my afternoon snacks down the toilet when I could finally get up and move around and then giving the finger to my tattling mother, and not buttoning up my gown before walking across the ward for weekly weigh-ins, I did get quite good at jigsaw puzzles and Scrabble. I made my own cheeky fun. I also befriended Heidi and Sophie, who I still keep in contact with today. Heidi La Paglia went on to become the women's officer of the Tasmanian University Union, and along with my other dear friend, Saffire Grant, who was president of the Women's Collective at UTas, she spearheaded the petition to have Bester removed from campus when my mother was a student there. Like me, both Heidi and Saffire received autism diagnoses later in life.

There's much to be said of the fine line in medical treatment. I am certain that what I experienced as a fourteen-year-old caused more harm than good. At the time, my mother asked the medical professionals if they had considered whether I might be autistic, as I seemed to be presenting some obvious female traits. Not only was she dismissed, she was condescended to.

Even a decade later, people would comment on the fact that I never left a crumb on my plate, or that I wolfed down food. I never stopped to make the connection that I'd been conditioned through fear. When I did finally join the dots, my desire to regain control only led to me wanting my childhood back, a thing which for more reasons than one I've fought for but will never regain.

Our History teacher, and my firsts softball team supervisor, Mrs Anning, came out to check on me after I ran out on the screening of *Iron Jawed Angels.* I don't remember saying anything at all but it's possible I was too wound up to notice I had mentioned Mr Bester. Either way, she said she would take me to him. I was choking on emotion and resurfacing trauma, both connected to the sounds I could still hear playing and visions of past abuses.

I was a sobbing mess in the doorway of Mr Bester's office. He rose from his chair as I stood with my head in my hands, and Mrs Anning left to go back to class. And he hugged me. Then, through the floodgates of pain, came everything I was seeing. I told him about the time I was abused by the older child when I was six. The cupboard. All of it. I could not contain the hurt that I felt.

What I had missed in my state of vulnerability is that in making physical contact with me in that moment, he had once again increased my unconscious dosage of dependency. His role had levelled up, but so had the fear. That day he did not comfort me, but rather tried to relate to me in the most warped way imaginable. He told me about his first erection.

I found myself locked in an impossible dilemma. I told my father that afternoon that I had disclosed to Mr Bester but I kept other parts of our conversation to myself. I could be honest with Dad about *my* behaviour, but did not feel like I could be honest about all of Mr Bester's behaviour. I mentioned the stories that he had told me about hazing. I could not bring myself to mention anything else. I still felt loyal to him – I was now well and truly stuck in his orbit.

I was trapped and conflicted beyond measure. At this juncture, I felt like I couldn't move backwards, even if it felt uncomfortable moving forwards.

I knew that I had another doctor's appointment coming up, and a potential second admission. I told Mr Bester that I wanted him to visit me if I did go. I was desperate to keep the peace.

Although I wasn't allowed a phone in hospital, Mr Bester had given me his number, and another patient's mother lent me her mobile. I can't recall if I even managed to reach him, to tell him he could pose as my grandfather if he visited. I just remember that I tried to call him one day from one of the bathrooms on the oncology ward, where I stayed with a roomful of other kids briefly during the week I was there because they had a shortage of beds in the paediatric unit. I barely slept, and at night as I traipsed the dimly lit corridor on my way back and forth from my bed to the tea room, I could feel the ghostly energy of the place.

Mr Bester didn't make it in. No one did. Unlike my previous stay, I wasn't allowed any visitors aside from my parents. For my own good. They knew more than I did then about what was best for me – including that inviting a child sex offender to a children's hospital was not a peacekeeping gesture.

When I was discharged on Friday, 30 April 2010, though, I learned that Mr Bester's absence was not for lack of trying. He had in fact attempted to visit me, but not as himself. He had posed as an uncle of mine. That very same day, the then-principal Robyn Kronenberg called my mother to tell her that she intended to hold a meeting with Mr Bester and me the following Monday.

By this point, my mother and father had already had two meetings with the school to request that Mr Bester stay away from me. My parents were horrified by this man and they wanted me to have nothing to do with him. They were very concerned about his inappropriate behaviour. However, the word 'grooming' hadn't been used. Not even Mum and Dad knew then the extent of the darkness within Mr Bester. My understanding was more naive again. All I could conceive was that I was in trouble once more; that I was being a nuisance to all the adults in my life, and it was my responsibility to repair the damage. That was certainly how I felt when I had the arranged meeting with Mr Bester and Mrs Kronenberg the day after my baby brother was born.

The atmosphere on campus was different from how it was before I had gone into hospital. I now know this to be the work of fear, conspiracy and gaslighting. I was terrified of upsetting Mr Bester. I didn't want him to hate me. In anticipation of the meeting, on the Saturday I bought a DVD of an ABC show I remembered him mentioning that he liked and I gave it to him before classes started on Monday as a gift of thanks for the support he'd shown me. DVDs are my go-to present. If you've met me, you probably own a DVD that I've given you. I told you, I am a Luddite. Please, spare me your fancy streaming platforms.

But the man who had been enthusiastic towards me was gone. In his place was someone standoffish, behaving as though he pitied me; as though I was ill, or even deranged. This from the person who had told me how smart he thought I was, who'd instructed me to dismiss my inner critic and professional health advice. When I sought reassurance from Mrs Ride in homeroom, she said to me, 'Mr Bester just feels like he is out of his depth.'

Yes, because he was swimming in his own *bullshit*.

Scarcity of attention makes us more desperate for it, whatever form it takes. Certainly, predators cruelly weaponise this. They groom an impressionable child's mind and body into unconsciously depending on something it previously didn't know it needed, only to withhold it so the child chases it more, and begins to believe they are to blame. Such is the stifling complexity of grooming that you don't know that it is happening to you. It is a life sentence of uncertainty and slow-burning chaos. Abusers will destroy others' trust in you, and yours in them, but above all else, they'll destroy your trust in yourself.

As I sat opposite him and the principal during the meeting in her office later that morning, I could not have felt more alone and confused. The power imbalance was heavily weighted against me. I didn't know Mrs Kronenberg very well, and I thought I knew Mr Bester, only now I wasn't sure. The embarrassment, shame and isolation I felt was crushing in that moment. No part of my people-pleasing DNA would have even considered the thought of mentioning that Mr Bester had an equal role in encouraging the time that he and I had spent together in his office, let alone the fact he had instigated it. All I could do was respond to the adults in the room, and accept their judgement of the situation at hand: that I was unwell and that it wasn't the correct thing to do to spend time with him. I was very apologetic. Mr Bester was very understanding. He echoed the principal's sentiments. That sticky, sticky voice.

He was very good at what he did. Not only did he rope the highest staff authority into his version of events, he guaranteed she would be unknowingly implicated in the broader ongoing conspiracy. If ever he sank, she would have to sink too. He coolly laid the groundwork for a narrative in which I was the supposed aggressor, and the mentally ill one that he felt 'sorry for'. This would, in fact, be his line of defence in court.

The meeting marked a clean slate on the official records, and in the eye of his boss. He was once again free to do as he pleased. Business, on his terms, on school grounds, as usual.

My 27-year-old self is writing this with heavy anguish, reliving my own naivety. It's stomach-churning stuff, it really is. At every turn, I was a lamb walking into a lion's den. I offered him my permissive good faith on a silver platter. I was the fawning fawn, running to him. To every survivor who sees themselves in these pages, know that *it is not your fault.* Nobody should ever have to live their lives in anticipation of sadistic abuse. It's true that in the end he groomed me into what I believed was infatuation. But he hurt me. He made me cry in front of him. And I never wanted to hurt that man.

I fucking do now. Fuck that cunning prick.

Terrified, I stayed well clear of Mr Bester. For over a month I didn't see him. I kept to myself. I had a newborn brother. And I was in another School of Performing Arts production, a musical version of *Cinderella*. My energies were elsewhere.

Then one Saturday rehearsal in late June, the show's director Ms Polley came and found me during a break to tell me, 'Mr Bester is here to see you.'

And just like that: adrenaline like mercury through my veins.

Ms Polley was none the wiser. There were too many things to explain. He was already here. So I went to him. And I followed him where he led me.

I trailed him all the way to the Science block on the other side of campus. We entered a classroom on the top floor, above his office. I don't know why. It wasn't a place that was familiar to me. It was to him, though. Maybe that's the reason. He needn't have reminded me that he was above me, if that's what he was trying to do.

He leant his tall body against the teaching bench near the doorway, and I stood quite away from him, in front of a desk beside the window that looked out over the courtyard. His being closer to the exit was not something that occurred to me at that precise moment. It soon would.

'I thought you hated me,' I said with a racing head, to which he replied, 'No, no, quite the opposite,' and smirked, but without even looking me in the eye. He was a coward then, with his cryptic talk, fucking with my young brain before he fucked my young body. Did he mean that he didn't hate me, and that it's okay, don't be silly? Or did he mean the *actual* opposite of hate?

Then he asked, 'Did you ever do that sketch of yourself naked?'

For every word I have ever learned, for every sight I have ever seen, for everything I have ever felt and understood, there is no way I know how to tell you what it was like to be there in that room right then.

'Yes,' I lied, now realising the game was well and truly up before we'd even got there.

'Good, I'd like to see it.'

I produced a naked sketch I copied from one of the books I had on how to draw nudes. That would suffice. I stopped drawing at the head anyway. It's just a body. The last time I saw that drawing, it was lying in the stack of evidence underneath the envelope of hair the police recovered. Why I was even given those things back, I'm not really sure. I assume one of my parents did the honour of binning them on my behalf after my detached self clearly walked off and never came back.

I had found myself in the midst of a dangerous game of chess. I was playing as a lonely pawn, against a man armed with a full set. And yet, he was drawing it out with twisted relish. All of sudden, Mr Bester, who had previously held to Mrs Kronenberg's word, stepped right over the line and was encouraging contact again.

At this point in my life, I was living solely with my mother for the first time ever. My stepfather was working long hours in a demanding job to support the family, while my mother was caring for my baby brother, Oscar, whose sleep was very disrupted for the first three years of his life. Needless to say, the immediate needs of a newborn were the top priority. What's more, as far as everyone was concerned, the Mr Bester matter had been put to rest.

The last thing I wanted to do was add more stress. I thought I could play the game alone. Only, I didn't realise that I didn't know the rules. I didn't know how much of myself I would have to sacrifice.

There were more conversations, and Mr Bester wanted to see the sketch, but he even put conditions around the way he wanted to see it. It was all so controlled. I couldn't just show him the damn fucking thing, I had to deliver it to his pigeonhole.

This. *This* is why the man preyed on people who weren't his own age: because an adult would have just scoffed at this childish tool.

I did wonder if this memoir would have been more powerful if I wrote less about the abuse and the man who perpetrated it, but then I realised that, after all this time, my self-esteem has rebuilt such that I believe I will write more books than just this one. And there will be more books that don't mention his name than those that do. My life is just beginning. I am standing up for the girl I once was, and still am, and always will be. This is how I say goodbye to that time, but not for him. For me. And for every other boy and girl whose shame should never have been, because no one ever deserves to be treated this way.

Synthetic love, especially under duress, is a perverse self-defence mechanism. When there's no way out, it's a way of turning something that's unbearable into something that's liveable. Children who are abused do it all the time. The fawning; the people pleasing. I was already doing these things with Bester out of fear.

Before that missed driving-school excursion in April 2010, if you had asked who Mr Bester was, I would have told you he was my Year 9 Maths Extended teacher, and maybe shared a funny anecdote or two. I was fond of him, sure. In the same way I was fond of many of my teachers. At this juncture, however, mere months later, a fifteen-year-old me was asking myself if I was in love with him. I was talking myself into a narrative I thought I needed to believe.

After I showed Mr Bester the naked headless sketch, he told me he wanted to 'repay' me, but, true to form, didn't say how. I said I didn't need repaying, but he insisted. I would have to wait and see. So I stayed back after school one day and we went up to the storeroom behind the classroom where he'd taken me that Saturday he turned up to our *Cinderella* rehearsal.

Intellectually, I was anticipating something physical. The thought seemed both outlandish and absolute in the one breath. I prepared myself to lose my virginity that day, despite not knowing what that really meant. I had not prepared myself for him to keep toying with me like I was a fucking dog. My anger now masks what I was then. Then, I was little *Gracie*.

I had not prepared myself for him to pull out a yellow piece of paper with 'yes' and 'no' written on either side. Nor had I prepared myself for him to ask me to undress in the supply closet, mirroring the abuse I'd disclosed to him in tears not months before, as he stood blocking the storeroom door.

I can't remember how long I was in the closet for, exactly. Before I went in, he'd explained that he was the only member of staff in the entire school who had a key to its door. He gave me the yellow piece of paper. That was supposed to be his cue to open the door, when I was ready. I had control, apparently. I was put into a fucking closet with a piece of paper by a 58-year-old man over six foot tall, who not only had the keys to the door I was behind, he was blocking another two, plus three flights of stairs, another entrance, a courtyard, a turning circle, a city, and a large body of water that separated me from home. I could've made myself an origami canoe, I guess, but it probably wouldn't have made it across the Derwent.

The brick walls surrounding the stairs in that old Science block, I just have to add, from top to bottom, were painted like an underwater seascape. It really was a case – a staircase – of the water I was swimming in, in that building. Or drowning in, depending on your perspective.

I knew there was an unclothed man waiting on the other side of the door. I wasn't that naive. And still, I couldn't undress all the way. I was shaking, and not from the winter cold. It was dark outside. And inside too. I stood there in my underwear, and bit the bullet that was waiting in my mouth.

The closet light was poor. The storeroom light was worse.

There he was, naked, with his arms outstretched. He walked towards me and pressed himself up against my body. I can still feel his cold hands on my bare skin.

And I gave him a peck. I couldn't bring myself to strip all the way, but the people pleaser in me couldn't bear to let him down completely. I could feel every beat in my bloodstream. You go along to get along.

There was a method to his extended mathematical madness. He had formatted a game that he orchestrated with geometric precision, such that I was forced into reciprocity. I had to keep making moves in order to keep up.

Each move was small enough that it looked like we were equal players. And with every move I made in response to him, I kept reflecting on my behaviour. Because when you have a fucking conscience, you assume responsibility. Only, there was not enough time to really think. I became convinced I was infatuated. That's all I understood at fifteen. That's what my wiring told me. You can't carry the baggage and unpack it all at once.

After that night, he knew he had me. I was his now. I was *his* little Gracie.

*

He created fake Facebook profiles to talk to me. There were more meetings; before school, after school, on weekends. Before Mr Bester's first attempt at penetration, he performed oral sex on me, although I didn't know what that was. 'I'm going to kiss you on the centre of your world,' he said. The police statement I made at sixteen, which was the document used to convict him, was absent of so many things – not least my adult ability to see that he simply revelled in my innocence. There was no way I could have expressed that back then, when I was still so young. For him to not only laugh when I said 'no', after he asked me if I knew where my clitoris was, but to then suggest I find it, is a clear indicator of cruelty. It makes me want to strangle him. And I write that knowing those are violent words. If you've got this far and you're worried about that, this is not the book for you. You're off my Christmas card list. No DVD for you.

That first day in the storeroom he had explicitly said there would be no sex, but that was the obvious next move, eventually. The conversations, as much as the physical interactions, were cryptic games. He would often throw out crumbs of ideas and I would be left to fill the gaps. It was his way of leading me to believe I had agency.

The ship had sailed before I knew I was on a fucking ship, and it was made by the same company who made my origami canoe.

For all my attempts to lean into the idea of love for Mr Bester, it never could stick. Believe me, I tried. And he will tell you that too.

I have spent countless hours in therapy. I have asked professionals if I am a psychopath, terrified that I am just like him. I have blamed myself for everything that happened. I have bashed my head on plastered walls and hardwood floors in the hopes of exorcising myself, to the point of blackout. I have read comments from people telling me I deserve all the abuse that I get. I have found myself wondering if they are right.

I will hide nothing. I will hide none of the manufactured sordid conversations we had. I tried to believe that it was a nice time we were having. It was not. I cut my wrists. I carved 'fuck' into my left thigh with a kitchen knife. I still have the scar, despite five laser treatments. I cried almost every night. I fought with my parents. I was hospitalised, medicalised and given Seroquel because it was assumed I had bipolar disorder.

He was everywhere. I would look up from my schoolwork during classes he didn't teach, and he would be talking to my teacher, while making eye contact with me. He thought it was entertaining, but it was exhausting. He had a free period during my English lessons and from the staffroom you could see directly into our English classroom, so he would often just sit and stare through the window at me.

He would message me on Facebook at all hours and I felt compelled to respond. Once my laptop wasn't working and I hit it in terror as I feared the consequences of not replying to him immediately. To this day I still feel a compulsion to respond whenever anyone contacts me, underpinned by an anxiety I can't quell.

I had gained weight and asked one day after he had just had his way with me on the floor, as I stood behind his desk naked, while he was fully clothed, 'Do you think I am fat?'

Mr Bester looked me up and down and said, 'You could do with some more exercise,' with no feeling at all. I burst into tears. Right after that, I started obsessively working out, much to his delight. It was two kilometres in the pool, straight after an hour and a half of hot yoga. It was anything I could do to please him.

I didn't know what love was. I wouldn't know what love was for a very long time.

He asked for my weight and height, and calculated my BMI. He told me the exact weight that I needed to aim for. The man who had feigned ignorance about eating disorders seemed to know an awful lot. One of his Year 12 students was recovering from bulimia. 'Don't be like her,' he warned, 'look at her yellow teeth.'

'I should've been a woman, I'm such a bitch' was one of his favourite lines.

'My daughter has cervical cancer,' he said, using her as a prop too. There was no one he was not prepared to use.

The things I did to humour and impress him will forever haunt me. One time he wanted to spend a night with me, so I packed my pyjamas and turned up to school on a weekend. He met me there but said he had to go out and would be back later. He left me in his office for an entire day, in my Tweety Bird pants. He didn't return until after 9 pm.

Not only did he forgo protection during my periods, and just put his old purple towel down underneath me on the floor, on one occasion he forwent it in the days after I'd stopped bleeding and insisted that it *should* be all right according to what he *thought* to be true of women's cycles. This from a Catholic man with children. Inside I was terrified; I knew even less than him, and had no one I could talk to. And then he said, 'Imagine all the little Gracie bunnies running around inside you,' and laughed to himself. I just stared. Both in public and in private, Mr Bester didn't seem to care if his 'jokes' – if that is indeed what they were – received a laugh from anybody else. He was as impervious to embarrassment as he was to guilt. He was impervious to the fear and shame that he drove so wantonly into the hearts of others. Or so it seemed.

If you'd like me to keep going my email address is theboiled-frog@fuckoff.iamkidding.com.

'There was no violence, there were no threats,' one supporter of Mr Bester's has argued online.

Tell me, what is all of this?

It has been twelve years. On 27 April 2022, a Twitter account under his name cited the email address that I used as the login to my old Facebook account, from when I was fifteen years old. It substituted the email address in place of my name to say, 'At last I shall come for [Grace] . . . in good time . . .'

I've mentioned in an earlier chapter that Mr Bester also came to my work. In late October 2010, Ms Patterson, another teacher – who was also tasked with identifying the students in the trophy images found on his computer during the police investigation – saw him there when she was passing one day. Knowing of my parents' concerns from earlier in the year, she reported his presence there to Mrs Kronenberg. At this point, Mrs Kronenberg rang the school's solicitor, and asked if this could be regarded as grooming. Despite this, there was no mandatory report, and no further action was taken.

It was also noted in Robyn Kronenberg's statement how kind Mr Bester was to her when he was first informed of the allegations levelled against him. They would offer leave with full pay while the investigation continued.

No Matter

'Why didn't you just say no?' is a question domestic and sexual violence survivors the world over are asked about their abuse.

What many survivors can also attest to in one way or another – provided that you weren't the ignoramus who asked the question (in which case, we reserve the right to tell you to 'fuck off' with your inane bullshit) – is that saying 'no' to an abuser is just as bad as saying 'yes'.

Abuse is, how do I put this, ABUSE. It is, by definition, a lose–lose situation.

There were three other locations where the rapes took place besides the floor of Mr Bester's office. One being Mrs Kronenberg's chair in the staffroom, because Mr Bester hated her. That was a fantasy he told me he wanted to fulfil: to 'fuck' me over the back of her chair. So he did. Another was a house at the end of Goulburn Street in South Hobart that Mr Bester looked after for an old man, who was an invalid. I remember walking there after school in my uniform. A mattress on the floor was a level up.

The fourth location was the Harrington Hotel, named after the street it's on in Hobart. Before Mr Bester had access to the Goulburn Street house, I had asked if we could go somewhere else besides school. Maybe it was an issue of comfort, I was telling myself. Maybe that's why it hurt. It wasn't the fact that he didn't use lubricant. Or that there was no foreplay.

In the years since, I have come to realise just *how* one-dimensional it all was. I couldn't even touch his penis with my hands. I did once. Once, on his request, with a single finger, before quickly pulling away.

He boasted about the size of it to me via an anecdote. He alleged that when he was fifteen his older female neighbour had seduced him and they had a relationship. Her words, according to him, when he showed himself to her, were, 'Oh, you are a big boy, aren't you?'

On the night we went to the hotel, he parked his car on Goulburn Street, just near the Harrington corner. I was still in my uniform. He gave me an oversized black hooded jumper to put on, gave me the room number, and told me to wait for a bit. Then I went inside. The room was white, yet somehow still dirty. I don't remember getting undressed. I just remember the pain being the same. No lubricant. His body over mine. Then after he had finished, he said, 'You weren't into that, were you?'

I said nothing. Not that there were any words I could say in that moment that would have made a difference. Then, he just answered himself, 'No matter, we are going to do it again.' He got up off the bed and went into the bathroom. I just listened and stared at the dirty, dirty white ceiling.

I hadn't even moved by the time he came back and raped me again in the exact same position I was in before.

Trust me, I thought I loved him. But it is impossible, I found out, to love someone like that.

Someone who loves you, they don't fucken do that.

*

Self-proclaimed 'men's rights activist' Bettina Arndt has a lot to answer for. 'This man is not a pederast,' she said, in an interview she gave with Bester in 2017. At the time she first posted the interview, it was illegal because it contravened Tasmania's victim gag law. It contained a picture of my face that identified me as Mr Bester's victim. It has since been reposted, and concludes with the sentiment that society must leave room in the conversation to consider the effect of provocative teenage girls 'who ruin the lives of men'.

It is now both a tragedy and a privilege to tell part of the story of a brave former student who also crossed paths with Mr Bester. She graciously consented for me to share this with you. We will call her A. She was a star student, and she is, without question, amazing.

Not long after Mr Bester started at Collegiate in 1992, A picked all her subjects for Year 11. She wanted to be a doctor. She was one of the best Mathematics students in the whole country.

Out of four classes, Mr Bester taught A for two. This meant 50 per cent of her grade was dependent on him. Early on in the year, he propositioned her, and she declined.

What followed was a cruel punishment of a different kind. At first, A continued to work diligently in class, but suddenly Mr Bester was giving her Ds for reasons she could not understand. He began to consistently humiliate her in class. To cope, A started drinking alcohol on campus. Her confidence deteriorated, her performance and life along with it.

The school said nothing, and A was forbidden to change classes, despite her request. She had no choice but to stay.

One afternoon, during a final lesson as end-of-year marking approached, Mr Bester dismissed every student except A. He told her to wait until he called her into his office across from the classroom.

'I waited for what felt like an eternity,' she recalls. Then, finally, he told her to come in.

'There is something we can do to fix your grades,' he said.

Again, A said no.

The following year, in 1993, Mr Bester had a 'relationship' with another student in A's year. I know this because Mr Bester himself told me about it. Let's call her Z. A and Z were friends. Z and Mr Bester allegedly sometimes held hands in the courtyard. At this time, there was also another Collegiate teacher, Ian Bartsch, who was abusing a student. He was sentenced to jail in 2017.

A did not go on to become a doctor. She did not have the grades. Mr Bester thwarted her chances. This would change the course of her entire life. She ran away from Tasmania, just like I did.

'When I heard what happened to you, I didn't sleep for several months because I thought that it was all my fault,' she told me on the phone.

It was not her fault. The only person responsible for his behaviour is him. He had a duty of care to the students he taught. He breached it in the worst possible way, repeatedly, voluntarily, cruelly and ever so coolly.

'He was notorious for inviting girls back to his office to drink wine from beakers,' she mentioned.

Notorious. It really makes you wonder.

Abuse can take many forms. There is no hierarchy. You can't analyse it through the lens of reason. The normal rules of life don't apply.

Let me leave you with these words from A:

'He made my life so miserable that I saw the way the other girl was and I wished I didn't say no.'

Chapter 14

Trauma Bonds

After I disclosed the abuse, there was a transition period where I didn't leave home for weeks, detached and despondent, watching *Flying Circus* reruns in my attic bedroom at Mum's. Bester was fired and charged, and I did try to return to Collegiate. It was never going to work, though. Among other discomforts, the only person I was allowed to talk to about the abuse at school was the chaplain. The same school chaplain who visited Mr Bester after he checked himself into a psychiatric hospital when he found out that he was being investigated by police.

Allow me to paraphrase Sixto Rodriguez, the mythical musician South Africans worshipped as a dead man for decades, not realising he was alive beyond their borders. As if the chaplain didn't realise this man's purpose was crucifying minds. As if he didn't realise this calculating child abuser was not tortured, he was the huntsman and the player, who was only sorry he got caught in the cruel act of causing harm to others, which he deliberately, willingly undertook. A man who assumed relaxed positions and prostituted the losses of everyone he met. He was only James the weak when it suited him. In reality, he thought he was the invincible, untouchable, almighty God. Even still, the chaplain went to him like a good Samaritan. I've always wondered how much of the child abuser's script he spoke to him then was just repetition of what he'd whispered to me too.

Whether the school chaplain was asked to visit Mr Bester by the school, or whether he went of his own accord is neither here nor there to me. He is a grown man. Although Mum did say that the chaplain's words to her were, 'He was only sorry he got caught.'

After this disastrous attempt to return to Collegiate, it was decided that I should move schools.

In the middle of 2011, I started at Hobart College and survived the next two years on a combination of the fumes of hope that I would get back to Santa Barbara, and the stalwart support of a handful of people who stuck by me in the darkest hours. Janet Upcher was one. She was assisting the teacher of the Hobart College Year 11 English Studies class, and she is the teacher I was visiting the day I broke my collarbone. Without her, I wouldn't have been able to complete my first year at College, which, I might add, is located at the top of the hill Mr Bester used to live on. Right before I disclosed the abuse, he took me to his house. One of the few bus routes to get to the College campus goes via the notorious Mount Nelson 'bends' that overlook Hobart's Sandy Bay. This meant for the final eighteen months of my high school education, in order to get to class, at least once a week I would pass the entrance of his home. Forget the sharp steep corners of the narrow roads, that alone was enough to give me the bends.

Over the next year and a half, I only did five subjects all up to count towards my ATAR: Economics, English, German, Art Appreciation and High Achievers German at the University of Tasmania. I had intended to do Mathematics Methods in Year 12 and was studying the foundation course when I first started at Hobart Collage. Although I had a mind for logic, though, I had lost the taste for Maths.

Like our Year 9 Maths Extended class, the Year 11 Foundation Methods class was very small. I made some good friends who I still have now, like Malcolm and Hugh. But I'll never forget the day the topic of the Collegiate 'scandal' came up in conversation. Nobody said anything awful, but I felt even smaller. 'You went to Collegiate,' the teacher said, looking at me as my gut dropped. 'Did he ever teach you?'

If looks could speak, I told her everything, but out loud I said, 'No.' It was too painful.

Not long after that I gave up on Maths and started to spend most of my time in the Art room, even at lunch and recess. I'd also found myself a new job at a cafe in the city called Blackcurrant, making sandwiches and coffee with a handful of lovely girls, Georgia, Bec and Beck. I took on as many shifts as possible to save my money, not that I was great at doing that. More than anything, I felt disenchanted with everything.

In Year 12, I became friends with a German exchange student named Selina who was living with a host family whose children both went to all-boys Hutchins, which meant she was alone during the school day. My German was semi-decent: I'd been studying it since Year 7, and I've always been somewhat of a parrot. In '72, Monty Python did whole episodes of *The Flying Circus* in German and you bet I can quote entire scenes of useless nonsense from them. Hobart College only offers a fast-track beginners' course before the pre-tertiary one, meaning I had four years on the rest of my peers when I took the class there, plus a bit of family background via Ron. I remember being approached by a College staff member at the beginning of 2012 who introduced me to Selina, another blonde runner, hoping that I would be able to show her around and befriend her. '*Natürlich*' is the German term for 'of course', translating (as you might have guessed by looking at it) to 'naturally'. Although I didn't vocalise it at the time, I was both flattered and happy to help.

Over the next year, a codependent friendship blossomed. Selina and I bonded in many ways. We laughed, we ran, but we also suffered. By the end of Year 12, I had returned to routine exercise punishment. At one point, I was running 14 kilometres in an hour every other day. I was also abusing marijuana and binge drinking at every given opportunity. Every escape I could see, I bolted towards. I strung out every distraction, as though it was the last time I might ever be distracted.

Somehow I graduated, although I didn't go to the formal. When I went with Maddie, Denise and Bob to the Falls Festival that year, which Selina also went to, there could have been another 13,000 attendees and still I would've been the loneliest soul in Marion Bay. The night before New Year's, Maddie went to bed early so I went looking for Selina at her campsite on the opposite side of the grounds. She wasn't there, but someone recognised me when I was chatting to Dan, her homestay brother. 'Is that Grace Tame?' a faceless voice asked from the shadows. Then a boy from my Year 12 Economics class revealed himself.

One thing led to another and we were in his tent. He'd told me that his friends had spotted me working out in the gym, and that he had noticed me before – that he and his friends had a group chat where they rated girls and I'd featured in it. I felt seen. This sort of validation from someone my age was rare and intoxicating, and I was drunk enough as it was. I voiced something to the effect that the majority of my previous sexual experiences were not positive. I was highly embarrassed by my lack of experience of youthful norms, but I also thought I was in the company of someone who was genuinely interested in me. All I knew was being open and honest. 'That's heavy,' he said.

Part of me looks back at that moment and feels like a fool. I hold great tenderness and sympathy for that girl. I have to. I owe it to her. In saying that, I also understand how little everyone around me knew. We were all young then. We were all young, raw and vulnerable in our own ways. Perspective and proportion are invaluable things. Children and adolescents will make mistakes, break hearts and take risks, but there is a wide gulf between these things and premeditated abuse.

We never ended up having sex in the end. In the early light of dawn, we walked through a sleeping campsite to the Valley Stage, and I continued alone to Denise and Bob's Winnebago. But such is Hobart's small-town intimacy that I would soon see him again, and many of his friends, boys who would invite me to spend time with them, and then wind back their interest when I became attached.

The only way I can reconcile some of the more painful interactions is to attribute it to a general lack of awareness. It's taken me the better part of twelve years to understand and accept the exceptional level of evil that belied the abuse at Collegiate, and I was as close as you could possibly get to it. I don't expect people to understand all the depths of it, and in many ways I wouldn't want that either. And the media's language was that I'd had an 'affair' with my high-school teacher. Over time the public narrative has certainly shifted, and it is now well known that it was actually the last of a number of abuses of power perpetrated by a highly skilled offender. Back then, though, this distinction wasn't made.

One night I was standing in a nightclub and the then-girlfriend of a mate said, 'I know you, everyone talks about you.' On another occasion, while waiting in line outside the same venue, a boy I liked said, 'Don't you know I have a girlfriend?' I didn't. We'd slept together twice and I liked him a lot. That same night one of his friends and I were chatting and he brought up the fact that he'd heard about 'the teacher'. He said we should grab coffee sometime, so I didn't understand why he didn't respond to my messages after we then spent the night together.

When you're as constantly discombobulated as I was then, what you think, feel and say can often wind up being unintentionally misaligned. There were a lot of things I did because I wanted to impress people and I thought I had to act in a certain way. Before I left for America, I gave a boy I thought I really liked a DVD. I did not know how else to tell him.

To thank him. The experience of intimacy I had with him was the first I'd had that was conventional. We were the same age. Maybe that was all there was to it. And maybe that was all that I needed. But back then, my traumatised mind did not understand that. My wires were very crossed. I got too attached, and wanted it to be more than it was. It wasn't.

I have often found that people assume many things about me based on the way I look. There have been insinuations that I don't fit the mould of autism, that I am more powerful than I am, or more self-assured, or more sexual. I'm not sure whether I was seen to be an easy target, a soft touch, a belt-notch, a good story or someone who would have sexual knowledge beyond their years. Sexuality isn't learned through abuse. I didn't have an orgasm until nine years after the abuse. Nine years.

Maybe it was none of those things. Maybe it was just thoughtlessness. Either way, my heart is big enough that it can both hold space for this and move beyond it.

There will be traumatised people seeing themselves in these attempts to reconnect and rebuild. You are seen. You are worth loving. There is no shame in surviving.

Before Christmas 2012, I had stopped getting shifts at Blackcurrant, but quickly found another job working at a shoe store in a shopping centre, walking distance from Mum's, called Betts, where I met my friend Holly who became another lifelong ally.

And then, then there was Georgie.

There are some friendships – some rare connections – that defy words. I can only try. It's your insides returning to base after the prolonged dip of a rollercoaster or an imagined fall in a nightmare. It's holding you and soothing you all the way down and back up too. It's the soft-landing pad that, no matter how hard the crash, is always there.

Georgie has known me since way back when, since before I even knew myself (still a work in progress). It's hard to distil her impact. She's one of only a few people I've ever met who can totally, effortlessly cut through shame. She steps through every ounce of pain and self-doubt that swirls around me and sits right next to my soul, gripping it tight, promising to never leave. And boy, does she crack me up. I've never met a better, faster pun-maker than her. What I would've done in some of the bleakest times without her, I hate to imagine. Thankfully, I don't have to. We've got a future full of love, laughter and late nights listening to loud music ahead of us to focus on instead.

After Selina left in 2013, I graduated and the structure of school was no more, and I'd also reached the legal drinking age. I cut sick with sickness. The lid came off the already ajar Pandora's box of trauma over the course of a rampant six months of drinking, dancing, drug-taking and short-lived relationships before moving to the other side of the world. I'd applied to attend Santa Barbara City College, but then had to wait for a response, then wait out the six months before the American school year started.

Enter: a blazing beacon of beach-goth hope with the biggest, brightest, most beautiful, long-lashed eyes you've ever seen. My angelic fellow anarchist. The one I want beside me when I'm riding high and when I feel like I'm dying on the inside. When I am lost for words, Georgie finds them for me.

Like me, Georgie went to Collegiate. She was in the grade above me, though, so we didn't know each other well while we were there. We had a mutual friend, Megan, but weren't close. We do share a mutual disdain for what the institution used to be. Thankfully, only fragments remain of the Collegiate we knew then.

On 31 January, we were both out drinking at a local pub, saw each other, then decided to catch up over a joint on Parliament House lawns. As we sparked the spliff, we sparked a lifelong connection. After that night we spent every spare moment together until I left the country.

While the unbreakable bond that Dom and I share was founded on an unspoken language, Georgie and I can talk about anything. Our conversations know no bounds. Perhaps because we're both people who've never had any – or, more to the point, we're both people who've had to put others' boundaries ahead of our own.

For hours we eased the violence of our minds in each other's company. Sitting on her doorstep smoking under the stars. Blasting Lana del Rey on late-night car rides down the Channel Highway in her violet Toyota Corolla. Dropping acid with my college friend Ben, placing the same takeaway order twice, winding up with six kormas and inspiring over a hundred curry puns in a single Facebook status thread. Eating fairy bread and wearing platform shoes. Ordering two packs of Tupac stick-on nails. Staging rap battles on the rooftops of Salamanca between just us two. Smoking a joint inside a Melbourne hotel supply room with Hudson and Jonno, while watching golf on a television that was playing inside it. Baffling convenience store clerks with our in-house jokes as we tried to buy every snack in sight while we had the munchies.

When it came time to make the move to America, my family said their goodbyes in Hobart, but Georgie flew to Melbourne with me for one last hurrah. We went to see Wavves and dropped acid when the band opened their set with 'Post Acid'. We had a final three-paper rooftop joint, which we wrote 'GOOD THANKS' on the side of.

The lasting image I have from before I left Australia is Georgie's face, in front of a window, looking over the tarmac. Just knowing people like her exist is my safety blanket.

I'll take sitting on Parliament lawns with Georgie over walking Parliament halls any day.

Chapter 15

Raw Red Whitewashed Blues

Disassociation is a powerful drug. It can cut through any sense. Sight, sound – it doesn't matter. When it strikes, it's nearly impossible to pull back from it.

I remember a time before I started having flashbacks that drilled through the present.

A time before I stopped being able to write chronologically without my memories dislocating and floating about. And I think I can also pinpoint when that stopped, too. It coincided with when my childhood sexual trauma began to surface in a time when I started to become able to understand it. When we were learning about sex in school. When I couldn't escape it. It was when I was fifteen.

I was never great at writing essays in a timed or pressurised setting. I now know that to be a symptom of autism. My friend Dom is like that too. We have talked and laughed about it. All I really had in my favour was hoping that my photographic memory would serve me well. But if the question or topic didn't fit the five-pager I'd stored in my brain computer, which I could only workshop to a certain degree, I was screwed. One time I literally quoted Monty Python's Protestant sketch from *The Meaning of Life* in a Faith and Life exam. '"When Martin Luther nailed his" 95 theses "up to the Church door in 1517" [something something something] "to challenge the autocratic power of the papacy..."' I wrote. That is textbook copy-and-paste autism right there.

However, I didn't have nearly as much trouble with assignments then as I do now ordering my thoughts. They've always been in a curvilinear washing machine like I have described, but at least they were connected. The particular coloured moments that I would focus on at any given time were merely separated by grey. Now, at random, without warning, when I am trying to concentrate, it's as if my memory is being hacked at with scissors when I am attempting to communicate. Where there was grey, there is now disjointed, shifting black. The memories I have are crystal clear and vivid but I struggle to hold them in place. Shards of thought, past and present, splinter off in all directions like a bone breaking inside a body, stretching skin and time. When this happens now, I have learned just to bend with my brain. I have to run forwards with the words that flow out of my head, because trying to retrace my steps is like walking on broken glass.

If I thought my life was hard and fast at home in Australia, when I moved to America for college it became harder and faster. Thanks to Julienne, who I stayed with for the initial two weeks after arriving Stateside, I found my first share house. There were ten of us in a small five-bedroom on East Anapamu Street in downtown Santa Barbara, a block from the courthouse. I used to sunbake there on my days off covered in Reef oil. You can take the girl out of Australia and all that. I think I got caught in the background of a family's wedding photos once.

My lovely roommate, Marquette, was a UCSB student too. I remember going down to the courthouse with her to watch outdoor screenings of Hitchcock movies, *Psycho* and *The Birds*, on the grass. Every summer in Santa Barbara they pick a different theme or director and have public weekly film viewings as part of a series.

I also remember sitting underneath the courthouse tower late at night with Celeste and Vicki, who shared one of the other rooms in the house, and bonding over a joint. Vicki and I would share another apartment together the following year. She remains one of my dearest friends.

There was a photographer in my Screenwriting 101 class who offered to take me to Disneyland, as a sort of American rite of passage, and I took him up on it, despite my reluctance. I love *The Lion King* as much as the next 90s child, but the actual corporate beast born of the antisemite that was Mr Walt Disney is just another predatory capitalist menace, in my jaded opinion. If I die and wake up at their theme park, waiting in line for two hours for a damp Cruskit of a ride that goes for twenty seconds, surrounded by the exaggerated veneers of shops full of overpriced useless consumer goods marketed to unsuspecting children who could be out in nature, I will know for sure that I am in hell. Yes, it's me, the Grinch. I'm just one big giant nugget of weed here to smoke your fun. If this sick, exploitative, claustrophobic nightmare is your idea of a good time, that is.

Look, to put it less cynically and more simply, in the case of Disneyland: the big guys get more out of it than the little guys do. Exponentially more, at the little guys' expense in fact. And the little guys are children, who don't have a clue. Not to mention the company is named after a *Nazi* and built on *lies*. Grinds my gears, it does.

Don't worry, I'll tell you how I *really* feel later. Where was I?

Not only did I go to this place with Joe, when we arrived in Anaheim, I came down with:

a) the flu, and

b) conjunctivitis.

I also had a very sore foot, which I later discovered was an ingrown toenail. (The doctor who removed it in Santa Barbara for a casual $500 fee said it was the worst he'd ever seen.)

Because of their dryness from the conjunctivitis, when my eyes started to close up, I had to remove my contacts. I hadn't brought my glasses with me, so this meant I was limping around my idea of hell on earth nearly blind, with a blocked nose and an aching foot.

Joe, on the other hand, loved the place. He sang every Disney song he knew on both days we were there.

Believe it or not, I went back after that. Spencer has an adorable son, Simon, who loves Disneyland. We took him there because he wanted to go. I will always put aside my needs for little ones, any day. I'm not that kind of curmudgeon. Not the kind that will go running through the crowd with a megaphone or stop you from entering against your will. Please, just please, don't make *me* go there again.

While on the one hand moving to a foreign country at eighteen, still in the throes of processing trauma, amplified my vulnerability in many ways, on the other, there was a newfound anonymity that made it possible for me to heal in ways that I couldn't back home. I felt free to move without oversight. I felt free just to be, on my own terms.

Downtown Santa Barbara is divided by the main drag of State Street, which runs south from the pier at Leadbetter Beach all the way north to the city of Goleta where it turns into Hollister Avenue. In the downtown precinct, all the streets that run perpendicular to it are divided into east and west sides.

I lived on the east side. My community college's campus was on the west, high up on the mesa, at the top of Carillo Boulevard, which would later be the go-to location that my friend Ariel and I would battle up for our hill workout sessions. My strength is flats, but she has the glutes for climbing. Many miles were spent trailing her, watching her steady gait, the angel on high above me. That is how I will always see Ariel, for more reasons than one.

On the corner of State and Anapamu is a yoga studio called CorePower. There are close to a hundred of them throughout the United States. Not long after I moved there, Julienne invited me to take a class with her because she had a Groupon and this Santa Barbara CorePower location had just opened. I went, and never looked back.

Not only did I become a 'black tag' member, and begin taking classes almost daily at 6 am before my college lessons, I signed up to do a teacher training course. This would be the first of two teacher training courses I would do with CorePower over the next five years, which have allowed me to teach in two countries.

At eighteen, I was the youngest among Santa Barbara CorePower's first-ever wave of instructors-to-be, but they all embraced me, and we became like a family. Having each other's backs in back-bend demonstrations. Partnering for partner-yoga workshops. Holding each other's hands in handstands. Seeing each other's pain in a blindfolded trauma exposure therapy class.

Dhyana hosted a viewing of *Kumaré* at her apartment on the mesa. Six years later, she and I and her roommate Katherine would go on a midnight hike to the Montecito Hot Springs to lie naked in the pools and be serenaded by a man bathing by the pipe. Shelby took me to her family's Thanksgiving lunch that year; and Shelley, who's since had three gorgeous boys, sent me a message to pre-order this book before I'd even finished writing it. Among the others was a bright, charmingly campy and handsome UCSB alumni from Portland, Maine, named Harrison, who would go on to work on Bernie Sanders' presidential campaign. He lived on Anapamu too, but on the west side, one block from CorePower.

At the end of 2013, after my first semester finished, I decided to find a new place to live that was more private. I was going home for the summer anyway, so logistically it made sense to pack up then. For the week between the end of my lease and my flight out, Harrison kindly let me stay on his futon. I was quite taken by him. He was 24, and very cool, with his obscure high-brow cultural references and underground European techno beats. I would become a fan of Darkside because of him. He was studying the LSAT, with hopes of becoming a lawyer, although he is too good to be a lawyer, if you ask me. That is not to say that lawyers are bad people. (Michael Bradley, don't sue me.)

He introduced me to Velvet Jones's loaded luxury of late-night mac and cheese, and taught me that knowledge is power. It was while talking to him in his kitchen one day, as he parroted my own words back to me, that I realised one of the harshest realities of my own abuse.

Harrison was also one of the few men who at least had the decency to tell me directly when the weight of my trauma became too heavy for him to bear.

Although I was decidedly disenfranchised by the experience I'd had in my English class with J. M. Coetzee's *Disgrace* as a set text, Santa Barbara City College had its gems. Their Screenwriting professor, John Shaw, had enough faith in me nine years ago, when all I knew to write about was my life, to pull me aside and tell me that I should pursue sharing my story in a creative way. For somebody with cripplingly low self-esteem, who was still ashamed of that very story in so many ways, that would be a defining moment. And here we are. I thank you, John.

Michael Gros, the former Head of Drama, would teach several of my classes as well as infinite lessons. In Michael's eyes, everyone was a star student. He is a big man, with a heart to match. Before I had figured out what to do about the *Disgrace* situation, I disclosed to him first because I felt more comfortable speaking to him than my standoffish English teacher.

Michael kindly offered to speak to him on my behalf. It didn't work out that way in the end because of timing, but Michael would nonetheless be one of my greatest advocates on campus.

In semester two I cemented more vital friendships.

Josue was in my Acting class, but if ever there was an authentic man, he's it. He taught me to drive – he taught me lots of things. How to look after myself. How to survive. We lived together, in two homes. We have driven for hours and hours on the wide-open freeways of California, going 90 miles an hour in his Nissan Micra. 'Liam,' he called it. Liam Nissan.

He is another brother. Another brother, from an amazing mother. We hit it off instantly. Our love of comedy and helping others, and our shared traumas. We have cried together as much as we have laughed together, although happy tears mostly. Our laughter often cracks the water well.

We have been through so much together. It's hard to know how to put it all down. There are few people whose compassion matches Josue's. When we met he was putting himself through school and working two jobs to support his family. When I had nowhere else to go, even though his home was already full, he and his mother welcomed nineteen-year-old me without question. When my pop passed, he went in search of a cricket set in a small American town so that I could play a game with my friends in his honour and send a video for his funeral because I couldn't afford to fly back for it. The gratitude I have for him is simply boundless and eternal.

Lazer will already be known to many Australians as my companion in the infamous 'bong photo'. No, he's not a 50-year-old man. He's just under ten years older than me, and is one of the kindest, goofiest, most self-deprecating people

I know, who spent four years of his childhood in Costa Rica, raised by his single father, who has only just passed. He was in the Directing course that partnered with my Acting class to produce short-form plays at the end of term. We connected over our twin wild spirits, and socialist hearts, taking regular day trips up into the mountains to Gibraltar Rock and Lizard's Mouth in his two-door, beaten-up, duct-taped RAV4, listening to Zeds Dead, during tarantula season, getting out along the way to watch the docile creatures crawl across the road. Or we'd go late at night, and I'd sit on the back of his dirt bike. Then we'd traipse through the mud to the hot springs, trying not to get stung by poison ivy plants, which Lazer has tattooed on his arm, just as a pisstake, along with – you guessed it – a marijuana leaf. Our first-ever unintentional coordinated political stunt involved Lazer wearing a T-shirt I'd bought him that said 'FUCK TRUMP' on it to a Bernie Sanders rally. Danny DeVito, also in attendance, spotted it and said, 'Not with my dick.'

Five years and a two-foot bong later, and Lazer, who has also been through hell, has helped me remind Australia that being human is not a crime. That children are not to blame for the abuse that is perpetrated against them, nor for the ways in which they cope with it. Lazer, like many of my friends, believed in me and the cause before I did.

Mahea was also in the Directing course. She is a warm hug, and became like another mother figure to me. When Robin Williams died that August, she brought dinners to my apartment. We went to the local DVD store and rented out all his movies that we could find, then bawled our eyes out watching them together.

Audrey was the roommate of Raul, who invited me on a date that didn't work out, but after which we stayed friends. They both worked at Peet's Coffee opposite CorePower and lived up on the hill above the city. We all hung out at their house, bingeing *Arrested Development* reruns. For a time, Audrey worked at the Santa Barbara International Film Festival. She has an eye for raw art. She is another misfit with no time for bullshit whose solidarity and love I treasure with all my heart.

Andrey, the Ukrainian-born ex-pat comedian, owns the Santa Barbara Comedy Hideaway, and his co-conspirator and fellow funnyman, Maximillian, hosted shows at local venues around town that Josue and I were regular guests at. That was how we would meet Camilla Cleese one night in February 2014, at the back of Petrini's restaurant in Goleta. There were about twenty of us in the audience of that show, and when we were mingling afterwards, Camilla recognised my accent. 'My dad was in Australia recently,' a six-foot-one, blonde-haired, dark-witted Cleese remarked. 'I know,' I replied. John had visited Bonorong Wildlife Sanctuary in Tasmania where my cousin Ryan worked. Camilla and I hit it off instantly and decided to stay in touch. Hers is another friendship that would become a lifelong, life-saving bond.

After five weeks at home visiting family and friends, I returned to Harrison's orange fabric futon in Santa Barbara. From there I moved to the black vinyl couch of a dumpster-diving, pottery-making, mechanically minded son of Christian missionaries named Ransom, whose brother, Mackenzie,

'Mack', was in my Voice Acting class. Mack lived with his brother too, and slept on the floor, voluntarily. Their other roommates were Ransom's German wife, Kadda, and Will, a softly spoken UCSB student who traded stocks in his spare time and kept semiautomatic guns in a safe by his bed.

A man of multitudes was the lean, curly-haired Mack, who rarely wore shoes, despised social conventions, and loved Martin McDonagh just as much as I did. For our end-of-semester duologue, he and I did a scene as Ken and Harry, from the blackly funny *In Bruges*, about two Irish hitmen who've botched a job. Once again, in Mack and his folk, I'd found common ground.

It took me three weeks to secure my own place, a studio apartment on Bath Street in a big, dilapidated pale-green weatherboard two-storey house. Mimicking Lazer, who had a pale pink and white–striped corn snake named Lily, I bought myself a baby ball python from the local Petco to keep me company. Marsellus Wallace I called him, after the *Pulp Fiction* character. No, he didn't look like anything. He used to sunbake in a coil on my chest.

My apartment was only a few blocks away from Mack and Ransom's. There was a little footbridge that went over the famous freeway that goes all the way up the Californian coast, the 101. It was rare for apartment blocks to have on-site washers and dryers but Mack and Ransom's apartment complex did. I would often carry my washing over the footbridge and get high with them while I waited for the cycle to end.

While I was staying at Ransom's, he held a party to welcome international guests. I couldn't tell you about a single person I met that day, aside from Christian.

The Christian of No Religion

I was deeply in love with Christian Uhler, and I didn't know that until he died.

Ours was a love that was not so much about possessive passion as it was about a mutual respect for the simple essence of life lived as wandering spirits who respected each other's freedom, eternally. We were star-crossed fireflies who knew each other inside-out. He died two days after I got married.

Christian will always remain a soulmate of mine. He was – he is – the freest person I've ever met, and I treasure the freedom of our friendship.

Christian was born in Hungary, but he lived in Portugal for a while and spoke Portuguese. Like Mack and Ransom, his parents were missionaries but he was agnostic. He was much taller than me. His cropped blond hair was bleached by the sun and sea and his tan was deep. He drove a 1990s white Volvo. His three prized possessions, besides his zest for life and all the people he loved, were a busted blue portable speaker that somehow still worked, his fibreglass shortboard and a bright yellow soccer ball. His favourite song was the Kygo remix of Marvin Gaye's 'Sexual Healing', which is the soundtrack of all my memories with him. I barely remember him wearing anything other than his red board shorts or blue jeans. His light and lean body somehow contained whole worlds of energy.

There is no story, no picture of smiling faces, not even an exaggeration that could possibly come close to doing any justice to the spirit of Christian Uhler. None.

It was Christian who somehow convinced my clinically depressed self to start letting go by trusting in his unmatched ability to find joy. I'm glad he did.

Without inhibition, I followed Christian wherever his thirst for life led him, whether that was into a hidden cave, to jump off a cliff into the sea, or over the fence of a well-to-do private pool in the middle of the night so we could dive-bomb into it with no clothes on. I followed him to Portugal, and I followed him to deserted pockets of Goleta Beach in Santa Barbara, where we'd light a fire and sit talking until the sun came up, then skinny-dip in the ocean and swing from trees at the top of the dunes. We danced, sang, hopped, skipped, swam in our clothes between classes and rode his skateboard together, back-to-chest.

Wherever we went, there was only laughter and warmth. There was no space or time reserved for anything else. We wouldn't look at our phones. We wouldn't talk about anybody else's business. In fact, in Christian's company, I'd often forget there was anybody else in the world at all.

Dearest Christian. I heard how it happened. You were on the train headed to the very same house we made our home during the summer of 2014 in Portugal. You were running away from the ticket man. We did that every day in Cascais; barefoot, laughing, sun-drenched and sangria-quenched, guarding the life of our €3.50, bursting-at-the-seams, scuffed-up soccer ball as if it were a newborn child.

You were not just a friend to me. You taught me freedom; you taught me how to see through fear and swallow it whole. You taught me how to love myself and everything around me even when I thought I'd never be able to do that again. You taught me life. And I know I am not the only one who has you to thank for these lessons. I won't ever forget that when I thanked you the last time I saw you, you told me that I had helped you too. I never would have known that, and now more than ever I am thankful that I do.

My thoughts will always be first and foremost with your wonderful family, but also with everyone you met, because I doubt there's a single person who crossed your path that wouldn't want to call you a friend. I love you. I always will.

It was the end of May when I arrived in Portugal. Christian met me at Lisbon Airport and we had a beer at the docks there. I remember the novelty of being able to drink in public. We bought a bottle of sangria and drank it on the train from Lisbon to Estoril, a place we would call home for the next six weeks. As we sat opposite each other in the train car, I remember looking out at the architecture and being so enamoured of it. Its worn history and muted colours, paired with the deep blue ocean, were warm and inviting.

Estoril is a beautiful place. Its winding cobblestone roads meet and hug the coastline where they become part of the beaches. The crafted staircases, rock pools and sand are all enmeshed. There are essentially castles in the sand.

Our share house landlord was a Chinese man named Bernardo who looked like he'd been pulled out of a 1970s safari and hadn't got changed since. His leather sandals were scuffed, his khaki vest covering a well-worn white T-shirt. He was never not smoking his rolled cigarettes, which he sometimes left hanging in his mouth while he talked with both hands. They would just cling to his bottom lip as if they belonged there.

The house itself was quite dated. Like Bernardo, I think the last time it had been done up was in the 70s. Initially,

Christian and I were put in the basement, but shortly after we arrived we were moved to a room on the second floor. It had a little balcony that overlooked the pool, a wooden closet, a desk and a double bed, which Christian and I shared the entire trip. Not once did we sleep together while we were there, though. Right before we left Santa Barbara, I told Christian about the abuse, and he always protected and respected me. He snored, though. Like a fucking tractor.

There were a mixture of locals and tourists in the share house. Some were just passing by, others lived there on a more permanent basis. There was a Brazilian guy called Wes who spoke Portuguese. He was tall, young and slender with curly hair. There was a Spanish man in his early forties. He was a rodent of a man who always wore a Ferrari polo shirt. There was another Portuguese guy, Arnold. And then there was Jorge who lived in the attic.

It was the 2014 Soccer World Cup during that time and Jorge had a satellite television. Arnold, Wes, me and sometimes Christian would pack like sardines next to Jorge on a tiny couch in his stinking hot room to watch the matches.

Jorge had a dinky little bright red Peugeot that was basically a toaster on wheels. We would go to Jumbo, the supermarket in Cascais, to buy groceries to make dinners for everyone. Like Bernardo, he smoked rolled cigarettes like a chimney. Inside too. His ashtray was a glass he always kept close by with a lick of water in the bottom.

One night, I had come home late by myself and started chatting with Jorge in the kitchen. The next thing I knew, the middle-aged Spanish man was in there with us, speaking to me from across the kitchen table. I did not understand him;

his phrases were both foreign and slurred. He was drunk. Before I could even reply to him, Jorge became hot with anger whiter than his hair. Spit flew with his words and arms.

Apart from my father and Ron after the abuse, and characters in films, I had never seen a man so angry as when Jorge exploded with rage that night. When the Spanish man left, he explained to me what had happened. The Spanish man was offering me 200 Euros to 'fuck'.

It was indeed an eventful time, of adventure both rapturous and rough – another brutal but beautiful rite of passage. From endless days of soccer and sangria with strangers on the beach to a short-lived fling with a tall German man who left me hanging. Like the cliff we jumped off while we were there, it was an exhilarating plunge into the wide open world.

The night before I left, we held a huge party at the share house. It was the first time I had ever tried cocaine. Jorge and I were high and having deep and meaningful conversations: he was always imparting wisdom but he also loved to party. He had a youthful energy even at his advanced age. Everyone was drinking and laughing and singing in the kitchen and Christian was playing the guitar.

I could put my hand on my heart and honestly say, without a doubt in my mind, that there was nobody on this planet who hated Christian. He was impossible to hate. Not because he wasn't flawed, like everyone. But because he was just so likeable and loveable and welcoming. He had a unique ability to put everyone at ease. It didn't matter who. It didn't matter where. He was magic. Magic man.

As the night wore on, we all jumped into the pool. I wore contact lenses and lost one when I dove in. I was going home the next day so I would eventually get other contact lenses but I couldn't let go of the fact that I needed to find it – my left eye is my dominant eye, so I had quite a different prescription in the two lenses. Everyone was looking for it. One of the men dove into the pool with me to search. Shockingly, we didn't find it.

My flight was at six o'clock the following morning. At three in the morning, I was still high and running late. Christian's friend Sam was quite wealthy and her family had a driver. I remember him driving me directly to the airport.

I had to fly from Portugal to London and then back to Los Angeles. It was around the time an ash cloud grounded a lot of planes in Europe and there were whispers through the cabin about something happening with the plane. I was sitting there by myself, with one working eye, coming down. I had never come down off cocaine before because I had never done cocaine before. All I could think was, *What the fuck is going on?*

It was a literally distorted, mostly self-inflicted reality of layered panic.

There will always be a tension between our inner and outer worlds. I was beginning to see, albeit murkily and subconsciously, that we needn't add any more through substances. Even for all the supposed heights they take us to. For if the sky's the limit, that might not always be a good thing. The sky too can be blackened with smoke. We can run, but we cannot hide in highs.

At this point of my journey, though, I was neither ready nor able to get off the ride. I was still so young. I was ill-equipped, without the tools to focus on the path ahead of me.

Buds, Bunnies, Bible-thumping Bosom Buddies

In semester three I worked on a weed farm, got kicked out of my apartment, and slept with a woman.

There you go, Rupert, there's your headline.

Things were getting more surreal, if you can believe that. My friend Vicki and I found an available room in an apartment at the bottom of the mesa, just by campus, with a girl who had four pet rabbits. Lazer's friends had after-hours work trimming bud on their rental property near Santa Ynez and I took it up. My World Religions class turned out to be purely Christian indoctrination, led by Theodore Faulders who spent almost the entire semester teaching from his chosen text of *The Language of God: A Scientist Presents Evidence for Belief.* There I met fellow anarchist Annaleeza. We showed up and did the work, but decided we preferred drinking apple ciders, philosophising, and getting to know each other in the biblical sense.

Beneath my light-heartedness is genuine feeling. Yes, I'm queer. I always have been. I think that's quite obvious. There's nothing contentious about it. And it brings pain to my chest to write that, in these soft moments with women, for the first time in my life, I felt like an equal intimately. I felt at home in my body. I did not feel ashamed.

Even though Vicki and I were at school full-time and our roommate only worked ten hours a week, she wasn't into chores. This meant there was bunny poo everywhere, and extra dishes that had to be cleaned up. On top of this, before moving in, we had been assured that her much-older aggressive ex-boyfriend was off the scene. When plates of 'seconds' of dinners I'd cooked kept disappearing into the bedroom, from where muffled baritone sounds could be heard, we began to suspect something was amiss. We were correct. He was climbing over the balcony.

We felt very unsafe. Never mind the floor covered in poo; there was a strange, volatile man in our home. The problem – added problem – being that, when we tried to politely address this and the other issues, we were met with fury.

For a time we tried to make it work. I brought weekly peace offerings of free marijuana and kief from my trips up north, where I'd sit for hours on end giving 'hair cuts', as I liked to think of it, to frosty dried plants.

I'll never forget the first night Lazer and I arrived at the ranch. We got there late when most of the house was asleep, so when we were shown to our digs, the bedroom light wasn't turned on. We just made our way to the rectangle shape of the bed. I assumed the marijuana smell was part of the general atmosphere of the business. When I awoke in the morning with the sunlight streaming in, though, I realised it was probably coming from the garbage bags full of pot that immediately surrounded us.

I had a great time at the weed farm, getting to know an eclectic mix of people, working into the early morning hours inside an old caravan, in California wine country. In between shifts we rode quad bikes through the vineyards, played with the farm dogs and cats, and ate Carolina reaper chillies.

In September 2014, I wrote a post on Facebook in response to an article I'd seen posted about a then-recent survey that revealed one in five Australian men thought that women who'd been raped were asking for it. It'd been four years since the abuse at that point, and I'd never said anything publicly about what happened to me. Not once. But now I felt like I had something to say. Not something defensive, just something from the heart.

Along with a link to the article, I posted some words about the psychological experience of losing innocence. I didn't write about the physical crimes themselves, just about what it felt like internally to experience them. I can't remember exactly what I said, but the underlying message I was trying to communicate was about what it was like to lose trust in humanity. That is not a kind of violence anybody asks for, especially when you have put your trust in the abuser themselves.

For a while, I had a different surname on Facebook. Bester used to stalk me on there. He also shouldn't have had a Facebook account, if Facebook and the police were doing their fucking job right. The man was on the sex offender register. Although 'man' is a debatable term for him.

Some friends requested that I change the privacy setting of the post so they could share it with a wider audience. Following that, I reverted my name back as well.

'You are not immune,' Bester wrote, citing the exact date of my post, on his own Facebook wall soon after. 'You are not unassailable,' I read, from my filthy apartment, surrounded by literal pellets of shit.

He also implied he had a revenge plan that involved 'harmless banter between friends'. 'Just a thought,' he ended it with. Five months later, in a public Facebook comment thread, while 'bantering', some might say, Bester committed the second offence.

At the time of his status update in late 2014, though, when my mother alerted the police, 'It's probably a veiled threat,' they said before doing fucking fuck-all about it.

In any case, it ended up being the least of my worries. Vicki and I made one final attempt at a civil discussion with our roommate; it didn't end well. Shortly after, we found our belongings outside of the building with no deposit back.

And just like that, midweek and midterm, we were sharing a motel room and figuring out our lives. I started another drawing to calm my nerves, this time a coloured portrait of John Cleese. Being from Long Island, Vicki was also far from home. In the end the upheaval was too much for her and she returned to New York. But not before we had a chance to clear out our rooms, and I gave our roommate's parents a piece of my mind. They paid her rent and were also the leaseholders.

To my surprise, while Vicki and I were still at the motel, we got a knock on the door and it was our now-ex-roommate's mother, who wanted to speak to me in the parking lot. What followed was bonkers. She'd heard from her daughter about my abuse, and she felt sorry for me. She returned my deposit in cash, in an envelope that she handed to me. But not Vicki's. No, just mine, because she pitied me. I was nineteen, and couldn't exactly afford to hand the money – my money – back. I thanked her perfunctorily, then went straight inside and told Vicki that she wouldn't believe what just happened. I was loyal to my friend, who was loyal to me.

The chaos only continued. From the motel, I moved in with my German teacher, Frangina, then with Josue and his whole family. Before the semester ended, I'd been offered a solo exhibition in a small gallery in North Hollywood. I spent the Christmas break drawing on Josue's couch.

Josue and I eventually found a studio apartment at the back of a house on the corner of Bath and Anapamu Streets, with an avocado tree in the backyard. On the night of our housewarming, I got a phone call from Mum. 'Don't go online,' she said.

Bester had reoffended by posting graphic details on Facebook describing the abuse, denying any wrongdoing, framing me as the aggressor – the 'demented weasel' who 'fucked' him – and boasting of how 'awesome' and 'enviable' it was.

I have run a lot of long races in my life, literally and figuratively. I had already been going for a long time at that point. I had been going hard, but I felt like I could see a rest in sight at the very least. But when I saw the second wave of press that began to break in 2015, it was as if someone had picked me up and put me right back at the very start.

The next day I was a raging mess. I was supposed to go to class, but instead I got into the leftover booze from the housewarming. I drank a sixpack of ciders in under ten minutes, while standing in the doorway, smashing the empty bottles on our concrete staircase. I chased those with absinthe, then started self-harming on the couch outside. Any progress I'd made got drunk with me.

I am lucky that there are so many people who care about me. I came to a while later on the couch, surrounded by familiar faces. Frangina, Josue and Audrey. I was very fuzzy.

Josue carried me to his car. I'd said something earlier about not wanting to be with men, not that I had any issue with Josue. Still, there he was carrying me.

All the good in the world outweighs the evil. Josue carries more than his fair share of it. So does Audrey. So do all of my friends. For I would not be here if it weren't for them.

I finished the semester. Mum flew over from Australia at the eleventh hour. She dropped out of all but one of her university classes. Ron took time off work to look after Oscar. There was a pending art show. It meant there would be no one at my graduation, but the support in the time of greater need was more important. We survived. We always did. Together.

Loose, And

LA markets specifically to people who are young, ambitious, unstable and insecure. I was that demographic. It was the natural unnatural next step after I finished school. I'd never planned to be an artist but I'd been asked to do a show at the last minute. It felt like a sign.

Soon, though, my cousin Gemma was staging an international rescue with my dear friend Nate. It turned out the man who'd offered me a place to stay was planning to seduce me. Nate's mother took me in, then Camilla, but then a friend of hers came to visit so her spare room was no longer available, at which point I began living out of my car. I decided to drive north up the coast to visit my friend Rachel in Burlingame, then all the way to Mad River in Humboldt County to stay with other friends. Without planning to,

I ended up being taken under the wing of a warm-hearted exotic dancer in San Francisco for a week on my way back down.

After the international rescue by my mother, who at first threatened to turn me in to the US police to try to get me home during a very public argument at a Marin County gas station, I eventually landed the job at Blue Rooster in September, where I met many a character. Including Gracie, who would later introduce me to Spencer. The night Gracie and I met, she invited me to her house, and I didn't leave until one week, one attended shift of work, one less tail-light and one less job later, in April 2016.

My next job, at the retail concept store Opening Ceremony, would only last two months, but it was during that time that Camilla commissioned me to do a Father's Day present for John, which would end up consuming seven weeks. I was drawing right up until I returned to Australia for two months in August 2016, before returning Stateside via New York to visit Gracie and meet my future ex-husband.

Between Thanksgiving with Russell Peters, a random invite to and attendance at an orgy in Beverly Hills, finding work as a personal assistant for actress Alexandra Shipp, and being commissioned to draw for Depeche Mode's Martin Gore (hands of all ages and genders signing the eleven letters of 'we are fucked'), things weren't getting any less weird. I rolled with the punches and punched with the roles. I even rolled in Russell's Rolls and I'll be honest with you, it wasn't my jam. I'm grateful for all the charmed experiences I had, but take it from me, that glittering scene isn't all gold.

Object of Permanence

Following my separation from Spencer, I moved back in with Camilla. I had nowhere else to go. She had a spare room in the condo she had just bought in the Valley, and Minnesota-born pop artist Kii Arens had an under-the-table job for me that could help me get by. I met Kii through my friend Jason Wisch. In August 2017, I contributed two original drawings inspired by *H.R. Pufnstuf* to Kii's group exhibition 'The Krofft Super Art Show', which paid tribute to the works of the legendary Canadian television producer brothers Sid and Marty Krofft. Having grown up watching Witchiepoo's countless failed attempts to pilfer Freddy the Flute, meeting the Kroffts was another full circle moment.

During that time I survived on minimum wage cash payments from working as a 'gallery administrator' at La La Land on Hollywood Boulevard, and maximum doses of true friendship.

Every Tuesday morning, I headed east to Silverlake, to my friend Jason's. He and I would start the day with a run, followed by a kettlebell workout in the driveway of his apartment building on Sanborn Avenue under the shade of towering palms. By high noon, it would be time to tan in the beating sun, on the baking asphalt. After that, we'd mosey to one of the cafes on the Sunset Strip to draw or write. At the time, Jason, whose animation credits include a decade supervising at DreamWorks, was working on an idea for a sci-fi series. Evenings were always reserved for a drink at Bar 4100, on the corner of the boulevard, or the famous Black Cat, just opposite.

From there on out, just like the rest of the day's activities, our watering-hole ritual was organic and uninhibited.

Jason would order a Moscow Mule, and I a French 75 – so-called, apparently, because the booze content gives you a hit that's akin to being shelled by a French 75-mm field gun. On the signal of a deep, booming 'skål', the Danish word for cheers, we would clink our glasses, take an unwieldy gulp and then try to keep a straight face for as long as possible without breaking eye contact. I can't recall there ever being a winner. We're both as goofy as each other.

And so on to our next dead-rubber game of 'squiggle', which nobody lost because the goal was laughter. One of us would draw a small freehand mark on a napkin and the other would have to create an image out of it. More often than not, it would devolve into a contest to see who could draw the most inventive cartoon dick. (My mother gave up reading this book a long time ago. I am really sorry, Mum, I love you. I also know she loves Jason.)

Much as I do, wholly and platonically. Jason is much older than I am. We met at Blue Rooster. He had come in to buy supplies one day while I was playing and singing along to Dire Straits. We struck up a conversation that followed a stream of consciousness that led us to realise we were cut from the same cloth, despite our external differences.

In Jason's company, I was completely and unashamedly myself, always. Among the gifts of his friendship was a similar albeit different lesson from Felix's reinforcement that I am not to blame for the abuse that has been perpetrated against me. There is the distinction of the age gap, and the time that Jason spent with me fostering all the parts of myself that I would have otherwise given up on.

There was no dream of mine, no passion, that Jason did not

believe in. He has had more faith in me than my own father at times, as much as that pains me to say. Whatever I wanted to draw, Jason believed I could draw. However far and fast I wanted to run, Jason believed I could run. He never laughed at me, but he was always laughing with me. Always.

I never feel embarrassed or stupid in his company. I just feel like a human, being.

Looking back on our memories always lifts me. Our paralleling pathways of perception were magnetic. People often remark on how animated my face is, and Jason is a literal animator. He was one of the original model makers for *Wallace & Gromit* at Aardman studios. I still have a Gromit paw he fashioned for me one day, and he has a hand I made him in return, 'flicking the vs', as joke. Much as Dom and I can spend hours in silence, so can Jason and I, but when we share ideas, our faces sparkle from the free-flowing connectivity. There's always so much light and life in our conversations.

It's sad that I should have to consider that some people will assume there was some kind of sexual element to our relationship, that I have to defend, simply because he is an older man. He didn't try to do anything to me, not once. Not ever. We spent a lot of time together, during periods of my life when I was particularly vulnerable. I behaved no differently around Jason than I did around the men who abused me, and he never took advantage of me.

When we would go back to his apartment to watch movies after the bars closed, or for our Friday night schlock-horror screening tradition, and I'd pass out on the couch, he would put a cover over me, and leave me to rest.

Like me, Jason has unconventional social filters. Perhaps that's a factor that strengthened our bond. In reflecting on this chapter with him, he speculated whether I befriended him because I was subconsciously looking to challenge the notion that 'all old men are bad'. In his view, this was unusual, because for most people it is easier to reinforce our beliefs than to challenge them, even if they cause us pain. That might have been it, I responded, if I did believe that all old men were bad. Only, that wasn't the case. There was a big difference between how I thought I was bound to receive the treatment of others, and how I viewed and treated people of my own accord. I wasn't prejudiced against Jason because he was an old man. I treated him, just as I treated the people who abused me, and everyone else, on a case-by-case basis.

Jason and I were often joined by fellow ragtags, who made our memories all the brighter: Colin Arens, Kii Arens' nephew, and his Bristol beauty Bonnie; the American Jason, who lived and breathed the town, and also took me in at various times of need throughout the years; Santa Barbara–based Alessandro, the soft-spoken, sharp-tongued son of a Peruvian mother and Hungarian father who would make trips down in his unreliable Saab; and my dear, dark angel, Scout, who I worked with at Opening Ceremony in 2016.

Scout. Whatever would I do without her. Her black hair and china-white skin, inked with subversive tattoos that hint at the depth beneath the surface. She's far too clever to be a cliché, and far too funny to care anyway. We were already close, but became closer in peculiar circumstances. Those being that she and I and her then-boyfriend had decided we were going to do something experimental together, that each of us thought we would enjoy, equally. Only, after Scout and I decided that we were no longer willing, he persisted with his expressions of interest, until Scout made it clear that doing so was inappropriate. She and I didn't want to participate. The three of us went to a party, which Scout's ex used an opportunity to go off and do something with someone else entirely.

Although we didn't have the tools to fully comprehend or express our hurt at the time, Scout and I had a mutual respect and understanding of each other's out-of-the-box individuality. We had shared quirks and questioning minds, born of a hybrid of heavyweight humour and hypersensitivity, that blossomed into an eternal sisterhood.

Even at the tender age of twenty, Scout had the wits to discern between genuine pleasure and that of the pressured kind. She also had the gumption to assert herself, which would take me a while longer to develop for myself. If it hadn't been for her taking the lead, I don't think I would have had the courage to speak up that night. What we had planned to do was similar to many things I've carelessly done in my life, thinking they might make me appear cooler, while not being fully aware, committed or understanding of their gravity. I aspired to Scout's self-assuredness, and the way she never allowed anyone to coerce or reduce her.

Both Jason's and Scout's are among the eleven hands I drew for Martin and Kerrilee Gore's commission. In the piece, they sign 'f' and 'e' respectively, two of the letters in 'friend'. They are two of my best, most definitely.

*

Giving comes in many forms. I am not one who is very good at receiving material gifts from people, unless it is a DVD. I'm incredibly object-sensitive because of my autism. Colour, shapes and textures have to align or else I effectively tune them out because their discombobulation overloads me. This isn't voluntary; it's a protective dissociative survival mechanism. Although I appreciate the gesture, I actually get quite anxious when I receive physical gifts, because they clutter my head and I don't know what to do with them. I worry that I might lose them, forget about or ruin them, because I am clumsy and not good at managing space.

This was one of the most damaging features of my father's household: the emphasis on materiality. It was crushing. And it has taken a long time to divorce myself from its underlying consequences. To get to the point where I now know that I do not have to be a shiny object to be a valuable person. To know that I can have blemishes and scars and still have worth. To know that how I choose to dress does not make me worse or better than anybody else, just different.

The most valuable gifts in my life are these human relationships with the people who love me unconditionally. I never misplace them, because they never misplace me.

Let me tell you something about how hardwired the narratives that abusers seed in our minds become – but also equally how easily they can be derailed with the help of perspective.

Right before I made it back to Tasmania in December 2018, I was scraping the barrel in every sense, financially and emotionally. At the advent of the #LetHerSpeak campaign,

I was still in the United States, and had to watch the anonymous interview with *60 Minutes* I regrettably did with just my friend Gracie and no one else to support me.

A friend of mine who was using a Sugar Daddy dating app suggested I join it as well. I had only ever used one dating app in my time, called 'Her', which I had for all of one day in 2016 in the hopes of meeting a woman, but my neurodiverse brain found it too hard to navigate.

I did meet a lovely brown-eyed New York artist who worked at the Taschen Gallery on Beverly Boulevard, and we dated for a while, and then kept in touch. She is married to a man now, with twin babies. Hers was a distinctly modern, aquatint style evocative of Hockney, and her nurturing warmth certainly made a Bigger Splash in my life. I remember when David himself came to town and she helped curate the exhibition of his works at Taschen. They gave up on trying to get him to smoke outside.

At this juncture, however, I wasn't looking for love; I was buying into what I was taught my worth was, purely in my body.

Reluctantly, I made a profile, secretly, silently. 'The Sound of Silence' plays once more.

I went on a date with a middle-aged man to the Getty Centre. We shared a sandwich then walked around and looked at the art. He liked Helmut Newton, and had bought a ticket to a Nick Cave concert in the hopes I would join him later.

After we left the museum and were descending the hill back to Brentwood in the cable car, looking out across the sprawl of the wealthier side of western Los Angeles, the man pointed to a building through the window. From where we were up on high, everything looked indistinguishably, deceptively clean. At least that's how I see it in my memory.

That might be because of what he was about to say, and my sudden clarity of sight that followed, as I was looking down at a part of my life that I was about to leave, so swiftly, and so easily, because it was never meant to be part of it in the first place.

'I almost worked there as a teacher.' I didn't see where he'd pointed to exactly, and I don't remember the name of the high school. But I'll never forget him telling me that he didn't take the job in the end because his wife said he would probably want to have sex with the fifteen-year-old students. And he agreed, *he would.*

He had said this out of nowhere. Out of nowhere, he had offered this confession.

It was not me. It never was.

I was horrified. I always had been. As a groomed teenager trying to make sense of what was happening all those years before, I had even asked Mr Bester if he found it hard working in a school with young girls. I had sympathised with him. He had danced around the question, in his usual cowardly way.

In that moment, as we were headed back to ground, as strong as the pull of gravity itself, the realisation that I wasn't bound by my past crystallised, brilliantly.

I wasn't a trope. I wasn't cast with a kind of Oedipus complex that was set in stone. The belief system that had been imposed on me shattered.

I was worth it. I deserved a good life. It didn't have to be like this.

I got off the cable car. I didn't see him again. There was no exchange of money, just a sandwich. Nothing happened, just a look at some art. I didn't go to the concert.

The seeds of terror that had been planted long ago, the vision in my brain that played to 'The Sound of Silence', had been destroyed.

I went home to Australia.

I left the broken dreamscape of Los Angeles for good.

There have been no older men ever since.

Chapter 16

Snakes and Ladders

Life is a game.

What goes up must come down.

I've spoken before about the pendulous nature of my life. It has indeed been a surreal, technicolour adventure of repeating rhymes marked by curious symbolism.

Extreme highs and extreme lows.

Encounters with saints and men, so many of whom are called Michael.

A sanctuary of self-expression that, true to life itself, only mirrored my vulnerability and rawness wherever I went to escape.

Just as friends can be foes and vice versa, the same is true for trash and treasure, and also snakes and ladders. Opportunities and failures, in some cases, are simply what you make of them. Ultimately, what defines us in any event are our actions and our character in the face of them.

I have learned these and many other hard truths the hard way. The best reason for cautioning against *wishing* for things lest you actually receive them is that nothing ever meets expectations, for better or for worse.

During the weeks of 2011 that I spent reclusively watching *Flying Circus* reruns in my room, before moving schools to Hobart College, my mum recalls that all she could hear if she walked through our hallway downstairs was 'The Liberty Bell'.

The Liberty Bell is a literal bell in Philadelphia. It has a message on it, promoting freedom, that has inspired the civil rights movement and women's advocates throughout the United States. On its inaugural ring, it was cracked.

Look, I can't find a metaphor in that. Answers on the back of an envelope, please.

I wasn't watching the Python episodes because they were making me laugh. I was cycling through the same familiar, completely different faces because they were the only things that comforted me, while I sat and drew. Our cat, Ralph, refused to leave my side, such that there was an imprint of his body marked by black fur on my throw rug at the end of my bed where he slept all day, purring like a motor.

When she could, Mum would sit with us too, and humour me with wild fantasies. 'Maybe you will draw for one of the Pythons one day.'

Not long before I left Australia, I drew a portrait of Lana del Rey for Georgie. During the first week of living in downtown

Santa Barbara, I met Lana del Rey, outside Wetzel's Pretzels on State Street. Her boyfriend kindly took a photo of us with my Canon camera. The coincidence was unreal.

On 31 July 2014, I drew a portrait of Robin Williams, inspired by his birthday, which is 21 July. News of his death gutted the world eleven days later, on 11 August 2014.

On 7 August 2014, I drew Jack Nicholson, because Tamsin's friend George had made a request from Portugal. Nothing happened to Jack because it's fucking Jack Nicholson. That one flew over the cuckoo's nest.

On 23 October 2014, after Vicki and I were unexpectedly thrown out of our apartment, I shared the finished portrait of John Cleese with my friends and family online. Camilla Cleese saw it, and asked if I would like to meet John and show it to him. She explained he would be in Los Angeles soon to advertise his memoir. I remember standing in the SBCC parking lot on the phone to her not long afterwards. She told me she had been following my story and reading some of the updates I posted.

Let me say this: people are people. The concept of celebrity is as mythical a construct as any other manmade idea. If you told me I could meet Justin Bieber or Ariana Grande, I wouldn't bat an eyelid. The point is not to make any particular commentary on them, but rather to say that I'm not interested in the work of individuals because of their fame. If you've got this far in the book, though, you'd be well aware of the significance of comedy in my life, and particularly Monty Python and John Cleese.

At this juncture, John Cleese had not outwardly aligned himself with J. K. Rowling. While the issue of trans rights is complex, and not one that I have the capacity to unpack as someone who cannot speak to the lived experience, I am a human being who has empathy. Our family will always grieve the loss of Kelly. I respect the need for women's only spaces, particularly as someone in a small body who has been repeatedly targeted physically, but I am a staunch believer in treating people on a case-by-case basis. What I do not believe in is casting blanket judgements about marginalised groups. I do not believe in false equivalences. From my own personal experience, the only people who sexually harm boys and girls, who claim to be something they are not – such that the consequences cause harm to others, deliberately or otherwise – are abusers. There is no stereotype. In fact, being part of a vulnerable community often makes you more compassionate towards other vulnerable people.

For these reasons, I am deeply conflicted about sharing my memories of John. I haven't spoken to him since 2018. He has some views that, in my opinion, are incredibly bigoted. He should not be platforming them. Is he commenting on something he knows nothing about? In my view, yes. Does it eradicate his and Camilla's generosity and support for me over the years? No. They gave me shelter. Both of the literal and figurative kind. To ignore and dismiss that would be ungrateful and dishonest. Moreover, and most importantly, John Cleese is just another human being. He is over eighty years old. He should not be put on a pedestal. Because nobody should be. People are complex, and they will disappoint you. Not everyone is an abuser. But no one is perfect. You have to set your own boundaries in each given circumstance.

On 19 November 2014, I took the three-hour train ride from Santa Barbara to Glendale and waited in a cafe for the afternoon, until I heard word from Camilla, who I was to meet up with at the theatre. The first thing I saw when I left the Amtrak station were the car yards that line the wide boulevard, which narrowed as I walked towards the town centre. The first car I would ever own I would buy from Glendale, albeit from a parking lot, and second-hand.

I had ice-blue hair. And I was shaking. I had my A3 sketchbook and backpack with me, and had taken the day off school to make the trip – that it was. The Alex Theatre in Glendale was small, and we sat close to the front. Eric Idle was John's interviewer, and I remember the depth of appreciation being very acute. In a positive way I was contextualising it with my past and the idea of karma. At the same time it kept me grounded in the present; I wanted to savour it.

At dinner after the show, 'You're a nice colour,' was the first thing a six-foot-five John said to me, surveying all angles of my head in a mannered way. I thanked him then ducked off into the corner. There are few people whose positive creative impact on my life at that stage could have topped his. Camilla came over to talk to me. I didn't want to bother him. She must have explained this to him. Now I want to cry: because the next thing I can recall is one of my childhood heroes, in a room full of friends who had come to see him, bending down to smile at an autistic kid from Tasmania. He gently grabbed my arms and told me to stick my fingers in my ears, before doing the same. Then he poked his tongue out. So I poked my tongue out. We were mirroring each other's silliness in a moment of pure joy.

In the following years, Camilla Cleese would become like a big sister to me, not just because she has over half a foot on me. She has taken me in, taken me out, stood up for me. We have survived several road trips across county and state lines together, and taken more midnight trips to Target than you can poke a useless piece of obsolete unicorn-themed junk at. We have also collaborated on a number of over-elaborate art projects.

In the lead-up to Father's Day in 2016, Camilla commissioned me to draw a present for John, who had five gigantic Maine Coon cats at the time. The original idea was to create a parody of something like Grant Wood's iconic *American Gothic*, except with the cats in place of the humans. Then it struck me that the perfect base image was *The Last Supper*, given that one of the Pythons' famous sketches was a send-up of Michelangelo's extravagance in which John played a very angry Pope berating the artist for putting 28 disciples, three Christs, a kangaroo and jello, among other things, into his work. It implied that was the reason Leonardo painted *The Last Supper* instead.

And so, we had our perfect canvas. I traded disciples for cats and characters from John's canon of work. On the table I added spam, a dead parrot, a glowing holy grail, cheese-shop cheese and fish from the fish-slapping dance. Among the feet is the famous Python foot. How'd they all die? The salmon mousse, of course. My personal favourite touch, which you have to squint to see, is the crucifixes from the closing scene of *The Life of Brian* in the windows behind them.

Upon seeing the completed drawing, Camilla's friend Kerrilee asked if I would do something for her husband, Martin Gore. Depeche Mode were releasing a new album and soon to be doing their Global Spirit tour. Kerrilee had also seen the drawings I had done for the North Hollywood show and was particularly fond of a piece featuring human hands signing the message 'this world has been fucked'. Her hope was for me to draw one of Martin's lyrics in sign language for a Christmas gift in 2016. It would be another year before I ended up handing it over.

I remember Christian brushing his own hand over the unfinished product the same day I dropped it off to Kerrilee. Despite two nights of no sleep trying to get it done, unsuccessfully, I agreed to pick Christian up from LAX after he got back from Portugal and drive him the 100 miles home to Santa Barbara, before driving back down to head home myself for Christmas. I was so tired, we pulled over halfway and he took over driving because he was worried about me. That night we talked about how grateful we were to have each other in our lives. It was the last time I ever saw him before he died.

I was listening to random streaming music the day I finished the last hand in late 2017, months after Christian's passing. Just as I was putting my pencils down, his favourite song came on. I am not a person of faith. But that moment got me.

After I handed over the completed commission, Kerrilee and Martin kindly invited Spencer and me to see Martin perform as an added thank you. On the night of the show, John, Camilla, Spencer and I had dinner beforehand. John wished to sell prints of the Last Supper drawing as merchandise for his 40-year anniversary *Holy Grail* tour.

As Camilla drove us all in the car to the Hollywood Bowl to see Depeche Mode play, John said, 'Last time I was here I was on stage.' He was referring to the famous 1972 live show, the recording of which I'd watched more times than I could count. Incidentally, it's also where he met Camilla's mother. 'I've got two artificial hips,' John told the security staff manning the body scanner he walked through at the entrance. 'And an artificial brain,' I sassed. Kerrilee had organised a throne for him, and when she led Camilla, Spencer and me to the side of the Bowl stage, it was enough to make anyone cry.

In early November 2017, I flew with Camilla to Florida, where I would become the sixth temporary crew member of the *Holy Grail* tour. The 'Tasmaniac' illustrator, as John called me.

There is nothing glamorous about living on a bus, no matter how 'rockstar' the image may appear. It is midnight truck stops. It is little sleep, close quarters and exhaustion. But it was an experience I wouldn't trade, if only for the insights into this reality. These were magical moments. These were personal – between people, in private. As ever, connection is king.

Camilla and I bought gorilla suits from Target to wear for a private tour of the lemur enclosure in Durham during our three-day break in North Carolina, only she got sick, so I chickened out. I couldn't bring myself to be a lone ape-apologist.

I was only supposed to stay with the crew for the Florida leg, after delivering a run of 100 prints for the merchandise team. But when 24 prints sold on the first night I joined in West Palm Beach, and when all of them were gone within five shows, I was asked to arrange for another shipment of 200 and stay until the tour reached Denver.

We signed the first lot all in one go. I had them printed with a one-inch white border where we could both sign our names. John had other plans. He autographed right underneath Jesus. 'That's supposed to be me, isn't it?'

I saw that I had a missed call from Mum one night while we were crossing state lines, I called her back, but when she answered I handed the phone to John, to surprise her. She was driving, but answered, albeit on speaker phone, and only a couple of blocks from home. I could hear her flustered cries from the other side of the bus, telling John she had to pull over, while complaining about the plovers in our street. He said he had just been looking at pictures of plovers and 'what an extraordinary coincidence'. He was very patient with her, and told her that the prints were 'the best-selling merchandise we've ever had'. The drawing has since been printed another several hundred times. It has been used as a backdrop for several shows in venues throughout the United States.

I stood in the wings watching the shows, looking after Camilla's chihuahua, Hercules – or Hercu-Cleese, as we called him – already feeling luckier than I could have ever imagined to be a part of this moment in time. Then, when I heard John mention my name, and saw the projection behind him turn to a giant image of my drawing, it floored me on a whole other level.

For all the happiness and pride I felt there and then, though, I was without anyone to share it. I was 22, and my family were on the other side of the world. Anybody who is reading this, let this be my greatest lesson to you. My gratitude in that moment is impossible to express. But so, too, was the power of the realisation that nothing means anything in this life without love around you.

I had run from my home. And all I wanted to do was run right back.

Such is the void of so many survivors; so many artists; so many people. It is unfillable. I have seen it from both sides. It is heartbreaking. I am sharing this with you because I want you to know that your worth is not measured in grand moments. They will not answer your questions. They will not heal your wounds.

I survived being Australian of the Year because I knew already that it wouldn't be a true reflection of my worth. I knew it would be ugly, at least in part. I came equipped with a glimpse of fame that made me realise two profound things. One is that people's ideas of it will always be warped from the outside and there's little that can be done to control that. The other being that you don't have to let it warp you if you hold on to what is most dear.

Speaking of saints and sinners, and false prophets at final dinners, throughout my life I have encountered the best and worst of humanity in all its forms, in unexpected ways, in unexpected places.

Saint Michael is the patron saint of paramedics, soldiers and police.

San Miguel is where my sickness took hold.

The monster who abused me at St Michael's Collegiate was a soldier.

When I was in America, I was abused and manipulated by an ex–police officer who learned of my history and used it against me. He traced his hands over my body. His had a single tattoo. It was Saint Michael the Archangel.

That makes three saints that turned out to be demons in disguise, all with the name of Michael.

Michael is also the name of my father, my college Drama teacher, and two of my dearest friends and allies, Michael Bradley of Marque Lawyers and criminologist Dr Michael Salter. They are not winged creatures. They are not perfect patrons. They are four great men who stand on solid ground.

Add these supporters to the fact that St Michael's Collegiate, the place that was once a hell for myself and so many others, is now redeeming itself, and we see that good can outweigh and outlast even the most insidious of evil. Mine is just one part of a bigger equation, but would that it be a message of hope.

I have since returned to the grounds of Collegiate. The Grace Tame Foundation was their chosen charity for the Year 12 annual fundraising project. As such, the logo is on their leavers' jumpers for the year. They even made me a personalised one. I didn't realise how much it would move me until I put it on. I didn't ever get a leavers' jumper or attend any of my formal education ceremonies – my family weren't there in Santa Barbara so I didn't go to graduation. I didn't take the jumper off for four days.

Mum's working-class upbringing didn't afford her the opportunity to pursue a university education straight out of high school. She's always been bright and curious, with a particular passion for behavioural science. In 2014 she began studying at the University of Tasmania.

In March 2013, a then-60-year-old Nicolaas Bester was released early from prison after serving only eighteen months of his two-year and ten-month sentence. He then almost immediately began studying Chemistry at the University of Tasmania on a federally funded PhD scholarship while living at their John Fisher College student accommodation, which has shared facilities including showers with teenage students.

Chorus: now stand for an internal scream.

For some reason, Mum was a bit uncomfortable with the idea of crossing paths with the man who had raped her child. As part of her course, she had to take a unit inside the building where Bester's office was. This was no way to study or live.

In February 2015, while still a student, Bester publicly boasted about his experience of abusing me, which saw him convicted of the crime of 'producing child exploitation material (in descriptive form)'. In January 2016 he was sentenced to four months in prison. By June that year he'd been released and was able to recommence his PhD studies.

At this stage, my mother's study became completely disrupted. The trauma was overwhelming.

She spent the better part of 2015 advocating for me in the court proceedings while I was living in America. Following Bester's sentencing at the beginning of 2016, Mum embarked on a battle with the university. Her belief was that Bester's recidivist criminal actions constituted a contravention of the university's Student Code of Conduct, and that his presence on campus posed a general threat to the safety of students, in particular those who were participating in pre-university courses from local high schools.

In April and July 2016, Mum and Ron met with a UTas representative, who insisted that no Codes of Conduct had been breached. Unable to reconcile this, Mum then sent a formal complaint to Vice-Chancellor Peter Rathjen. Still, the university held their ground and no meaningful action was taken until the current Vice-Chancellor eventually restricted Bester's studies to an online capacity. Incidentally, in August 2020, Peter Rathjen was found guilty of sexually harassing two women at the University of Adelaide.

With the help of End Rape on Campus Australia (EROC) founder and director Sharna Bremner, she wrote a formal complaint to the Tertiary Education Quality and Standards Agency (TEQSA).

The university consistently maintained the position that to prevent Bester from studying would be discriminatory.

Because you'd let him babysit your kids. It would be discrimination otherwise.

In 2017, the UTas Women's Collective created a petition to have Bester removed from campus. His presence was widely discussed, with students expressing how uncomfortable it made them. Heads up to all the UTas Women's Collective members who turned up to hold banners in the rain and present the UTas VC representative with the petition. I would later hear directly from a member of staff that Bester would allegedly sit on the university gym's exercise bikes for two hours at a time because they overlooked the early learning centre – which, incidentally, was where Collegiate students did their work placement.

On 16 May 2017, I received a message from my friend Heidi, who shared details of contact she had received from New South Wales–based freelance investigative journalist Nina Funnell. Nina's focus throughout her career has primarily been on rape and sexual assault, particularly in institutions. Amid the press surrounding the petition, Nina was eager to report on the story, including providing anonymous quotes from me if I was willing. After receiving communication from Heidi, who had passed on Nina's expression of interest, I responded with confirmation that I was happy to talk and that she should get in touch. Nina also reached out to Mum via Heidi.

So began an ongoing relationship, and the seeds of unanticipated and unprecedented advocacy were planted.

After Mum told Nina that I needed to apply to the Supreme Court for permission to self-identify in the media, Nina passed this onto News Corp's Senior Legal Counsel, Gina McWilliams, who found there was indeed a gag law. Nina then made sure that my case was taken to the Supreme Court in the hopes of being granted an exemption to Section 194K of the *Tasmanian Evidence Act 2001* so that I could tell my story under my own name.

I had never disclosed my experience of child sexual abuse to a journalist before, save for the earbashing I gave David Killick the day it first hit the press in 2011 when I was sixteen. I didn't know how to speak of it other than to get mad. As such, my mother connected me with a man named Steve Fisher. Back in 2017, Steve Fisher was the only survivor of child sexual abuse who was legally able to engage in public advocacy. He had been granted an exemption to Tasmania's gag law by the Supreme Court, after the *Mercury* newspaper paid his legal fees. His story of clergy abuse was deemed in the public interest.

I was living in America while all this was happening, mind you. All of a sudden I went from seven years of unnameable feelings, to an explosion of understanding, but with like minds an ocean away. It was painfully paradoxical. The double-edged sword of revelation: equal parts trauma and validation. I could talk to Steve and Nina for hours on end and months upon months of emails flowed between us. But I was not on the ground, in more ways than one.

It would take a year, a separated marriage and a cross-country move before the Supreme Court's verdict was handed down. In the meantime, in November 2018, the #LetHerSpeak campaign was launched. Nina's idea was to change the entire law and grant all survivors a voice, using my case as the foundational example. She pulled together a coalition that included Marque Lawyers, news.com.au, the *Mercury* and EROC. The campaign would soon grow and include sixteen other survivors from a total of three jurisdictions: Tasmania, Victoria and the Northern Territory.

In April 2019, I opened a letter while standing at the kitchen bench containing the Supreme Court's verdict in my case. It said I had a voice.

The tears you cry in those moments don't weigh upon you. They don't resist you and you don't resist them. They are meant to be. Because they are just free.

I didn't attend the first trial but I did go to court when Bester was sentenced to his second prison term. He, in his most honest moment, could not look me in the eye. When the judge read the verdict, it was clear he wasn't expecting more jail time. I saw his knees shake as I sat just behind. The tears I cried then were the exact same kind.

I fucking hate the term 'he said she said', if only for the fact that he had every word in court. I was still a minor when I reported the abuse. Children should never be made to testify in front of their perpetrators, nor should they be cross-examined. But nor should they not be given a right of reply. Eight years it took.

I spent 2019 and 2020 running, in more ways than one. I lost weight I couldn't afford to lose, and with it my period. As I pushed myself under 47 kilograms, I thought I'd pushed my trauma under too. Advocacy and activism had unwittingly become one of the primary focuses of my life. Only, my life and advocacy were the same thing. When I wasn't dealing with trauma on a conscious level, I was living it on another. It was coursing through my body. Subconsciously I was starving my emotions and pounding out my fears.

I was home for the better part of 2019. With my newfound ability to speak, I had done some local media, and was motivated by glaring gaps in public understanding of grooming and child sexual abuse. I was eager to help in whatever ways I could to educate and raise awareness. At the same time, though, I wanted to leave. My home in Santa Barbara was calling me.

On 11 November 2019, I returned to the United States, and moved in with Andrey, right by the mesa cliffs in Goleta.

I started doing yoga at CorePower again. Then I met Leo. And then I met Ariel.

Leo, Ariel, Nora and I ran together almost every Saturday for the few short but sweet months that I was back in Santa Barbara before COVID hit in March 2020. We called ourselves the 6:30 Squad.

I could run all day with Ariel and it wouldn't be long enough. Before I met her, the longest I had ever run was 21 kilometres. By the time I had to make my unexpected return home, we'd run the better part of a marathon together, and regularly covered at least 25 kilometres of the Santa Barbara coastline or the winding hills of Hope Ranch.

I had been effectively celibate for about a year before moving back. I had become very protective of my body and myself after my break-up, and amid the unrelenting background pressures of advocacy. I had a lovely boyfriend who was living in San Francisco, but we only slept together twice and, because I was bony and had no oestrogen, I found it uncomfortable. This wasn't a reflection on him; it was because, even while I was deeply unwell on one level, on another I was realising that I wanted to sit with my childhood body, and I wanted to be untouched.

Ariel's arresting purity was something I could not relate to, such that I felt like I did not deserve to be around her. The day we met, we ran thirteen kilometres from Leadbetter to Butterfly Beach and back with Leo. Anyone who's ever shared company on a long run knows that, even if you begin as complete strangers, it's impossible to finish as anything other than friends. The conversation is unrestricted, raw and honest. The solidarity is irrefutable. And the silent miles are some of the most binding.

Not long before meeting Ariel and Leo, Bettina Arndt had just been given her OAM, and the media had been probing me. What was beneath the surface inevitably rose above. Ariel and Leo just listened, absorbing every detail with love and compassion. The day Arndt's award was announced, Ariel turned up at my work with a bag of homemade cookies.

'Smooth,' I call her, and she calls me 'Squoosh'. For all her gentleness, she has seen unfathomable harshness. By 24, she had helped nurse and rescue displaced people in the Middle East. And she rescued me.

I was hoping to run a marathon. She had already run a few, and she and Leo were training for the Boston Marathon. One day we set out to run for three hours. I'd never felt transcendence like that before. It mirrored our friendship.

We said our temporary goodbyes in a cave on the bluffs, eating fresh papaya with a spoon, crying, laughing, knowing we loved each other forever.

In March 2020, I went home for good.

The COVID quarantine on my return might have been the most freeing two weeks of my life. I stayed at Nan and Pop's old place on South Arm Road, savouring the full-circle moment, honouring their memories. I sat at the breakfast table looking out across the highway at Rokeby Vinnie's bin, imagining that I was the new torchbearer, and pottered around in Pop's old room.

While I was sunbaking one day in the backyard, my friend Matt, wearing a motorbike helmet, dropped off a fresh catch of fish in a Woolies bag on the end of a rod.

Ron and Bob set up Jenny's treadmill in Pop's shed, so I was as good as gold to keep on running. And that I did.

After leaving quarantine I lived at Jenny's, and Eloise and I ran almost every day together. She would pick me up in the morning, or we would leave straight from Jenny's. My friend Milly would often join us too.

On 20 May 2020, a 46-year-old African American man named George Floyd was killed after a police officer in

Minneapolis knelt on his neck for almost ten minutes. The numbers '846' became a symbol of the Black Lives Matter movement, and of police brutality, signified by the originally reported time of eight minutes and 46 seconds that the officer spent asphyxiating him. The world erupted in all manner of protests, commemorations, and acts of solidarity.

Ariel and Leo ran for eight hours and 46 minutes without stopping, as a gesture of unspoken solidarity. Knowing it wasn't my place to speak, I took a leaf out of their book, and committed that year to putting my money where my legs were. For every race I ran in 2020, except for the half marathon I won in Santa Monica just before I left to come home, I donated a dollar per minute that it took me to run the course.

Eloise and I created a little fundraiser called Minutes for Movements with a more local focus. We wanted to honour the global issue, while specifically acknowledging Australia's damning history of police brutality against First Nations people. At that time, there had been 437 Indigenous deaths in custody since the 1991 Royal Commission into Aboriginal Deaths in Custody. Translated to hours, 437 minutes is seven hours and seventeen minutes. On 28 June, Eloise and I ran 72 kilometres in one go, only stopping for bathroom breaks. At the end of the project we'd raised over $9000, which we split three ways between the NAACP Legal Defense and Education Fund, Sisters Inside and the Tasmanian Aboriginal Centre.

It was also through running that I met Max.

Chapter 17

Max

I am very grateful for the men in my life. And this brings me to Max Heerey.

When I stayed at the clinic in Rokeby earlier in 2022, there was a man there whose name I can't mention lest I identify him; we became friends because we both liked playing table tennis. I will call him S because he loves the sea – now, whenever he sees dolphins while he's out on the water, he makes sure to send me a picture to cheer me up.

When I told him the following story after a hit in the gym, we both cried.

'I am proud of you, and I don't even know you,' were the first words Max ever said to me, the day I won the first marathon race I ever entered, ten years after the abuse at my high school, eleven years after I was too weak to walk, after being bed-bound in hospital recovering from anorexia.

I knew who Max was. I'd known his name for thirteen years. He went to Hutchins, the brother school of St Michael's Collegiate. We'd never met in person, though; we only knew of each other, and followed each other on social media like many Hobart contemporaries.

He was the most handsome man I had ever seen. Why he would want to have anything to do with me was beyond me. From what I remembered, Max was very well liked at school. I, on the other hand, got by with my clowning antics, but was never part of the 'in' crowd. I certainly wasn't by the time I left. I was a nerd. Then I was a rumour.

Only weeks before Max reached out to me, I had been blindsided by a blind date who led me on for two weeks of intense flirting, during which I shared with him my strung-out history of being used for sex. Lo and behold, this man, who'd said, 'That's the record player we'll put in our house,' as we passed by a music storefront after one of our dates, and invited me to meet his parents, decided it might not be a good idea to keep seeing each other, just after we had sex for the first time.

As much as it pained me, all I could say in response to Max's first message was 'thank you'. I wasn't ready to get hurt again. I had also just run a marathon, literally.

And I had done it alone. I had coached myself to a victory, all on my own. And you bet your fucking arse I am proud of that because I know what that takes to do.

It wasn't the fastest time. It wasn't a strategic race. But I set myself a goal, and I did it. For me. On my terms, on my turf.

On 10 October 2020, Mum and I got up at dawn to drive to the midland Tasmanian town of Ross. Mum brought her book and a chair, and set herself up at different spots over the course of the four-lap race route. All I wanted to do was crack three hours.

At the start of the gun, I flew. Too hard, too soon. That would be my first lesson. For the opening three kilometres, I ran alongside the man who won in two hours and 37 minutes.

I ran the first ten kilometres in 39 minutes, but I had no concept of how to race for longer than 21 kilometres – and I'd only done that once, seven months earlier in Santa Monica, where I'd finished my first half marathon 58 seconds shy of 90 minutes. All the longer training runs I'd done over that distance were tempo speed at best.

Seeing Eloise line up for the half marathon and hearing cheers at the 21-kilometre mark, which I made in one hour and 25 minutes, gave me a much-needed lift, but I also heard myself say, 'I have to do that all over again,' as I entered the third gruelling lap. By that stage, the sun was high, and I was already cramping. Earlier, I hadn't been able to take in the fuel I'd brought. All I had was my handheld water pouch. The next female runner was fifteen minutes behind me, and the male leaders were way out ahead. I was running alone.

I stopped looking at my watch. It wasn't making me any faster. The only thing I could do was run.

By lap four, I wasn't running with my body. If I had listened to the pain, I'd have stopped. I was moving with my mind.

With seven kilometres to go, I found myself at 'the wall' marathoners speak of, which would have you defeated in an instant.

What happened next would stop me from falling to my aching knees and ultimately get me across the line.

Suddenly, I was surrounded.

Ten years before that, just the sight of one tall man would have made me freeze.

In that moment, a whole group of them circled me so that all I could see was their bodies and the pavement beneath my feet. It was just little me, walled in by giant men.

They told me that they had my back. They told me to stick with them.

Ten years after I had been stripped of my love of running by one man, isolated, terrified, lying on my back wishing I didn't exist, I crossed the finish line as the clock ticked over two hours, 59 minutes and 31 seconds, smiling through tears, embraced by my mother and cousin and friend Milly, buoyed by the solidarity of a community who believed in me and helped me believe in myself.

The victory that day was not the race. It was survivorship, transforming and transcending through love.

Max reached out to me a second time unprompted shortly after the marathon. He sent me the Instagram profile of an objectively attractive, über-tanned Danish hurdler with the disclaimer that he wasn't meaning to be 'weird', but insisting, 'This must be your twin.' Being the literal autist that I am, I wasn't sure if this was clumsy flirting or he was simply making a statement. Having never really spoken to Max, I responded literally, saying, 'She is far too symmetrical,' and once again thanked him. I then asked my friend Milly what the hell was going on. Was this man single? Is this how people flirt?

Let's be honest, my initial frame of reference for interacting with men was with a sadistic child abuser. From there I got off to a bad start because my criteria for intimate partners was effectively: not a rapist – tick. Following that, I had a series of short-lived relationships, many of which were also abusive, troubled or complicated at the very least. Add to this my awkward humour and neurodivergence. I say this with a light and open heart, having never given up on trying to find love, but with a justified track record of trials and trauma that ultimately led me to self-protection in my later years. My baggage is something I've never hidden, but I know it has driven people away. I don't begrudge anyone that. In life we have to take care of ourselves first. I don't want to hurt anyone. I don't mean any harm. But hurt will spark hurt, accidentally and unknowingly. It ricochets down bloodlines and transfers vicariously from ear to ear.

Before Milly responded to me, Max sent me another message saying that he'd heard word was going around that he was messaging me. Anyone who's seen pictures of my face knows I can't hide my feelings for very long. I simply told him that I wasn't complaining about it.

For the next two weeks, Max and I spoke, effortlessly, every day. There were no drawn-out pauses. There were no games. Neither of us left the other hanging.

Back then, Max was working a nine-to-five job in finance. For our first official date, we arranged to meet at 7 pm on Saturday, 24 October 2020. I suggested a local restaurant called Dāna Eating House that I'd just been introduced to, in the hopes of impressing him. I had also just discovered sloe gin, which I intended to order confidently, even though I know next to nothing about alcohol besides how to drink it.

In the days leading up to that evening, I voiced my deep anxieties and internal shame with Milly as we jogged together. Did he know I wasn't anything like the Collegiate girls he grew up with? Did he realise how weird and goofy I was? That I listen to daggy dad rock like Dire Straits and AC/DC? And that he was out of my league? How familiar was he with my story? Did he realise I was *me*?

I could take off my faded Rolling Stones jumper, but I couldn't hide the cut-up arms and worn tattoos that covered my naked body. *'Nobody's Girl', that's me,* I thought, and so say the words still inked on my core. I always cry when I hear those Bonnie Raitt blues.

I didn't want to scare Max. I didn't want to hurt him.

In my experience, time stretches in moments of fear. And in the face of true love.

I didn't want to be late, so I got to town ten minutes early on the night of the 24th, and drove around the block until just before seven. At 7.01, I entered the restaurant.

Max was wearing a maroon knitted hand-me-down jumper his gran had given him. He didn't want to take it off because he was embarrassed about the crinkles in his shirt.

He didn't notice me walk in. But when I saw him, he was the only person in the room I could see.

*

Max is just like me.

Beneath his conventional exterior is another scrappy, misfit child, making mischief, making do.

We were born six weeks apart.

He loves ginger beer and ocean swimming. Jumpsuit Elvis and red meat. Helping others and running free.

Both he and I have lived our lives in bodies that draw assumptions and projections from strangers that don't reflect our realities.

I was wrong. For not believing in either of us before we had begun.

Max was also a hybrid of the public and private school systems, having done four years at Hutchins and two at Taroona, where my dad taught. Another thing we share is a subversive sense of humour. That said, I never shuffled the shape of a 100-metre-long penis onto the school oval during a morning frost, leaving a permanent work of oversized phallic art after all the grass blades snapped off.

On that first date, we talked all night and were finishing each other's sentences. The AFL Grand Final was on, but he chose to meet me instead. We stayed at the restaurant until it closed, then continued on to his friend's house, where the last quarter of the match was playing, and then to Max's parents' house. They were away for the weekend.

We were transfixed by each other, but I knew I had to leave. I didn't want to rush things. I didn't want to repeat mistakes of the past. I had also made plans to run with my friend Meriem the next day. Max insisted that I didn't drive home, though, because we'd been drinking.

I was as stiff as a board when we got into bed. I kept my

clothes on, and my distance, flat on my back. This was going to be the death of it, I thought to myself. Previously, I had been disarmed by subtext too many times. It was not my native tongue, being autistic and behind the age-appropriate eight ball when it came to intimacy. So I armoured up, and cut to the chase. 'You're going to have to tell me exactly what you want from me,' I asserted. If his reciprocal conversation was just a ploy to get me into bed right there and then, I needed to know.

'I just want human connection,' he replied, as his hand gently brushed mine, in an offer to hold it. He didn't try anything more than that.

Still, I was telling myself it was too good to be true. Our second date was a run six days later, at 6 am on Friday, 30 October. That was the day of the 2020 Tasmanian of the Year Awards, but I hadn't prepared myself very well. I didn't write a speech down on paper, and was more preoccupied by the thought of seeing Max again. I'd almost forgotten to tell him about it.

I'd pre-booked a dinner with close friends and family for the evening to mark the occasion regardless of the result, because there was cause to celebrate the milestone and I wished to thank everyone who had helped make it possible. I also arranged for a local make-up artist to come over mid-morning as a treat for Eloise and me. Otherwise, I was still in my own world as usual.

I didn't think Max would turn up for the run, so I got to the Fish Bar at Bellerive Beach early and ran four kilometres just in case to make sure I got a workout in. I was so excited when I saw Max jogging towards me on the path that, for the next six kilometres, I effectively sprinted with joy the whole way along the shoreline and around the bluff, past the houses overlooking Howrah Beach. Max was breathlessly keeping pace, but to his credit, stayed the course. Afterwards, we decided to swim out to the Bellerive pontoon, in just our running gear. I was so taken with Max and the simple joy of the moment that I forgot my phone was in my pocket.

Of all the noise and voices that would drown me later that day, his was the soothing sound I wanted to dive into headfirst after. And I did.

I remember sitting at the restaurant that night, speaking to him on the phone, surrounded by buzzing chatter. He was welcome to join us, I told him, but he didn't want to impose. We would celebrate privately the following evening.

My godmother's daughter, Lizzie, works with Max's friend Liam, and word spread that my favourite meal is slow-cooked lamb.

On the afternoon of 31 October, I picked Max up from a birthday party, and we drove to his place to spend the evening together. He had prepared lamb as a surprise, and said he wanted to watch my acceptance speech from the day before. I was okay with the first part, but the latter made me nervous. I'd confirmed by then that he knew my story. We'd talked about it in general terms, but the speech I made was off-the-cuff and confronting. I'd cried. I knew there was something special between us by this third date. I was nonetheless scared and defensive.

Max insisted. We sat on his couch and played the speech on one of our phones. For the whole eight minutes, he kept his arm around me, and didn't say a word. When he looked up, he was crying.

I've heard many words. Sorries. Pity. Everything from prayers and thoughts of how bad it must have been to how it could have been worse. I don't need that. Max was the first man to be strong enough to just be vulnerable with me without trying to say or do the right thing.

And that makes Max the manliest man of all the chest-beating, punch-throwing, voice-raising, finger-pointing men I've ever met.

None of those things make a man, or anyone, for that matter. What makes a person is the person themselves.

Strength isn't the absence of vulnerability; it is the ability to face it without fear or shame.

After that turning point, when Max suggested we watch music clips on YouTube, I didn't feel up to contesting any of his song choices. Only, I didn't have to. Right off the bat he played 'Money For Nothing', followed by 'Highway to Hell'. He was the daggy dad to my daggy dad. He was my home.

I didn't stay that night, but it wouldn't be long before I effectively moved in with Max and his best friend, Howy, to their share house in Clarendon Vale, the suburb next to Rokeby. In fact, the end of their street linked up with Mockridge Road, which runs all the way behind Nan and Pop's, and joins with Princess Buildings Parade.

Another literal and figurative full circle that Max and I would often run together in the mornings to start the day.

*

We went on a double date with my friends Maddison and Declan. That was going to be the night.

For the first time ever in my life, there were all the ingredients of a perfectly imperfect moment. It combined each of the things I'd lost and re-imagined, but never experienced all at once.

I was nervous. Out of practice. We had waited. He was my age. And I knew that I was in love.

At 25, that was my first time of really getting to know a man as an equal, without rushing. Just fumbling and feeling.

After that it was long runs all around Hobart. Road-tripping together up the east coast, singing Red Hot Chili Peppers and Paul Kelly the whole way. Cooking steaks on the camp stove and picking up huntsman spiders with our hands. Exploring Maria Island as a team of two on foot, greeting wombats, jumping fences, swimming and climbing trees. New Year's with Max's school friends at the Bay of Fires, dancing for days in op-shop costumes. Returning to a steadying base that would be pulled out from underneath us in a matter of weeks.

Another thing that Max and I have in common is that we are strangers to rest. If we are not moving or working, we're out of place.

From Year 8 onwards, Max has worked as a dish pig, pumped petrol at a servo, was a bartender, laboured with his grandfather who was a builder, ran a business with Howy called '2 Mates and a Mower' – 'You grow it, we mow it' – and was also employed at MONA as a groundsman and landscaper.

He is a chartered accountant with a bachelor of business, and a master's in financial planning. Besides one budget holiday to China with two school mates, Max hasn't had more than a week off since he finished school.

In the tumult of 2021, Max was the one who was there behind closed doors to pick me up whenever I fell.

He was the only constant the entire year. No matter how brutal the outside world got, no matter how strained its weight threatened to make us, we did not break.

He showed up for me, for us – not for him.

We moved three times. We house-sat and stayed in two short-term rentals – the first we found on Gumtree and the second on Facebook marketplace, because nowhere would take two newly self-employed 26-year-olds. Before 25 January 2021, I was an unemployed advocate. I'd lived with Mum for six months, and my aunt Jenny for a few months before that.

To go overnight from obscurity to extreme media scrutiny, demands on your time, confected politicisation and relentless, magnified re-traumatisation is not something you can prepare your nervous system for, even with ample warning.

The National Australia Day Council provided a PA at the beginning of the year, an assistance that was given to the previous recipient, James Muecke. Though grateful, I went in another direction because she was based in Canberra. At first, my mother's friend Lynnette managed the influx of requests, but while still working a full-time job and living in Sydney. We hired an EA, Chloe, to help see out the year.

But the support was as fragmented as my mind.

When I wasn't travelling, I spent my days at home alone, writing and giving speeches, interviews and attending advocacy meetings via Zoom.

Australian of the Year is an award, not a paid role. The National Australia Day Council, via Australia Post, caps out at $40,000 worth of travel reimbursement in exchange for free gigs for their sponsors, including Australia Post and Chevron.

Yes, the very same, grubby Amazon-poisoning Chevron. You know when you see a picture of a spider and suddenly you feel like there's one on you? A similar thing happens when you're sitting in the audience at the Australian of the Year Awards lunch and amid the celebrations of our Indigenous history and red earthen outback landscapes, a video message starts playing brought to you by the drawling, suited American CEO of a wallet-bleeding multinational OIL COMPANY, as if that is completely normal, or everyone just got hypnotised by something in the food for 30 seconds. Afterwards you're left feeling a little sick, like there's slick on your back.

Later that year I was asked to do a public talk for Chevron in Perth while I was there to do other speaking events. I said no.

In June Max quit the job he'd worked his whole life to find so that we could become a team of two.

Neither Max nor I had ever experienced that level of stress before, but we were determined, and we had each other.

The physical body doesn't have a schedule. It can't wait for the mind to catch up with processing and compartmentalising. It just feels what it feels. The axis of autism and complex trauma crescendoed at unseen heights. I'd never had such intense panic attacks, coloured by flashbacks cut with criticisms so violent that all I could hope to do was knock myself out in the hopes of knocking them out of me.

One night, I did knock myself out, but when Max called the ambulance, it didn't come. This is a big problem in Tasmania; the strain on services down here has been reported on. He received a call two hours later from the paramedics apologising that they were unable to make it. I'd hit my head on the kitchen floor.

Max would be there every other time since, walking with me in the pain that no one saw. What everyone saw is just what I presented to cover it all.

Max stood by me that day, and he stood up for me too.

The day before Australia Day 2022, a News Corp journalist sent a barrage of texts to him, in which she questioned repeatedly whether my autism had something to do with why I frowned at Scott Morrison. Max told her more than once to never contact either of us again. Despite this, she kept going, refusing to acknowledge the pain she was causing by sending ableist comments on a day already overwhelmingly stressful.

'This is a strange question but some people on Twitter have suggested that might be a factor in PM meeting – I have no idea if that's offensive or true or what but just wanted to ask as it's discussion being raised,' the journalist sent, followed by screenshots, including one of a tweet from commentator Peter van Onselen stating he was prepared to retract his comments and apologise if I frowned because I was autistic.

'Grace is autistic, it's incredibly offensive: please don't contact me again,' Max replied.

With complete disregard of our boundaries, the journalist continued: 'OK – but I'm not trying to offend you – it's a genuine question. People on social have asked the question in a supportive way – not a critical way'

Text: 'People who also have autism have asked the question'

Text: 'But I have no idea if that was a factor in the interaction which is why I asked the question'

Text: 'I have read interviews where she's spoken about that in terms of interactions. It's not a criticism – it's something people who have Autism have raised'

Text: 'Like this'

Then the journalist sent another screenshot sampling an essay that cited autistic 'so-called "social-deficits"'.

Text: 'She's basically saying it's a break down in understanding from people who see the world differently'

'I said please don't contact me again. This is all incredibly offensive,' Max repeated. 'Grace is autistic but not stupid,' he added.

'But nobody is saying that,' the journalist kept on.

Text: 'Nobody thinks she's stupid. I assumed she did it purposefully and that's what I wrote'

Text: 'But because a lot of people raised issue today I thought worth clarifying'

The journalist then sent another screenshot, this time from Geoff Trappett stating that not all disabilities were visible and remarking how I had talked at length about my autism diagnosis.

'Please don't contact me again,' Max said for the third time.

'No problem,' the journalist replied, ironically. 'I'm sorry if I offended you but I think that's unfair – I'm trying to clarify something people with autism people [sic] have raised in support of her. Not a criticism.'

If anyone has ever wondered what ableism looks like, it is an abled person speaking on behalf of the disabled community without permission. It's an abled person patronising a disabled person and telling them how they should feel. It is an abled person repurposing support, disingenuously, for their own agenda. It is an abled person not accounting for the harm they have caused after being called out. It's an abled person disrespecting boundaries put in place by or on behalf of a person with a disability. Worst of all, it's an abled person repeatedly denying the experience of a disabled person because they think they know better, despite never having walked a single day in their shoes.

We all have our limits based on our own values, informed by our past experiences. I didn't frown at the prime minister because I can't control my face, because I'm disabled, because I have some kind of deficit, or because I need help. Spare me, and spare the rest of society the insults to our collective intelligence. I might see the world differently, and I am loath to hide my feelings, but there is no 'breakdown in understanding' of who Scott Morrison is, and what he has and hasn't done for the people of Australia. I didn't frown at him because, in his words, I've 'had a terrible life'. Certainly, like everybody who has ever lived, I have seen some strife. On the whole, though, I have had a wonderful life.

I frowned at Scott Morrison *deliberately* because, in my opinion, he has done and assisted in objectively terrible things. No matter what your politics are, the harm that was caused under his government was some of the worst in our nation's history, including but not limited to survivors of domestic and sexual violence. To have smiled at him, to have pretended that everything was all right, would have made me a fucking liar.

That there was more outrage that day directed towards me over a momentary death stare than towards many of Scott's political acts, reflects how disturbingly skewed our national media's perspective and priorities have become. If people are more upset by the way you look than what you're exposing, it says more about them than it does about you.

They're the emperors without any clothes on.

Max is no emperor. He is a humble hero, helping in the background. A gravitational pull. At once lifting me up, and pulling me back down to earth.

Your head on my head. Your hands in my hands. Us. Together, in each other's arms. Finding our feet. Side by side. Equal parts rebellious and romantic. Double trouble. Ridiculous, and real. Wholesome. Whole. Lovers. Friends. Family. Sharing everything. Facing the world. Thanks for standing by me, and carrying me safely home, finally. Max, I will always love you.

Epilogue

Black and Blue Fingerprints

After everything I have been through and everything I have seen, I have realised that truth telling is bigger than individuals.

It is certainly bigger than me.

I have a lot to lose in sharing these words. I can attest, from experience, to how immeasurably hard so much of what is covered in these chapters is to process. I've provided as much unedited information as possible. Ultimately, what each of you makes of it, is up to you.

My roots are in my heart, and here they are.

Personally, I can't make exceptions because certain people are my family or my friends. I have to be able to look fellow survivors in the eye. I can't permit my grandfather.

I have joined the dots. I have borne and sat with the immense grief and pain that has been passed down to me that has led me to my own conclusion.

And that is: every perpetrator of abuse is someone's someone, but every survivor of abuse is someone's someone too. For far too long we have prioritised and protected the wrong people. Out of fear. Shame. Guilt. Whatever received, inherited reasons. To the detriment of ourselves, and to the benefit of abusers who will continue to abuse us if nothing changes.

I believe there is a difference between a person who makes a mistake and accounts for it, and a person who makes a choice to keep harming others for their own gain, denying any wrongdoing.

Forgiving the latter in the same way we forgive the former isn't an act of compassion or kindness, it is an act of ignorance. It is an act of social sabotage that perpetuates the cycle of abuse by granting blanket acceptance to those who exploit our good faith in the same way they exploit their victims.

I am aware that this book will draw varying responses, including brutal backlash, and undoubtedly more than ever before. It is heavy, explicit, confronting and emotionally charged. It is my unfiltered, unfinished life, written not only upon reflection, but while still realising some of the deepest darkness I've seen. In order to do that, at just 27, I had to armour myself with anger, because the only person there with me was me.

No matter who we are, our words and actions will always draw criticism. None of us is immune. But we don't live and work for the critics. We work for the people who find themselves in our words and stories of truth, and are empowered by them.

I know child abusers despise people like me. They don't like how direct we are about the subtleties of their murky ways. Naturally, they deny, they attack, and they cry victim, while attempting to cast us as the offenders. Watch how long it lasts before they inevitably implode. Usually, the only people they can keep fooled until the end are their irretrievable selves.

I believe it is important to help show others that there are links between traumatic pasts, behaviour patterns, psychosocial disabilities and coping mechanisms that stem from abusive incidents and relationships.

People must comprehend that there is no such thing as the perfect victim. This is the last frontier in understanding survivors. Our missteps should not be used against us, to shame and blame us. They are manifestations of the trauma that became us, but which doesn't have to stay in us.

If nothing else, if this book is a blueprint for one person that helps them in some way, whatever that may be, my work here is done. If there is a chance my being vulnerable will permit the vulnerability of another, quell shame, encourage a disclose, bridge gaps in understanding or ignite a conversation, it is worth the risk of pain.

No amount of hatred, doubt or vilification attempts can detract from that.

This isn't martyrdom; it is a realistic acknowledgement that nothing worth doing is easy.

Evil thrives in silence. In each of us is a powerful story that could be a catalyst for the change we need.

*

The album *Charcoal Lane* was a defining part of the soundtrack of my Australian childhood. Gunditjmara and Bundjalung elder singer-songwriter Archie Roach is one of my all-time favourite storytelling heroes. He performed until the day he died, taking the stage with a ventilator, but making music as profoundly moving as ever.

His unaffected words give us a raw history that will forever dance through the hearts and veins of our nation.

Uncle Archie epitomised storytelling at its most pure, teaching, as always, by humble example. It's bearing the torch for the crowd. It is putting the work before the self and knowing that, in and of itself, will give back the energy needed to sustain the message.

In the words of my dear friend, First Nations artist and fellow Tasmanian Rulla Kelly-Mansell – whose own uncut musical magic will be immortalised forever with Marlon Motlop in Triple J's Like A Version for NAIDOC Week 2022, making up Archie Roach's last-ever Like A Version recording – we must simply 'carry on, there's a life to attend to'.

The captivating force of Rulla, a proud Tulampanga, Kooparoona niara Pakana man from Lutruwita, and Marlon, a proud Darwin-born Larrakia/Kungarrakany and Erub/Darnley Islander from the Torres Strait, supported by their band, isn't something you encounter often. It's at once grounding and transportive. Hard and soft. Fast and slow. Dark and light. Bitter and sweet. Art imitating life, effortlessly. A perfect balance of raw talent and cutting-edge style. These creatives have no need of extravagant outfits or set designs. Just as they are, they transcend everyday mastery of musical skill. It's a very rare palpable power that covers the skin, pierces the soul, fills your heart and lungs with hope and belonging with every breath as you listen and move to its pulsing, honest beat. It's dancing with the past, present and future in a single moment. It's returning home.

After coming off ten back-to-back, eighteen to twenty–hour days to finish this book, Max and I had to fly from Sydney to Melbourne, then drive to Geelong so I could deliver a 30-minute speech immediately followed by a 30-minute Q&A. I didn't think I could do it. Before I took to the lectern, a teenage song-and-dance group performed a piece they had written and choreographed called 'No Means No', inspired by my Australian of the Year Awards acceptance speech. Within seconds of the number starting, I was trembling with tears. There was nothing I could do to hold myself together. Every last scrap of strength I felt I had was gone. I was terrified that I would not be able to face the audience.

Yet, when I found myself looking out at a crowd of fellow human beings moments later, I allowed myself to accept their trust, remembered why I was there, and who I was there for, and I was regenerated in an instant. I was there to serve and to pass on my lived experience. I was there as a conduit for truth and learning. I could feel the pure connection in the room, coursing through me and back out again.

There's always more good to go around.

None of us would be here if it weren't for storytelling.

I spent my entire life running, trying to find secure ground, searching for a home in other people and places, only to discover that my home was with me all along. It is in the innate voice I have; that each of us has; that grounds and connects us with others by way of sharing truth. It is our collective power that breaks the walls of silence.

May these words bring you home.

Acknowledgements

To all the diamonds whose value I can't put a price on, who have helped along the way, I am indebted to you, and will treasure our bonds forever:

I have already mentioned my family, but they are worth an encore. The Matriarch, my Nanny Pat, all my mum's sisters, their former and current partners, my cousins and their children. All the Tames, the Carmichaels and the Plaschkes.

My Fairy Godparents, Jane Melross and Rod Arnold, and their two children, my adoptive siblings Lizzie 'Schmimpm' Arnold and Joe – my gratitude for each of you is as bottomless as our ability as a whole to find laughter.

Karen Molhuysen, who has worked alongside my mother in the pursuit of elusive justice.

The heroic Heerey family: Andrea, Paul, Matilda, Sam, Moose et al, thank you for grounding Max and me in the whirlwind.

Max's dear friends, who have welcomed me into their circle. I would like to start with Sophie Murfitt, who played softball with me in high school. She is a warrior. From one to another, this is a special nod to a true champion, in every sense. Rose Burbury, thank you for the long phone calls and late nights. Liam Blue, thank you for the long rides, the sweet treats, the laughs, and the 2021 New Year's resolution after all those years. Jack Turner, Holly Smith, Allie Shearman, Lewis Nettlefold, Tom Howard, Sam Heron, Emily Crawford, Angus Balcombe, Fraser McCreary, Lewis Noye, Georgie Limmer, Maddy Ingles, Xavier Deveraux, Isabelle Sutton, Michael Burgess, Nick and Sally Boon, Alec Willing, Kate Mundy and Alistair Edwards. To be included among such a crowd is truly heartwarming.

Emily Marriott, you are a gem. As are our private moments. Thank you.

Miranda Allender, thank you for reconnecting with me in England. I see a side of you that many others may not, and I know you see me too.

Likewise Ebony Abblitt and your lovely father.

The Cutler family, a home away from home. You know.

Brynne Beck, who sat with me in the courtyard of my high school, the day the disclosure of the abuse bubbled to the surface. Renee Shepherd, who sat with me when I finally shared as much as I could with the school principal. Bill Simon, who I told first, and who believed me. Glenn Carmichael, who did too, and who did the right thing. Alannah Roach, Liz Harper, Katie Stanley, Jane Polley, Katie Walker, Charles Kemp, Christiane Zander, Judy Davis, Julie Kemp, Julie Brock, Sandy von Allmen, Anne Morgan, Vicki Patterson, Dale Anning,

Brian Denne and the other staff I met at Collegiate who I trust did their best, despite the odds.

Jill Lambert, for all your confidence and the coffees in the mornings before college after I left Collegiate. Thank you.

Linda Burrows and Rhys Leeming, your ongoing support and presence is greatly appreciated.

Brave Georgia Bennett. Never underestimate your strength. I draw courage from your being.

The MacDonald family. Lucy and Rosie, our mischief was made of love.

Dear Lauren Eagling, you shine ever brightly.

Elisha Burton, so do you.

You too, Rhi Hamilton.

Liam Firth, you taught me how to express myself. I love you, my friend.

Fotti Porihis, you free and funky soul. You too.

Dan Peacock. What I couldn't say then, and what I hope I am not out of line in saying it now, is that your kindness is something I didn't know how to accept or respond to. It will nevertheless stay with me.

As will yours, Ochre Frohmader.

Kade Hull, your friendship was an *Escape from L.A.*, literally. It was an escape from everything. I appreciate you so much.

Zac Romangoli-Townsend. The light in me sees the light in you. You are a beautiful human being. Thank you for always listening and understanding, and for your decency and respect.

The family at Equalise studio in Hobart, led by Benjamin Korkmaz, who fostered my passion for teaching yoga, and gave me another home to breathe through decades of stuck pain. Rox, Grace and the rest of the team, I adore you.

The Running Edge family: Allan, Kim and Jay, who gave me a dream job that reignited a dormant passion. Annabel, Geoff, the three Rubys and the rest of the team who would help that too. Ben Covington for all those early morning runs. Alex and Sarah Robb for the delicious meals and company.

Josh Harris, who coached me to a half marathon personal best of 1:23:21, but more importantly through the ups and downs of life outside of training.

My fellow Australian of the Year nominees, the mighty forces of Tanya Hosch, Dr Wendy Page, Dr Dinesh Palipana, Dr Helen Milroy, Brendan Murphy, and last but not least Shane Fitszimmons, who also stood up to the inaction of Scott Morrison.

Ashley St. Pierre Martin, Sven Martin and Lynsey Shaw, for keeping Jason Wisch afloat, and me as well.

The beautiful Uhler family. Although I am not a woman of faith, I am eternally spiritual, and I believe in everything you do. I am blessed to know you.

The Santa Barbara and Hollywood studio CorePower families. Cara Ferrick, Vesper Gray, Laura Rebecca and all the teachers in training I learned alongside in 2013 and 2015.

Dan Ilic, who believed in my humour. The little autistic kid who found comfort in Robin Williams' hotdog impressions was beside themselves on the 2022 Melbourne Comedy Festival stage. Thank you, Dan. And you too, John Delmenico, for keeping this very real Tasmanian on her toes.

Charles Firth and Dave Milner, who've given me a space to write at The Shot. Ronni Salt for being a mentor and guiding light.

Jess Hill, where I would be without your influence, support and friendship, I shudder to think. The world is better for having you in it.

The O'Donovan family. You are one of a kind, and kind above all else. Thank you.

Ben Kowaluck, and the rest of the Society quiz night stragglers who made 2019 Tuesdays a win regardless of our abysmal performances. Long live 'Bob Hawkes Beer Brewers', 'Harold Holt's Swimming Coaches', and 'Scomo's No Homos'.

Purdie Day. Your courage knows no bounds.

Lynnette Edmonds and all of your gorgeous children, Grace, my namesake, especially. Lynnette, your brother Brian as well.

Erika Flynn, the effervescent expressionist. Thank you for launching my illustrating career. You modelled for me in both human form and by your grace, your boldness and your eternal brilliance. You are a revolutionary.

As is Gary Bradley, an artist ahead of his time.

Güstavo Stebner too. Thank you for all the cinematic adventures.

Speaking of cinematic adventures, I can't forget Gregg Briggs. Or Craig Riggs, his alter ego.

Nor Preston Pope, and our nights singing karaoke in Sherman Oaks.

On that note, Jane and Jimmy Barnes, thank you for the sparks of joy you brought in a difficult year, my family are grateful to you for your generosity.

Jock and Lauren Zonfrillo, yours too.

Artist Kirsty Neilson, your talent matches your heart. It was as much an honour to be painted by you and hung in the 2021

Archibald Prize as it was to simply sit and listen to your own story. Thank you for the gift of your friendship.

Holly Rankin, my sparkly soul twin, to be immortalised in song is something I something I never imagined. Your talent is endless, just like our bond.

Tarang Chawla, you are as great a private advocate as you are a public voice in the fight against sexual and domestic violence.

Luna Robledo, your intellect and heart will take you far.

Zoey Dwyer, yours too. You're a powerhouse, and you crack me up.

To Phoebe Hawthorne, Amelia Johnston, Stef Macgeorge, Cleo Thomas and Isabella Maxwell; gentle souls, whose quiet support has been some of the loudest.

Georgia Eade, my Blackcurrant babe. Thank you for standing up for me when few people would when we were young, and for looking after me.

Tanya Murphy, you are indeed True to Heart. Your magic, it works.

Max Barnett, my friend and fellow inquiring mind, whose thirst for all things real and realpolitik is as unquenchable as mine.

Magda Szubanski. You might be a national treasure, but to me you will always be a down-to-earth human being, just like the rest of us. Thank you for reaching out when I needed it most.

And finally, to Cate Blake and Emily Brooks for helping bring this book to life. My inner fatalist perfectionist would not allow for a ghostwriter, but if it weren't for you stalwarts, I would be nothing but a ghost myself.

If I have missed anyone, it's not for lack of appreciation, truly. As you can see, I've crossed many a path, each as meaningful as the next. Thank you, everyone. My heart is overflowing with love and gratitude. I want nothing more than these riches.

The Grace Tame Foundation

The Grace Tame Foundation (GTF) is a not-for-profit philanthropic organisation established by the 2021 Australian of the Year, Grace Tame, to campaign for and help fund initiatives which work to prevent and respond to sexual abuse of children and others.

The Grace Tame Foundation aims to ensure the Australian Government and governments of states and territories take appropriate action by enacting laws, delivering educational programs and encouraging social behaviours. It also promotes attitudes that fulfil obligations to ensure the right of children to be safe no matter where they are as per the UN Convention on the Rights of the Child (CRC).

The Foundation also raises funds to support other projects and initiatives through grants. It seeks to partner with and support existing organisations and programs which align with the Foundation's purpose.

One in five Australian children experience sexual abuse. Our vision is of a future free from the sexual abuse of children and others.

thegracetamefoundation.org.au

Resources

If you think you need immediate assistance, call 000.

If you would like to speak to someone about your situation, you may wish to contact one of the following services.

Blue Knot

Blue Knot provides information and support for anyone who is affected by complex trauma. Complex trauma is repeated, ongoing, and often extreme interpersonal trauma (between people) – violence, abuse, neglect or exploitation experienced as a child, young person and adult.
Call: 1300 657 380 – 9 am to 5 pm (AEST), 7 days a week
blueknot.org.au

1800RESPECT

1800RESPECT is the national online and telephone counselling and support service for people who have experienced, or are at risk of experiencing, sexual assault and/or domestic and family violence, their family and friends, and frontline and isolated workers.
Call: 1800 737 732 – 24 hours, 7 days a week
1800respect.org.au

Kids Helpline

Kids Helpline is a 24-hour telephone service that is available for young people (aged between five and 25) who need advice, counselling or just someone to talk to – no problem is too big or too small.
Call: 1800 55 1800 – 24 hours, 7 days a week
kidshelpline.com.au

Lifeline

Lifeline is a non-profit organisation that provides free, 24-hour telephone crisis support services in Australia. Volunteer crisis supporters provide suicide prevention services, mental health support and emotional assistance, not only via telephone but face-to-face and online.
Call: 13 11 14 – 24 hours, 7 days a week
lifeline.org.au

QLife

QLife provides anonymous and free LGBTQIA+ peer support and referrals for people in Australia wanting to talk about sexuality, identity, gender, bodies, feelings or relationships.
Call: 1800 184 527 – 3 pm to midnight (AEST), 7 days a week
qlife.org.au

Beyond Blue

Beyond Blue provides information and support to help everyone in Australia achieve their best possible mental health.
Call: 1300 22 4636 – 24 hours, 7 days a week
beyondblue.org.au

Suicide Call Back Service

Suicide Call Back Service provides free counselling for suicide prevention and mental health via telephone, online and video for anyone affected by suicidal thoughts.
Call: 1300 659 467 – 24 hours, 7 days a week
suicidecallbackservice.org.au

MensLine Australia

MensLine Australia offers free professional telephone counselling support for men with concerns about mental health, anger management, family violence (perpetuating and experiencing), addiction, relationships, stress and wellbeing.
Call: 1300 78 99 78 – 24 hours, 7 days a week
mensline.org.au